ESSAYS IN EARLY FRENCH LITERATURE

PRESENTED TO BARBARA M. CRAIG

ESSAYS IN EARLY FRENCH LITERATURE

PRESENTED TO BARBARA M. CRAIG

Edited by

Norris J. Lacy

and

Jerry C. Nash

French Literature Publications Company
York, South Carolina
1982

Copyright 1982

ISBN 0-917786-28-9

French Literature Publications Company, Inc.

Printed in the United States of America

CONTENTS

FOREWORD

In 1978, the editors of this volume and the editors of *Chimères* (the graduate student journal in French and Italian at the University of Kansas) began planning a volume of essays as a tribute to Professor Barbara M. Craig, whose retirement, after more than thirty years as a Kansas faculty member, was expected within a few years. We subsequently solicited contributions, both financial and scholarly, from a number of her colleagues, former students, and professional friends. The response to both appeals provided gratifying evidence of the esteem in which Barbara Craig is held. Financial contributors are listed elsewhere in this volume, and it is our pleasure to acknowledge their substantial assistance.

Our invitations brought us the fifteen essays published here, divided between medieval and Renaissance literature, Barbara Craig's two primary interests. We chose not to impose a theme or subject, and as a result, the essays exhibit a healthy variety of topic, approach, and method. The articles range from analysis to synthesis; from treatments of specific works (*Cligès, Aucassin et Nicolette, Le Moyen de Parvenir*) to authors (Marie de France, Rabelais) to genres (fabliaux, farce); from French to Provençal to the Latin of Erasmus. A specific focus for the volume was sacrificed in favor of diversity, and authors were free to pursue their own interests; we trust that readers will approve the decision.

We owe a special debt of gratitude to a number of people, and especially to the staff of *Chimères*. In the course of preparing the volume, we decided not to publish it as a special number of *Chimères*, as we had originally planned. Nonetheless, we received invaluable assistance from the journal staff, both before and after this decision was made. In particular, we wish to thank Lee Gerstenhaber, Paul Homan, and Raymond Whelan, three successive editors of *Chimères*, whose enthusiastic and capable support made our work much easier. Our thanks as well to the College of Arts and Sciences of the University of Kansas, which generously provided the additional financial support that permitted us to proceed with the publication of this volume.

N.J.L.
J.C.N.

DEDICATION

Barbara M. Craig was educated at Queen's University (Kingston, Ontario) and at Bryn Mawr, where she prepared her Ph.D. dissertation under the direction of Grace Frank. She first taught at Mt. Royal College and then came to the University of Kansas in 1947. She has taught at Kansas since that date.

Professor Craig has devoted most of her scholarly efforts to editing and studying medieval French dramas. Her editions include *L'Estoire de Griseldis* (1954), *La Vie Monseigneur Saint Fiacre* (1960, co-edited with M.E. Porter and James Burks), *La Creacion, La Transgression and L'Expulsion of the Mistère du Viel Testament* (1968), and her *The Evolution of a Mystery Play: A Critical Edition of "Le Sacrifice d'Abraham" of Le Mistère du Viel Testament," "La Moralité du Sacrifice d'Abraham," and the 1539 Version of "Le Sacrifice d'Abraham" of "Le Mistère du Viel Testament,"* soon to be published by the French Literature Publications Company. Among her recent articles are "Prefiguration and Literary Creativity in the *Sacrifice d'Abraham* of the *Mistère du Viel Testament*," in *Voices of Conscience* (1977), and "The *Moralité du Sacrifice d'Abraham* of the *Recueil Trepperel:* a Literary Assessment," in *Jean Misrahi Memorial Volume* (1977). In 1978 she was chosen to deliver a lecture in the University of Kansas Humanities Lecture Series, a group of presentations by distinguished scholars, only one of whom may each year be a Kansas faculty member. Her lecture was "The *Mistère du Siège d'Orléans* and Joan of Arc"; a related article on "The Staging and Date of the *Mystère du Siège d'Orléans*," can be read in *Res Publica Litterarum*, no. 4.

Barbara Craig is also a devoted and highly successful teacher. That success is indicated by her having received, in 1973, an award for distinguished teaching given by the University of Kansas and by Standard Oil of Indiana. The following year, she was named an Outstanding Educator of America. Her imposing command of her discipline, her profound concern for her students, and the fact that she demands as much of herself as of them, inspire equal measures of learning and admiration—not to mention the many friendships that last long after degrees are earned and careers begun.

As she is a dedicated and capable scholar and teacher, so was she, however briefly and reluctantly, a dedicated and capable administrator. In 1975 she yielded to the wishes of her colleagues and her deans and became Chairperson of the Department of French and Italian. Her state of health, aggravated by the pressures of her duties, forced her to relinquish the position after two years, but her administrative tenure was marked, predictably, by fairness, firmness, and efficiency.

In 1979, she was honored by election to the University of Kansas Women's Hall of Fame, a group of university women designated as exemplary models for women students.

A rather impersonal listing of her accomplishments cannot convey a notion of her dedication, her sacrifices, her influence on large numbers of students, both undergraduate and graduate; in short, her value as teacher, scholar, colleague, and friend. It is thus to Barbara M. Craig that this volume and the essays in it are dedicated.

TABULA GRATULATORIA

ANDERSON, Robert & Corinne

ARGERSINGER, William J. & Marnie

ARMITAGE, Isabelle

BENARROUS, Edgar & Judy L.

BERNARD, Robert W.

BOOKER, Tom & Karen

BOON, Jean-Pierre

BOWEN, Barbara

BOYD, Beverly M.

BRYANT, Lucie M.

CARMAN, Mrs. J. Neale

CAWS, Mary Ann

CLEVELAND, Mary L.

COBB, Robert

COLBERT, Ann

COMEAU, Raymond

CONNELL, Mary Ellen

CRIVELLI, Joseph D.

CRUMRINE, Mattie E.

DAVIS, Jacqueline Zurat

DEAM, Anne S.

DeGEORGE, Fernande M.

DEHON, Claire L.

DINNEEN, David A & Nancy L.

DIORIO, Mary Ann

DONALDS, Marjorie Bordenave

DOUCETTE, Clarice

DOWNER, Shirley I.

DOYLE, Brigitte

DUGAN, Mary

ERICKSON, John D. & Inge F.

FISCHER, Dr. Billie Thompson

FREEMAN, Bryant C.

GAGEN, Jean E.

GERSTENHABER, Lee D.

GOWAN, Patricia

GRIGSBY, John L.

HAMILTON, Suzanne

HANDLEY, Joan

HENDERSON, Judith M.

HENDRICKSON, William L.

HOMAN, Paul

HORNER, Channing & Louise

JODOGNE, Omer

JONIN, Pierre

JOHNSON, J. Theodore & Mary G.

JOHNSON, Simone A.

KNIGHT, Alan E.

KOZMA, Janice M.

LACY, Faye Tison

LACY, Gregg F. & Margriet B.

LACY, Norris J.

LAZAR, Moshé

LOCEY, Michael & Lenita

LYNCH, Juanita L.

MADDOX, Donald

MAGERUS, John E.

MASON, Alexandra

MAZZARA, Richard A.

McKERNAN, Susan A.

MEYER, Kathleen J.

MORDY, Murle, Jr.

MUNDIS, Martha F.

NAI, Ton-Thât Dong

NASH, Jerry C.

PATTERSON, William T.

PERRIGAUD, Martha

PINET, Christopher E.

REED, Mary B.

ROBSON, Walter W., III

RUNTE, Hans R. & Roseann

SALIEN, Jean

SCREECH, M. A.

SHANKEL, Delbert M.

STOKSTAD, Marilyn

STONE, Donald

STURM-MADDOX, Sara

SYMONS, Eleanor

TARR, Kenneth R.

TOBIN, Ronald W.

VAUGHT, Diane M.

WAGGONER, George R.

WARREN, Glenda

WHELAN, Chantal & Raymond

WHITE, Kenneth S.

WILLIAMS, John R.

WOLFF, Geneviève M.

A NOTE ON THE GENRE OF THE *VOYAGE DE CHARLEMAGNE*

John L. Grigsby

A brief glance at the library's card catalogue or a bibliography of medieval literature will remind us that the famous story of Charlemagne's *gabs* lacks a definitive title.[1] The one heading this note often includes the words *en Orient,* while Gaston Paris, and many of his followers, have preferred *La Chanson du Pèlerinage de Charlemagne,* or simply *Le Pèlerinage de Charlemagne.* The MS bequeaths us the lengthy incipit: "Ci comence le liver cumment Charels de Fraunce voiet in Ierusalem et pur parols sa feme a Constantinnoble pur veer roy Hugon,"[2] which identifies accurately the story and has generated the awkward *Voyage de Charlemagne à Jérusalem et à Constantinople,* adopted for two recent books: Aebischer's edition and Tyssens' translation.[3] Good fortune has obviously befallen German scholars blessed with the brief and noncommittal *Karlsreise,* for no French- or English-speaking historian has adopted Francisque Michel's mercifully short, but cryptic, *Charlemagne.* Neuschäfer is correct in noting that "pèlerinage" adds an interpretation to the poem which would please few critics today.[4] If Bédier could plead for a neat transfer of relics along pilgrimage routes, and Coulet could preach that the poem was a sermon against sin,[5] most would agree with Neuschäfer (p. 89) and others that the so-called pilgrimage camouflaged the real purpose of Charles' trip: to measure his stature against the rival named by his wife. The fluidity of the poem's title is, however, minimal compared to the flow of interpretations which it has inspired. One need only to consult Horrent's dense summary of studies in the introductory pages of his *Essai d'explication littéraire*[6] to recall the variety of reactions that this poem of only 870 lines has engendered.[7]

Such multiplicity of evaluation is symptomatic not only of a masterpiece but also of its indeterminate genre. Humor is of course present in almost every *chanson de geste,* surely in the *Roland* (witness Roland's and Ganelon's bantering or the apple anecdote), though perhaps not in the blood and gore of the Vivien songs. Charles' voyage stands out, however, as something different. If the grandeur of the great emperor is being ridiculed, if the heroic Twelve Peers act like drunken fools, one suspects that the notion of epic has been replaced. But by what? The genre of parody springs to mind first, since parody must depend on a previous work, and one thinks of the *Chanson de Roland,* or with Walpole of the *Descriptio,*[8] or with Neuschäfer of both the Charlemagne and Guillaume cycles.[9] Horrent vigorously objects to the arguments for parody set forth by Moland, Stengel, Koschwitz, and Neuschäfer, *inter alios.* He sees no "déformation burlesque des procédés courants de l'épopée" (p. 111), and insists repeatedly that the poem is "un simple conte à rire" (pp. 121, 122), "comique et non satirique" (p. 125). Neuschäfer's effort to classify the work as a parody is one of the most exhaustive, but is seriously damaged by his desire to make it an angry French reaction to the canonization of Charles on January 8, 1166,[10] and above all by the deeply troubling aspect of genre classification itself. More than once he and other literary historians have bogged down in definitions, generic "rules", and in the case of parody, the problem of parody's object. Aebischer goes so far as to claim that the *Voyage* is "une parodie d'un poème que nous n'avons plus"[!].[11]

Do genres exist? If so, how are they created? Why study them? These questions are seriously posed by contemporary critics and have evoked rather discouraging replies. Let us examine some of the answers (as well as the validity of the questions themselves) to discover how they might apply to the *Voyage.* We must admit that the *concept*, at least, of genre exists, that people *believe* that genres exist, whether or not the works we study fit neatly into the frameworks we think we perceive for each. The maker of a literary work— *jongleur, trouvère,* poet, novelist, playwright—does not, it would appear, set out to create a genre, but instead relies on rules perceived in his predecessors' productions. Genres seem to be existential, that is, created after the fact: "Toutes les espèces, tous les sous-genres, genres, ou super-genres sont des classes empiriques, établis par observation du donné historique, ou à la limite par extrapolation à partir de ce donné".[12] Genres come not from nowhere, but through empirical observation, from institutions which function as "horizons of expectation" for the public and as "models of writing" for the author.[13] The path followed by the author of the *Voyage* is more clearly outlined than, say, the one taken by the genius who composed the first *chanson de geste,* for his model is apparent to us, whether it be the *Descriptio,* the epic tradition in general, or the *Roland* in particular. When our poet undertook his composition, he had a ready-made vehicle, an assonanced song divided into laisses, which he guided in new directions. His change in form, from decasyllabic to dodecasyllabic verse, is minimal in comparison to the modification in content. From the reverent glorification of Charles, Roland and the peers, he takes us through episodes where the great warriors are humiliated by tumbling like bowling pins in Hugon's rotating palace, blunder themselves into drunken insults of the host, and must be rescued by a surely overindulgent Father, the same God who stopped the sun to assist Charles' vengeance of the martyred Roland. The battles in the *Roland,* each preceded by a series of threats, are deadly serious events. In the *Voyage gabs* replace the ceremonious boasts; sexual prowess (Olivier's) and circus performances are substituted for bloody combat, while the tone of deadly seriousness, Hugon's threats, is not only removed to the background, but caricatured.

Roland and Charles are no longer sacred: the genre has changed. "Le principe. . . créateur de genres n'exige aucun changement dans la disposition d'esprit; son rôle est bien plutôt de contraindre une seule et même disposition à s'orienter vers une fin nouvelle, essentiellement distincte de l'ancienne."[14] Few can fail to notice the shift in attitude which these episodes betray. Much more subtle is the narrator's manipulation of his audience. In the *Roland,* indeed in most epics, the narrator warns us of a tragic outcome, so that esthetic pleasure derives not from suspense, but from vicarious participation in history. Such characteristics of the epic narrator explain why critics so often label Béroul as a *jongleur:* He imitates the epic manner by belaboring his public with outcries announcing the sorrowful end of the lovers. In contrast, the *Voyage's* narrator constantly keeps his audience in suspense. We suspect that Charles will finally prove to be the greatest emperor (in reputation and in actual height),[15] but the narrator never discloses the *dénouement.* He portrays Hugon ambiguously, perhaps even misleads us, when he notes that the emperor "Sages fud e membrez mais plains de malevis" (Aebischer ed., v. 438). Hugon seems to be innocent and well intentioned as he asks his spy if Charles will remain his friend,[16] and even more so in Koschwitz's understanding of the line as he inquires whether Charles intends to accept his cordial invitation to remain in Constantinople awhile longer.[17] The author justifies the spy's presence as a national "custom", hence exonerating Hugon of malevolence. But as the story progresses, we wonder if the joyous knights will meet with disaster: "Le public se demande si la farce ne va pas tourner au drame. Le poète le tient en haleine avec l'habileté d'un homme de métier," exclaims Horrent (p. 81). Humor, suspense, and the imaginative, inventive, mockery of the *gabs* are a far cry from the ominousness of the *Roland,* or the pathetic sincerity of the elogious remarks with which these French knights shower each other: Roland for Olivier, vv. 2207-14, for Turpin, vv. 2252-58; or Charles' lament, vv. 2402-10,[18] which so reminds us of Villon's "Ballade des seigneurs du temps jadis."[19] While the warriors portrayed in Digby 23 are close to God (Gabriel takes Roland directly to Paradise "non-stop" and Charles often appears to be God incarnate), in Constantinople, God reprimands them for "gabbing" ("Ne gabez ja mes hume, ço cumandet Christus!" Aebischer ed., v. 676), as if they were naughty children, and although he promises to aid them by means of the relics to perform their *gabs,* neither Olivier nor Guillaume need divine assistance to seduce the emperor's daughter or to shatter a large portion of the castle walls respectively. Only Bernard, with a quickly formed Sign of the Cross, obtains help from heaven to make the waters rise. We can assuredly observe that the existential attitude, the mental disposition, the "schéma imaginatif,"[20] have changed, but if the *Voyage* represents a new genre, what is it?

The often preferred designation "parody" is anachronistic, refers to another day and another land, and too often, I insist, leads to problematic definitions. The word is Greek and belongs to the literature of antiquity. We have mentioned that one source of genres is previous works, and for our poem, scholars have proposed the *Roland*, the *Descriptio*, and epic in general. Let us examine three further potential sources.

Theorists are fond of noting that society itself is the breeding ground of literary genres. Wellek and Warren provide an analysis of the now conventional view that genre is an institution,[21] and Todorov, more recently, has again underscored the social origins: "Chaque époque a son propre système de genres, qui est en rapport avec l'idéologie dominante" (*Genres*, p. 51). The social link is even more important to Marxist critics, as Goldmann corroborates in his comments on the novel: "On savait, en effet, depuis toujours que le roman était la principale des formes littéraires correspondant à la société bourgeoise et que son évolution était étroitement liée à l'histoire de notre société."[22] Is there any hint in the *Voyage* at what type of literature corresponds to the warrior society of the eleventh or twelfth century? Charles, in his famous apology for the tall tales his knights have invented, has recourse to a "custom in France, Paris, and Chartres" (v. 654).[23] The inventive, exaggerated boasts at bedtime (and in the *Roland* the elegies pronounced over fallen knights) are, then, discourse clearly tied to recognized social institutions. The *gab* requires imagination, an object (Hugon is the target of 7 of the 13 *gabs*),[24] and an audience: a desired one, the French, and an unwanted one, the spy, who will carry the message to the butt of the mockery. The poet's audience, like the chivalric audience in the *récit*, takes pleasure in the banter, but surely another audience, churchmen, believers in Charles' saintliness, were likely to take offense at the irreverent treatment of sacred elements, as does the spy. The social setting for the *gabs* within the narrative corresponds to the living audience outside the poem. We begin to perceive some relationship between the *gab*, an ingredient of the narrative, and the narrative in its entirety.

If society is a source of genre, so also is language, or more precisely, discourse. Speech for its own sake cannot, however, produce literature. Todorov, in his investigation of psychotic discourse, reports that victims of paranoia are capable of fabricating a coherent world. Their syntax is correct, contradictions are avoided. Their stories lack only a signpost such as "Once upon a time" to be transformed into a literary genre. But the discourse which he labels (perhaps arbitrarily) as schizophrenic, lacks referents. The syntax occurs only to maintain the discourse itself, not to link it with identifiable antecedents, so that it abounds in incomplete clauses, contradictions, and reversals of transitivity. Anaphora, syntagmic repetitions of severals sorts, and conjunctions tie the segments to each other, but to nothing outside speech. In contemporary English, we might call it, ironically, gabbing, or blabbing. It is "verbal intoxication", talk for its own sake (Todorov, pp. 81ff.). Language alone is incapable of giving birth to literary genre; it must be guided toward some goal. A "speech act" (used loosely here) can, for example, yield a genre. It may coincide with a genre, as in prayers. It may share characteristics: The novel derives from the speech act of "telling." But no verbal activity in normal, everyday communication corresponds to a fixed form of lyric poetry, say a *rondeau*, despite the many properties a *rondeau* may have in common with talking.[25] We observe that the *gab* as speech act has the same relationship to the *Voyage* as that of telling to the novel, i.e., *l'acte de gaber* resembles the act of composing a story about *gabs*.

The final source we must note for our purposes is the work itself. A new genre can spring from a single work, as the fortune of Montaigne's *Essais* can testify. Todorov, relying on Lessing, Blanchot, and others, calls into question the very notion of genre. We cite with Todorov a pertinent observation by Blanchot: "Seul importe le livre, tel qu'il est, loin des genres, en dehors des rubriques, prose, poésie, roman, témoignage, sous lesquelles il refuse de se ranger. . . . Un livre n'appartient plus à un genre."[26] Todorov, exploring several texts, attempts to show that each has forged its own "generic rules" and is thus a genre unto itself. Even though Novalis' *Heinrich von Ofterdingen* presents itself as a novel, it betrays "poetic" characteristics. It abounds in parallelisms, repetitions, allegories, and an opaqueness which might best be described as a manifestation of Jakobson's poetic function. Its "events" are moods, or stories within stories (*enchâssements*) where the *énonciation* is more important than the *énoncé* (Todorov, pp. 104-116). In other words, the elements necessary to describe the genre of a work are hidden in the work itself. Such is, I believe, the situation of the *Voyage de Charlemagne*.

The *gabs* occupy, quantitatively, the major portion of the poem. They are pivotal in the narrative action. Horrent among others has commented on their indispensableness to the total meaning: "Les Français recourent aux gabs pour se dédommager de leur humiliation devant la cour d'Hugon, Hugon recourt aux gabs pour se venger des Français, et ce seront les gabs qui feront triompher les Français" (p. 84). "Dans l'économie du poème, les gabs exécutés sont le ressort de l'action" (p. 105). These observations describe the narrative action but cannot suffice to identify a genre. Deeper structural homonymities must be uncovered. Let us offer then the following correspondences between the characteristics of a *gab* and the narrative structures of the *Voyage*.

In the opening lines, Charles sets a tone of comic vanity, but only after the narrator with a straight face imitates a serious initial situation typical of a *chanson de geste.*[27] Charles boasts: "Dame, veïstes unkes hume dedesuz ceil Tant ben seïst espee, ne la corune el chef? Uncor cunquerrei jo citez ot mun espez!" (Aebischer ed., vv. 9-11). His vaunt is already a *gab:* It follows the *gab's* grammatical framework with its interrogative, an object pointed out (here the crown, the sword and the man himself like the gabs were a sphere [v. 508], a pillar [v. 521], or the Emperor's blond daughter [v. 486] are indicated), and a claim to accomplish a feat. The syntax of both the *gabs* and of Charles' boast requires quite logically an interrogative (or an imperative), a subjunctive and a future usually of the verb *veir,* to emphasize the visual. Charles has expressed himself with idle talk, which must have irritated his wife, who enters into the game with idle but dangerous discourse when now she boasts that she knows of a greater king. Upon recognizing her spouse's anger, she confesses that she was playing: "si me quidai juer" (ed. cit., v. 33) and offers to swear at the risk of her life that she was jesting. Her "jest," too, was a *gab,* part of that custom to which her husband will later refer, but perhaps denied to women, especially empresses who speak publicly.[28] The punishment with which she is threatened is decapitation, the identical sentence which faces Charles and the peers should they be unable to make good their own idle talk: "S'or ne sunt aampli li gab que vus deïstes, Trancherai vus les testes od m'aspee furbie!" shouts Hugon in rage (ed. cit., vv. 646f.; cf. Horrent, p. 85). Charles is forgiven by God (vv. 674ff.), and reluctantly by Hugon who offers him treasures (v. 839) and embraces at his departure (v. 848). Charles, with the roles changed again, pardons his spouse: "Sun mautalent li ad li reis tut perdunet" (v. 869). In sum, Charles brags; his wife replies; he threatens her; she begs forgiveness; he pardons her. In macrocosm, the narrative mimics the microcosm of the *gab:* a knight brags; others try to better the boast; the leader threatens punishment; Charles petitions God; all are forgiven. The *gab* is the mainspring of the entire narrative movement.

The *gabs* pervade the poem, its spirit, its structures. The *gab* mocks, is spoken in jest, delivers a boast, tells a tall tale. The poet embellishes his *gab* with the fantasy of the relics, the imagined trips to Constantinople and Jerusalem, which betray his "mental disposition." These are supporting episodes which form part of *his* boast. Aebischer hinted some time ago that one might call the *Voyage* "un gabet",[29] but only Guido Favati has dared to label outright its genre as a *gab.*[30] With the corroboration of recent critical theory we can now justifiably claim that the *Voyage de Charlemagne* created its own genre, and that it is indeed a *gab.*

Washington University in St. Louis

NOTES

[1] Cf. Hans-Jorg Neuschäfer, *"Le Voyage de Charlemagne en Orient* als parodie der Chanson de Geste," *Romanistisches Jahrbuch,* 10 (1959), 78nl.

[2] *Karls des Grossen Reise nach Jerusalem und Constantinopel,* ed. Eduard Koschwitz, Altfr. Bibl. (Leipzig, 1913), p. l.

[3] *Le Voyage de Charlemagne à Jérusalem et à Constantinople,* ed. Paul Aebischer, TLF (Genève: Droz, 1965); *Le Voyage de Charlemagne à Jérusalem et à Constantinople,* trans. Madeleine Tyssens, Ktéma, no. 3 (Ghent: Editions Scientifiques, 1978).

[4] Neuschäfer, p. 78nl.

[5] Jules Coulet, *Etudes sur l'ancien poème français du Voyage de Charlemagne en Orient* (Montpellier, 1907).

[6] Jules Horrent, *Le Pèlerinage de Charlemagne: Essai d'explication littéraire avec des notes de critique textuelle,* Bibl. de la Fac. de Phil. et Let. de l'Univ. de Liège, no. 158 (P., 1961), pp. 9ff.

[7] Tyssens summarizes Horrent's compilation in pp. v-vi of her critical translation. To these lists should be added Sara Sturm's interpretation that the poem is a comic expansion of a literal measurement. See her "Stature of Charlemagne in the *Pèlerinage,*" *Studies in Philology,* 71 (1974), 18.

[8] The full title is *Descriptio qualiter Karolus Magnus clauum et coronam Domini a Constantinopoli Aquisgrani detulerit qualiterque Karolus Caluus hec ad Sanctum Dionysium retulerit,* ed. F. Castets, *RLR,* 36 (1892), 439-474. Ronald N. Walpole develops his argument in "The *Pèlerinage de Charlemagne:* Poem, Legend, and Problem," *RPh,* 8:3 (Feb. 1955), 181ff.

[9] Neuschäfer, esp. p. 93.

[10] Neuschäfer, pp. 100ff. Cf. Horrent's refutation, p. 126nl.

[11] Paul Aebischer, *Les Versions norroises du "Voyage de Charlemagne en Orient,"* Bibl. de la Fac. de Phil. et Let. de l'Univ. de Liège, no. 140 (p., 1956), p. 161.

[12] Gérard Genette, *Introduction à l'architexture,* (P.: Seuil, 1979), pp. 70f.

[13] See Tzvetan Todorov, *Les Genres du discours* (P.: Seuil, 1978), p. 50, who relies here on the notion of "Erwartungshorizont des Publikums" coined by Hans R. Jauss in *Untersuchungen zur mittelalterlichen Tierepik,* Beih. zur ZrPh, no. 100,

Tübingen, 1959.

[14]Georges Lukacs, *La Théorie du roman,* trans. Jean Clairevoye (n.p.: Editions Gonthier, 1963), p. 32.

[15]Cf. Sturm cited n. 7 supra.

[16]"Oïstes les parler si remaindrum ami?" v. 624, ed. Aebischer.

[17]"Oïstes les parler s'il remandront a mi?" v. 624, ed. Koschwitz.

[18]See for ex., *La Chanson de Roland,* ed. Georges Moignet (P.: Bordas, 1969).

[19]The second of the triad on the theme of time gone past in *Le Testament.* See for ex., *Poésies complètes,* ed. Robert Guiette (P.: Gallimard, 1964), pp. 67f.

[20]These terms are commonly used to characterize genre. See Genette, p. 72.

[21]René Wellek and Austin Warren, *Theory of Literature,* 3rd ed. (N.Y.: Harcourt, 1962), ch. 17, esp. p. 226.

[22]Lucien Goldmann, "Introduction aux premiers écrits de Georges Lukacs," in Lukacs, *Théorie,* p. 173.

[23]In the *Roland,* the narrator explains that the hero laments Turpin's demise "a la lei de sa tere" (v. 2251, ed. Moignet). See also the discussion by Guido Favati, ed. *Il "Voyage de Charlemagne,"* Bibl. degli Studi mediolat. e volg., no. 4 (Bologna: Libreria Antiquaria Palmaverde, 1965), pp. 46ff.

[24]For details on the special semantic problems of the *gab,* see my forthcoming "The *Gab* as a Latent Sub-Genre."

[25]These remarks paraphrase Todorov, p. 53.

[26]Quoted from *Le Livre à venir* (P., 1959) by Todorov, p. 44.

[27]Neuschäfer (p. 82) offers a sensitive interpretation of the poem's opening lines.

[28]On the notion that *gabs* were games see the 17th-c. anecdote reported by Godefroy, s.v. *gab,* pp. 197f.

[29]*Versions norroises,* pp. 9, 161.

[30]Favati, pp. 79f.

PSEUDO-HISTORICAL DISCOURSE IN FICTION: *CLIGES**

Donald Maddox

It has been said in countless ways that in his writings "Medieval Man," whoever *he* was, made no significant distinction between history and fiction. Alluding to the synonymy of *story* and *history* in medieval narrative, C. S. Lewis bluntly asserted that "the distinction between history and fiction cannot, in its modern clarity, be applied to medieval books or to the spirit in which they were read."[1] Modern scholarship has disclosed to what a great extent medieval historiography, despite its frequent claims to veracity, valorized rhetorically polished, edifying commentary over documentation.[2] In medieval literary texts history and fiction may also combine for exemplary or edifying purposes. In the lives of the saints and the *chansons de geste* great legendary figures and events are often commemorated with a blend of documentable fact and fictive detail and offered candidly as true accounts. Conversely, in works for which no protestation of veracity is made, as in some narratives drawn from the *matière de Bretagne,* fantasy may be diluted by elements that promote a strong sense of the mimetic and of the historical.

It is the intent of this essay to suggest, using the example of *Cligés,* that if "history" and "fiction" do not normally constitute a pertinent opposition in medieval narrative, it is not because medieval authors were incapable of distinguishing between them. The example drawn from the works of Chrétien de Troyes would suggest that these writers were no less aware of the difference than their descendants, but that they were less concerned with veracity *per se* than with the effects that might be achieved through selective integration of mimetic and historical detail with fictive elements. Prior to consideration of what specific effects Chrétien appears to achieve in *Cligés,* some general comments are in order with regard to the relative significance of "truth" and fiction in contemporaneous writing.

In general, we find that medieval vernacular texts reflect a tacit assumption that historiographic writing and fiction share the same mode of representational "telling." The utterance identified by Roland Barthes as fundamental to all historical discourse, one which asserts simply that in fact *this happened,* occurs in romance no less than in saint's life, epic, or chronicle.[3] Likewise, extra-literary referents and fictive detail co-exist in all of the narrative genres. For example, consider a few lexical items from the categories of proper names and toponyms, such as Alexander and Babylon, Eufemiiens and Rome, Charlemagne and Aix-la-Chappelle, Arthur and Cardigan. All were potentially receivable in the twelfth century as terms with historical referents. Yet each, in varying degrees depending on texts, is at one time or another assimilated to the context of narrative fiction. In modern conceptualizations of narrative, one determinant of the distinction between historical and fictive writing is the manner in which such historically referential terms are predicated.[4] Charlemagne at Roncevaux and Charlemagne arguing with his spouse are familiar situations to readers of the *Geste du roi,* yet to even the most casual modern observer of Carolingian history, the former is evocative of a more fully historical referential field because of its predication. The fact that both types of situation often occur in the same medieval narrative context would seem to corroborate assertions that medieval authors were inclined to blur the distinction between documentable and imaginary events.

There is also evidence that protestations of "truth" were made as readily for the one type of situation as for the other. It will be recalled that Jehan Bodel drew a distinction between the *voir* narratives of the *matière de France* and the *vain et plaisant* stories based on the *matière de Bretagne.*[5] The issue of "truth" also concerned Wace who, following the lead of Geoffrey of Monmouth, presents his translated pseudo-chronicle of Britain as true: "Maistre Wace l'ad translaté / Ki en conte la vérité."[6] Yet these two examples show that "truth" is not a matter of documentation and fact, for neither the *Chanson des Saisnes* nor the *Roman de Brut* and its Latin prototype is remarkable for the veracity of its account. Other criteria of "truth" are clearly involved.

Such "truth" may in these two instances designate a legendary nucleus, that element of factual or "eyewitness" detail around which fiction has been elaborated in the reworking of sources. Yet with reference specifically to the distinction drawn by Bodel, Douglas Kelly has suggested that "truth" designates "the truth of topical invention as Material Style, a truth whose validity is determined by established social typology rather than by documentation."[7] Truth is thus a matter of the correct generic representation of social hierarchies, so that persons, as well as their attributes and actions, consistently conform with high, middle, or low styles. "The identification of such properties aids the reader in finding the work's context, and through the context the author's intention in inventing it."[8] By appealing allusively to the expectation of a certain generic coherence, or intrinsic "truth" to the *matière,* the author may create what Hans Robert Jauss has called a narrative that "wants to be believed" on account of its inherent verisimilitude.[9] Hayden White has argued that modern historical writing owes its coherence and effect less to the veracity of its content than to the way in which generic norms of narrative are maintained so that, in effect, historical and fictive writing have a closer kinship than is often admitted.[10] Likewise, generic and stylistic coherence is more important than veracity in determining the "truth" and "verisimilitude" of medieval narrative.

Verisimilar "truth" is frequently no less ethical than descriptive, however. In both historiographic and fictive narrative of the twelfth century, a familiar exordial commonplace extols the circumstances of an earlier, ethically superior age and introduces a narrative exemplary of this claim.[11] In terms of genres, verisimilitude and veracity most often coincide in the *chanson de geste* and the historiographic text, according to Zumthor, while in the romance, verisimilitude is restricted to a moral *sens*.[12] Wisdom and moral truth are perennially to be found in even the most extreme forms of the fabulous and the fantastic, as storytellers and romance authors have always known. That these could be emphasized in romance more effectively by a *bele conjointure* was Chrétien's refinement of this tradition, by recourse to the rhetorical premise that one must "teach well" by "speaking well," as he reminds us in his prologue to *Erec*, v. 12. The concept of access to covert higher "truth" by means of an attractive esthetic surface is central to Chrétien's project, and in *Erec*, the *Charrette, Yvain,* and the *Conte del graal,* we find a vast array of fictive elements in service to a chivalric and courtly ethos. This view of "truth" as the kernel overlain with a beautiful integument finds expression in contemporaneous Latin writings as well.[13]

It seems, then that verisimilitude, whether it be at the level of *sensus litteralis* or of *sensus moralis*, is a stronger criterion of "truth" than is veracity, in both the production and the receptin of narrative of this period. And, without in any way implying that "Medieval Man" was credulous, it is evident that his admissible spectrum of the verisimilar was far broader than ours, certainly during the pre-Aristotelian twelfth century.

A case in point is *Cligés*. In contrast with the other works of Chrétien, we recognize in this romance a kind of nervous preoccupation with extra-literary referents, yet these are woven into a folk narrative replete with fantastic elements.[14] Scholars have discussed at length the apparent allusive distortion of historical and contemporaneous circumstances in Constantinople, Saxony, and Germany, identifying it with a kind of so-called "realism" which has repeatedly been foraged for information pertinent to the chronology of Chrétien's works and to suggest that *Cligés* reflects thinly-disguised real-life circumstances.[15]

As early as 1908, W. P. Ker in *Epic and Romance* said that *Cligés* is the romance which "best corresponds to the later type of novel . . ." because it lacks what Ker called the basic "machinery" of romance, such as ". . . enchanters, dragons, magic mists and deadly castles . . ."[16] More recently,

Anthime Fourrier has maintained that *Cligés* is one of a select few Old French romances that might be called *romans-miroir* because they reflect more aspects of extra-literary reality than do the *romans-évasion.* The latter category includes the majority of Old French romances because they presumably "make us forget our own situation . . . . "[17]

Paradoxically, however, reminiscences of historical events and descriptive realism pervasive early in *Cligés* eventually thin out and give way to *évasion.* As the story moves into the later events leading up to, including, and following the *fausse mort* of Fénice, we watch the fictive *conte* unleash its potions, torture, suspended animation, and convenient sudden death with a sense that mimesis has largely ceded to fantasy. If hair-pulling is not among the tactics used on Fénice by the three physicians of Salerno, the story itself begins to seem increasingly *tiré par les cheveux.* One begins to wonder if the production of a "reality effect" early in the story would have sufficed to suspend the disbelief of the medieval listener as effectively as the potion suspends the animation of Fénice.

Because of its Janus-like profile with regard to extra-literary reality on the one hand and fantasy on the other, *Cligés* would seem to be an appropriate text with which to consider how non-legendary, non-historiographic narrative might deal with mimetic and historiographic properties.

Fourrier has already addressed himself to this problem. While his distinction between *évasion* and *miroir* usefully brings into opposition criteria of fantasy and those of mimesis, his study of *Cligés* does not extensively focus on intrinsic aspects of this work. Instead, he compares *Cligés* and Byzantine relations with the West during the 1170's, adducing textual reminiscences of possible historical counterparts.[18] By maintaining the focus of his study primarily outside of the text, Fourrier does not adequately show the extent to which the narrative, in its intrinsic development, departs from the norms of the so-called *roman-évasion.*

A more serious problem inheres in the tacit assumption upon which the *évasion / miroir* distinction is based. By attaching the substantive "roman" to these epithets, it is implied that the *roman-miroir* is a generic entity completely distinct from the *roman-évasion.* It would have been better to acknowledge that one may find *évasion* in the *miroir* and vice-versa. The magic of Thessala, the feigned death of Fénice, and the molten lead of the physicians all coexist within a text otherwise laden with realia of every sort, while in *Yvain,* for example, *évasion* toward the magically animated events at the castle of Laudine nonetheless retains many aspects of twelfth-century feudal life. There is a *courant réaliste* in each of Chrétien's romances, which the terms *miroir* and *évasion* are *both* descriptive of discursive features in *Cligès*.

Rather than pursue an unduly rigid classification of romance into subgenres represented by specific texts, we might do well to adopt a more flexible approach by asking what types of discursive properties inform octosyllabic romance. By basing our classification on categories of discursive properties rather than by categorizing specific works within a genre, we can preserve a critical sense of generic integrity while at the same time disclosing the extent to which the genre is transformed by each new work that brings with it a fresh combination of discursive properties.[19] Expressed in the terminology of Fourrier, this would mean that instead of making an inventory of works under such rubrics as *roman-évasion, roman-miroir, roman idyllique, roman picaresque, roman fantastique*, etc., we might instead identify constituent features of the *discours-évasion,* the *discours-miroir,* the *discours picaresque,* etc., as they occur in the diachronic transformations of the *roman*. This approach would enhance the results of hermeneutics and further the inductive elaboration of a descriptive poetics of vernacular narrative.

Such an enterprise is obviously beyond the scope of a single investigation. In what follows, we shall examine discursive features in *Cligès* which, by virtue of either their mimetic or historiographic qualities, create a level of coherence exemplary of pseudo-historical discourse. This term is descriptive of a coherence perceived in critical reception. With regard to literary production, it designates the modulation of fictive sources so as to heighten the sense of extra-literary referentiality while diminishing, either intermittently or throughout a work, the sense that what is being told is fiction and not fact.

Already in the 44-line prologue to *Cligès* we find oscillation between images of fictive writing and historical subjects.[20] In the first seven lines we are told what the author has already written: *Erec et Enide,* translations of two Ovidian treatises, vernacular versions of two stories from the *Metamorphoses*, and something entitled "king Mark and the blonde Iseut." The narrator then says that Chrétien is beginning a "novel conte," a term which, because of the epithet "novel", implies that *Cligès* may be classified with its fictive predecessors. Yet this is followed in verses 18 through 27 by a claim of veracity: "The story I intend to tell you, we find written in one of the books of the library of my lord Saint Peter at Beauvais. Therefrom was drawn the story (*conte*) which attests to the truth of the account (*estoire*). For this reason it is more worthy of belief."[21] Of this passage, Fourrier has remarked that "the author himself indicates that the book was a sort of chronicle . . ."[22] Note, however, that the claim of veracity is embedded; it is neither the narrator nor the author, but the source, the *conte,* which made the claim of veracity in the *estoire.* Moreover, the antecedent of "this" in "For this reason" remains ambiguous. We are therefore uncertain if the account is worthy of belief because of the claim of veracity made for it in the source. It could just as well be because of the masterful way in which Chrétien has extracted and refashioned the story in which the account is related, as he had done with the source of *Erec.*[23] Chrétien exploits this ambiguity to counter-balance the generic, stylistic, and ethical "truth" of the poetic vocation to which this catalogue of his writings attests, with the factual, referential, extra-literary "truth" which is the formulaic objective of the historiographer.[24] The two images conflate in this protestation. In fact, Chrétien tips the balance in favor of the latter when the narrator says that "by the books that we possess, we know the deeds of the ancients and of the world in former times" (vv. 25-26). This topos casts new light on verses 8 through 13, where we were told that the story is about a Greek youth of King Arthur's lineage, prefaced by the life and lineage of his father. This particular book, then, takes us back to the lifetime of one of the Nine Worthies, thus to a moment recognized in the Middle Ages as historical, and to the deeds of a particular family during the lifetime of Arthur, the seventh of the nine.[25] On balance, the prologue subtly implies that an established author of fiction has realized a work of historio-graphic significance in his latest venture.

Despite these historiographic indices, critical reception of *Cligés* has shown that Chrétien's *conte* is in fact a composite reflecting a considerable array of sources, including intertextual play with the *Tristan,* the *Brut, Enéas,* and other works.[26] We find broad hints at the fictive background throughout the text. One such introduces the second part of the story dealing with the exploits of Cligés: "This is Cligés," says the narrator, "in whose memory this account was put into the Romance idiom" (vv. 2345-46). As Frappier has suggested, the tenor of these lines could be construed as introductory of the authentic source, which might not have included the story of Alexandre and Soredamors.[27] Did Chrétien, perhaps to emulate the bipartite *Tristan,* fabricate the story of Cligés' parents? This notion is reinforced by the fact that the thirteenth-century story of Cligés in *Marques de Rome* contains no trace of the parents, and if Chrétien's alleged source at Beauvais—provided even this is not a fictive representation—was the same version of the *fausse morte* found in *Marques de Rome,* then Chrétien has indeed fused two separate accounts and attempted in the prologue to present them as one true, historical narration.[28] Whatever the case, the prologue is clearly an effort to dissimulate the heterogeneity of sources by an appearance of historical authenticity. Antici-pation of the believable and the historical could thus be awakened in the mind of the hearer, who might either suspend disbelief of more implausible elements, such as magic and molten lead, or else view these fantastic details as part of a deliberate contrast with earlier mimetic and historical elements. One function of pseudo-historical discursive elements in fiction would perhaps be to manipulate the quality and effects of reception.

So as better to recognize the pseudo-historical type of discourse, let me revert momentarily to the hypothesis of Jauss concerning the use of sources.[29] Jauss identifies a progressive "fictionalization" of exotic traditions whose original legendary import was lost through transposition to an alien cultural context. On foreign soil, epic and legend tend to be read as romance because understood apart from their original ideological coherence, as Nathaniel Griffin suggested.[30] Accordingly, the Byzantine and Celtic varieties of the *merveilleux* in romance are symptoms of the perceived alterity of its sources, and the predominance of these elements helps to confine verisimilitude to the level of ethical significance.

In the concept of "fictionalization" as in the distinction between *évasion* and *miroir,* there is an implicit norm, whereby the inherited exotic traditions of romance characteristically shift toward fantasy and away from mimesis on a spectrum created by the antagonism between these two terms. Yet in certain texts like *Cligés* we find a shift toward the opposite, referential polarity. This is not the result of a quantum change in the genre, however. It reflects what Franz H. Bäuml has recently identified as "the development of an illusionistic function in narrative texts" beginning in the second half of the twelfth century.[31] The advent of a vernacular written tradition made possible the "manipulation" of writing so as to achieve new effects. Chief among these was the creation of an "illusion that the fiction is not a fiction" by breaching the boundary between the text and extra-textual 'reality'." Bäuml traces "the increasing use of the fictional structure of space and time in terms of extra-textual 'reality' " from "the classical Arthurian romances of Chrétien and Hartmann von Aue."[32] At or near the inception of this trend is *Cligés,* which contrasts with the earlier *Erec* precisely on the basis of its "illusionistic" tendencies and its use of a variety of properties identifiable with pseudo-historical discourse.

The norm of a specific topographical locus of events is established in the 400-line account of the siege of Windsor Castle (vv. 1625-2035). The detailed description suggests first-hand familiarity with the area. Moreover, the Arthurian army consists of men from England, Wales, Scotland, and Cornwall, rather than from a variety of realms, many of which are fantastic, as in the Arthurian court at Pentecost in *Erec* (vv. 1884-1954). The Thames is crossed, not by a sword bridge, but at a ford, made possible by the severe drought of that year. With the help of the Greek warriors, the siege unfolds in phases characterized by a specific, premeditated strategy, conceived in deliberation, or *porpensemanz,* 1802-03. (This term is used often in a similar sense by Villehardouin in *La Conquète de Constantinople.*) There is a clear division of labor among the Greeks, and the action is seldom restricted to the point of view of one hero, as in much romance, but is constantly shifting perspective from one group to another. The moonrise that reveals the ambush of the traitors is attributed to divine intervention. Although reminiscent of the epic *merveilleux,* attributions similar to these, reflecting the causation of providential history, are widespread in historiographic texts from the time of Bede through the fifteenth century. While occasionally reminiscent of the style of the *chanson de geste* or of the classical epic, treatment of geographical and topographical detail betrays an affinity with vernacular historiographic writing of the late twelfth and early thirteenth century.[33]

The Saxon ambush of the Greeks and the Germans later in the story is also highly detailed, and Jacques Stiennon has shown that the marvelous tower created by Jehan is remarkably similar to likely Byzantine prototypes.[34] Mimesis is also evident in the wealth of toponyms scattered across a large portion of the known twelfth-century world. The detailed prospect of Windsor or of the Danube from Regensburg fosters an impression that because environment is extensively depicted in these instances, but for reasons of economy it would have been equally possible to describe London or Constantinople in minute detail.[35]

Along with a kind of spatial mimesis unparalleled anywhere else in Chrétien, we find that temporality is used to heighten the referential illusion. In contrast with the exclusive use of the Church Calendar to indicate temporal segments in *Erec,* time in *Cligés* is reckoned by months, weeks, days, and hours.[36] While the Church Calendar imposes upon *Erec* a cyclical sense of time as being periodically abolished and renewed according to the rhythms of the Christian paradigm, secular time systems in *Cligés* suggest a linear conception of human history. Perhaps the best example of such a conception in *Cligés* is the one already implicit in the exordial *translatio:* "Our books have taught us that in Greece there was once pre-eminence in chivalry and learning. Then passed chivalry to Rome, and highest learning, which now has come to France" (vv. 28-33). Here the concept of time is historical, acknowledging a cyclical rhythm in the rise and fall of civilizations which are displaced in irreversible chronological succession.[37] The narrator hopes that France will always remain the center of learning (vv. 34-37). Yet the example of earlier Greek and Roman decline (vv. 38-42) is no assurance that the honor of France, in its turn, will not one day be displaced.

In the narrative, there is an acute sense of the precariousness of military dominance among world powers. England boasts the Arthurian chivalric ideal, to which Alexandre and Cligés strive to conform, yet the influence of Greece is nascent. The Byzantines save the kingdom for Arthur and later outbid and outfight Saxony while seeking a marital alliance with Germany. It is frequently apparent that the balance of world power is fragile and subject to change because of military success, weak leadership, or a realignment of powers. Throughout all of this, chivalry abounds, yet of learning there is scant evidence, presumably because, according to the prologue, *clergie* resides in France which is within the twelfth-century temporal context of the author, well after the allegedly Arthurian events in the story itself. Projection of current Greco-German relations, altered in various significant ways, onto a remote past imposes recognition that historiographic referents are being assimilated to the pseudo-historical irony of anachronism.

Of capital importance to the constitution of pseudo-historical discourse in *Cligés* is the predominance of action over event. Jauss has evoked the Hegelian distinction between epic action (*Handlung*) and the type of event (*Geschehen*) characteristic of romance. According to this distinction, events in the *chanson de geste* are typically consequent upon "the conscious decision and action" of the hero, who acts on behalf of the "Christian and national community" as the agent of "supra-personal and objective events . . ." By contrast, events in Arthurian romance more often result from fortuitous occurrences encountered by the lone itinerant knight, and these events derive their exemplary significance "uniquely with regard to the central character . . ."[38] While *Erec* compares favorably with this scheme, *Cligés* is totally at odds with it. At no time do the chivalric heroes journey without specific itineraries, nor do they ever encounter fortuitous adventures significant to themselves alone.

Alexandre's confrontation with Angrés is motivated by the civil war in England, while Cligés encounters the Duke of Saxony as an agent of the combined forces of Greece and Germany. Nor is "bride-winning" the fortuitous result of a quest. Alis marries Fénice in order to bring about an alliance between Greece and Germany, while the Duke of Saxony had apparently had a similar goal in mind in seeking the hand of the German emperor's daughter. The marriage of Alexandre and Soredamors is not motivated by political ambition, but it does come about as a result of Alexandre's consciousness of a political and social order greater than that of his own empire, which he leaves behind in order to augment his political and social standing. With the exception of the retreat of Cligés and Fénice into the tower, which is in complete disregard for the political and social establishment, the characters behave as beings who are conscious of their situation within a social structure that imposes action and displacement from one realm to another. Absent are the dark forces that propel the questing knight in a pattern of separation from and return to a particular court.[39] Adherence to the epic model of action brings *Cligès* much closer to the type of causation and motivation typical of historiographic narrative. Indeed, it is precisely this aspect of *Cligès* which has prompted the search for analogues in contemporaneous historical situations.

As this partial sampling of pseudo-historical elements in the text already suggests, their distribution is very uneven. Initially, segments rich in pseudo-historical discursive properties seem to alternate with other types of narration, ultimately shading into the events surrounding the ruse of the "false death." Yet the pseudo-historical mode returns with a flourish in the epilogue, where we learn that because Fénice deceived Alis, subsequent Byzantine emperors confined their empresses to constant attendance by eunuchs, whence pseudo-historicism in service of aetiology. By attributing the origin of such a practice to the reign of Alis, the story locates a new pseudo-historical niche. It is thus once again devalued as pure fiction as it appears to refer to a certain span of historical time.

Like any type of discourse, the discursive mode identified here as pseudo-historical is not necessarily tantamount to an aprioristic category at the disposal of an author. It may well be a common denominator in contemporaneous writing, whether it be purportedly fictive or historiographic. Chrétien certainly did not invent it, nor does *Cligès* by any means exhaust its potential devices. Just as analysis of the *discours amoureux* in *Cligès* reveals a substratum composed of a wide variety of elements, notably those bearing the imprint of Ovid, one might perceive in the pseudo-historical discourse of Chrétien traces of the *Enéas,* the *Brut,* as well, perhaps, as those of Virgil, Statius, Vegetius, Boethius, Geoffrey of Monmouth, and who knows how many others, faintly limned? Yet discursive coherence is more than an intertextual palimpsest or a mosaic of sources. It is the cumulative result of a *combinatoire* of widely disparate elements. Pluralistic in terms of production, it is the coherent effect of reception, both in modern criticism and by Chrétien's contemporaries.

To what purpose did Chrétien repeatedly establish and then subvert extra-literary referentiality in *Cligès?* There can be no doubt that he was manipulating some aspects of what was known about historical reality, as Hofer, Fourrier, Misrahi and others have argued.[40] It would seem that, not unlike other types of discourse in *Cligès,* the pseudo-historical variety is part of the author's ironic play with sources and conventions.[41] The high frequency of more or less distorted resemblances to Byzantine and Germanic political life may result from an authorial desire to adopt an ironic attitude toward current events by creating the anachronism of an Arthurianized 1170's and by using pseudo-historical elements to evoke well-known contemporary issues, but in a critical or satirical vein. Rather than assert that *this happened* and have it received as if it indeed had occurred, Chrétien is perhaps saying to his public: "*What if* that which we all know about had happened this way instead?" Such an attitude is not unlike the kind adopted by modern novelists as they indulge in fictional explorations of possible universes suggested by current events. If *Cligès* was to have fulfilled an instructive function for the contemporary public, as did *Erec* according to verse 12 of its prologue, depiction of a meaningfully altered facsimile of real-world events may have played a vital role in such an objective. Any significance these alterations acquired in the ethical verisimilitude or *sens* of the work may be forever lost to the modern reader in the "insuperable alterity" of the Court of Champagne.[42]

Whatever the unique intent of Chrétien, the repeated flagrant subversions of pseudo-historical referentiality by elements of fantasy ultimately disclose the illusory nature of historical discourse itself. The naive assumption of a transcendental historical signified is a mirage. Chrétien illustrates what Barthes would much later say about historical discourse, that "reality is nothing but a meaning, and so can be changed to meet the needs of history, when history demands the subversion of the foundations of civilization 'as we know it'."[43] Whether Chrétien met the needs of history and, moreover, of *whose* history, are open questions perhaps forever to remain unanswered. Yet why should we even ask them? Is this a political discourse, after all? By cultivating a level of coherence which we have identified as pseudo-historical discourse, the poet has met the perennial needs of FICTION to renew itself within its potentially narrow generic prison cell. In so doing, he has by no means created a new twelfth-century genre or sub-genre—no *roman-miroir,* no pseudo-chronicle or pseudo-historical romance. Rather, by exploiting the potential of a relatively new genre of discourse by contrast with what we find in *Erec et Enide,* he has multiplied devices that he will employ in his own later romances while broadening the twelfth-century generic "horizon of expectations." He has also unwittingly ensured that twentieth-century literary scholars, faced with accounting for the generic eccentricities of such a work as *Cligès,* will sooner or later be forced to accept the fact that if in their discourse on genres there are no archetypal generic forms, as was once maintained, there is nevertheless a potential infinity of genres of discourse.

University of Connecticut, Storrs

NOTES

*An earlier version of this essay was presented at the Twelfth International Arthurian Congress, Regensbury, August 13, 1979.

[1]C. S. Lewis, *The Discarded Image: An Introduction to Medieval and Renaissance Literature* (Cambridge: Cambridge Univ. Press, 1967), p. 179.

[2]See the useful survey by Roger D. Ray, "Medieval Historiography through the Twelfth Century: Problems and Progress of Research," *Viator, Medieval and Renaissance Studies,* 5 (1974), 33-59. On the similarity of twelfth-century romance and historical writing, see I. D. O. Arnold and M. M. Pelan, eds., *La Partie arthurienne du Roman de Brut* (Paris: Klincksieck, 1962), p. 17; and Paul Zumthor, "Roman et histoire, aux sources d'un univers narratif," *Langue, texte, énigme* (Paris: Seuil, 1975), pp. 237-48.

[3]Roland Barthes, "Historical Discourse," in *Introduction to Structuralism,* ed. Michael Lane (New York: Harper, 1970), p. 154.

[4]On the difference between strictly fictional statements and statements about reality as a difference in predication, see Hector-Neri Castaneda, "Fiction and Reality: Their Fundamental Connections," *Poetics,* 8 (1979), 31-62.

[5]Jehan Bodel, *Saxenlied,* F. Menzel and E. Stengel, eds. (Marburg, 1906-09), vv. 6-12.

[6]Ivor Arnold, ed., *Le Roman de Brut, de Wace* (Paris, 1938), I, vv. 7-8.

[7]Douglas Kelly, "Topical Invention in Medieval French Literature," in *Medieval Eloquence: Studies in the Theory and Practice of Medieval Rhetoric,* James J. Murphy, ed. (Berkeley and Los Angeles: Univ. of California Press, 1978), p. 238.

[8]Kelly, p. 237.

[9]Hans Robert Jauss, "Chanson de geste et roman courtois (Analyse comparative du *Fierabras* et du *Bel Inconnu*)," in *Chanson de geste und höfischer Roman. Heidelberger Kolloquium. 30 Januar 1961* (Heidelberg: Winter, 1963), p. 65.

[10]Hayden White, *Tropics of Discourse: Essays in Cultural Criticism* (Baltimore and London: The Johns Hopkins Univ. Press, 1978), esp. pp. 27-134.

[11]Two well-known but quite different examples occur in MS L of the *Vie de Saint Alexis* and Chrétien's *Yvain*.

[12]Zumthor, *Langue, texte, énigme*, p. 246.

[13]As in this passage from the *De planctu Naturae* of Alain de Lille:

> in superficiali litterae cortice falsum resonat lyra poetica, sed interius, auditoribus secretum intelligentiae altioris eloquitur, ut exteriore falsitatis abjecto putamine, dulciorem nucleum veritatis secrete intus lector inveniat. Poetae tamen aliquando historiales eventus joculationibus fabulosis quadam eleganti fictura confoederant, ut ex diversorum competenti junctura, ipsius narrationis elegantior pictura resultet. (Ed. Migne, ccx, 451)

See Claude Luttrell, *The Creation of the First Arthurian Romance, A Quest* (Evanston: Northwestern University Press, 1974), pp. 67-68, who relates the passage to *conjointure* in Chrétien. On the theory of *integumentum,* see Brian Stock, *Myth and Science in the Twelfth Century: A Study of Bernard Sylvester* (Princeton: Princeton University Press, 1972). As it applies to *Erec,* see Luttrell, and my "Nature and Narrative in Chrétien's *Erec et Enide," Mediaevalia,* 3 (1977), 59-82. On the role of topical invention and Material Style in the production of *conjointure,* see Kelly, pp. 236-49.

[14]For the background of the folktale, see Henri Hauvette, *La Morte vivante* (Paris: Boivin, 1931).

[15]Space does not permit a discussion of studies that present hypotheses concerning the historical sources of *Cligès.* (For a partial list, see note 40.) Most of these are based on the depiction of relations between Germany, Saxony and Constantinople and possible historical prototypes. For a survey of work in this area, see my "Critical Trends and Recent Work on the *Cligès* of Chrétien de Troyes," *NeuphilMitt,* 74 (1973), 740-41.

[16]W. P. Ker, *Epic and Romance* (London: MacMillan, 1908), p. 359.

[17]Anthime Fourrier, *Le Courant réaliste dans le roman courtois en France au Moyen Age* (Paris: Nizet, 1960), pp. 11-15.

[18]Fourrier, pp. 111-78.

[19]Tzvetan Todorov has defined a literary genre as "a codification of discursive properties." See "L'Origine des genres," *Les Genres du discours* (Paris: Seuil, 1978), pp. 44-60.

[20]All citations of *Cligès* are from the edition by A. Micha, CFMA, 84 (Paris, 1968).

[21]My translation. "Ceste estoire trovons escrite, / Que conter vos vuel et retraire, / En un livre de l'aumaire / Mon seignor saint Pere a Biauvez; / De la fu li contes estrez / Qui tesmoigne l'estoire a voire: / Por ce fet ele mialz a croire."

[22]Fourrier, p. 159.

[23]*Erec et Enide,* vv. 13-14: "et tret d'un conte d'avanture / une molt bele conjointure . . . "

[24]I cannot agree that Chrétien in this prologue "has extracted the myth from the context of historical truth and transposed it so that it is completely circumscribed and defined by the world of romance fiction," as maintained by Michelle A. Freeman, in *The Poetics of Translatio Studii and Conjointure: Chrétien de Troyes' Cligés* (Lexington, Ky.: French Forum, 1979), p. 36. In the guise of historiographer, he is creating the illusion of an historical truth which he will repeatedly subvert with the devices of romance throughout the work. On the significance of the *translatio* in this prologue and elsewhere, see Douglas Kelly, "*Translatio studii:* Translation, Adaptation, and Allegory in Medieval French Literature," *PQ,* 57 (1978), 287-310.

[25]On the Nine Worthies, see Lewis, p. 181, who identifies them as part of a conventional historical past in medival thought.

[26]See my "Critical Trends," pp. 730-37.

[27]Jean Frappier, *Le Roman breton, Chrétien de Troyes, Cligés* (Paris: Centre de Documentation Universitaire, 1951), pp. 43-46.

[28]*Le Roman de Marques de Rome,* J. Alton, ed. (Tübingen, 1889).

[29]Jauss, p. 67.

[30]Nathaniel E. Griffin, "The Definition of Romance," *PMLA,* 38 (1923), 50-70.

[31]Franz H. Bäuml, "Varieties and Consequences of Medieval Literacy and Illiteracy," *Speculum,* 55 (1980), 264.

[32]Bäuml, pp. 249-62.

[33]Descriptive passages of armed warfare in *Cligés* compare especially favorably with similar passages in the *Conquête de Constantinople* of Villehardouin, whose style has been characterized as "epic". See Jeannette M. A. Beer, *Villehardouin, Epic Historian,* Etudes de Philologie et d'Histoire, 7 (Geneva: Droz, 1968). The accounts of Villehardouin abound with the formulae of providential history, e. g., "Dieu lor dona

bon tems . . ."; "au tierz jor lor dona Dieu bon vent . . ."; "se Dieu ne amast ceste ost, . . . il ne peust mie tenir ensemble . . . ," etc. *La Conquête de Constantinople,* in *Historiens et chroniqueurs du Moyen Age,* Albert Pauphilet, ed. (Paris: Gallimard, 1952), pp. 119; 121; 115. On providential historiography in the Middle Ages, see Ray, pp. 53-59. An example of the use of *porpensemanz* by Villehardouin, with reference to the planning of the Fourth Crusade: " . . . la somme del conseil si fu tel . . . le lundi iroient a l'assaut . . . assaudroient deus nefs a une tor . . . cil de la tor estoient plus que cil de l'eschiele. Et por ce si fu bons *porpensemanz* que plus greveroient deus eschieles a une tor que une" (*Conquête,* p. 144).

[34]Jacques Stiennon, "Histoire de l'art et fiction poétique dans un épisode du *Cligés* de Chrétien de Troyes," in *Mélanges Rita Lejeune* (Gembloux, 1969), I, pp. 659-708.

[35]On the descriptive "realism" of vernacular narrative and analogous developments in pictorial imagery, see Bäuml, pp. 259-65.

[36]For an extended discussion of the temporal dimension in *Erec,* see my *Structure and Sacring: The Systematic Kingdom in Chrétien's Erec et Enide* (Lexington, Ky.: French Forum, 1978), pp. 155-63. On chronology in *Cligés,* see Peter Noble, "Alis and the Problem of Time in *Cligés,*" *Medium Aevum,* 39 (1970), 28-31.

[37]Pierre Duhem distinguishes between two fundamental theories of time in Western thought, one reflecting a neo-Platonic preoccupation with absolute, extrasensory temporality, the other a neo-Aristotelian perception of temporality in the movements of the phenomenal world. The temporal context of *Erec* would be a variety of the neo-Platonic view which was current in the twelfth century. See Pitrim A. Sorokin, *Social and Cultural Dynamics,* vol. II. *Fluctuations of Systems of Truth, Ethics, and Law* (New York: American, 1937), p. 368. The temporal dimension in *Cligés* anticipates the "progressively linear conception of human history" which becomes widespread only after the beginning of the seventeenth century. See Sorokin, II, p. 375.

[38]Jauss, pp. 71-72.

[39]On this pattern see Erich Köhler, *L'Aventure chevaleresque, Idéal et réalité dans le roman courtois,* trans. E. Kaufholz (Paris: Gallimard, 1974), pp. 77-102.

[40]Stefan Hofer, "Streitfragen zu Kristian: eine neue Datierung des *Cligés* und der übrigen Werke Kristians," *ZfSL,* 50 (1937), 335-43; Fourrier, pp. 160-78; Jean Misrahi, "More Light on the Chronology of Chrétien de Troyes," *BBIAS,* 11 (1959), 89-120.

[41] See Peter Haidu, *Aesthetic Distance in Chrétien de Troyes: Irony and Comedy in Cligés and Perceval* (Geneva: Droz, 1968), for an extended treatment of this attitude. See also by the same author, "Au début du roman, l'ironie," *Poétique*, 36 (1978), 443-66.

[42] The nature of medieval alterity is discussed at length by Hans Robert Jauss, "The Alterity and Modernity of Medieval Literature," *MLH*, 10 (1979), 181-229. See John F. Benton, "The Court of Champagne as a Literary Center," *Speculum*, 36 (1961), 551-91; on the relations between this court and Germany, Saxony, and Byzantium see, in addition to items in note 40, Maurice Halperin, "The Duke of Saxony and the Date ad quem of *Cligés,*" *RR*, 31 (1930), 239-41; Henry and Renée Kahane, "L'énigme du nom de Cligés," *Romania*, 82 (1966), 192-203.

[43] Barthes, p. 155.

LE ROI DANS LES *LAIS* DE MARIE DE FRANCE:

L'HOMME SOUS LE PERSONNAGE

Pierre Jonin

Pourquoi penser à étudier le roi chez Marie de France et en particulier l'homme sous le personnage? Parce que nous baignons avec les *Lais* dans une littérature essentiellement aristocratique et qu'il est naturel de prêter attention au plus haut représentant de cette classe. Mais surtout parce qu'il est intéressant de se demander dans quelle mesure Marie a su dépasser le social, de chercher à découvrir jusqu'à quel point en montrant les rois elle a voulu atteindre des hommes et quelle valeur elle a jugé bon de leur attribuer.

Ces rois seront présentés successivement en raison de l'importance qu'ils me paraissent avoir dans le récit. Le roi Hoël nous est signalé dans *Guigemar* comme une sorte de jalon chronologique. C'est une grande figure locale bien connue destinée à situer le lai dans un certain climat. Dans les premières pages le roi de Petite Bretagne remplira ses devoirs de suzerain, ce dont je n'ai pas à m'occuper ici. A première vue il n'y a pas d'autre roi qu'Hoël dans *Guigemar*, puisque les seuls personnages masculins socialement importants sont Guigemar, fils du seigneur Oridiol, Mériaduc possesseur d'un château fort et le vieil époux jaloux qui ne porte jamais le titre de roi comme le font Arthur, Marc, Equitan, le roi du *Bisclavret,* des *Deux amants* ou ceux d'*Eliduc*. Mais cela n'est pas une preuve suffisante car si le vieillard est appelé sire (v. 209), terme polyvalent, il est aussi présenté dans un contexte précis. Il possède "une antive cité / Ki esteit chiefs de cel regné" (v. 207-208).[1]

Les termes "capitale de ce royaume" ne laissent subsister aucun doute et il s'agit bien d'un roi. Pourtant les effets de son autorité se manifestent seulement dans le cadre très limité d'une chambre à coucher dont il fait défoncer la porte (v. 589). Si l'on excepte, comme il se doit, la suivante et le prêtre affectés à la garde de sa femme on ne voit auprès de lui qu'un chambellan transformé en surveillant de l'épouse et trois de ses familiers appelés précipitamment pour faire voler en éclats ("despecier") la porte de la chambre où se trouve Guigemar. Il manque à ce roi tous les attributs de la fonction royale dont la cour, les vassaux, les jugements, etc. En fait le roi s'efface complètement devant le mari et plus exactement le vieux mari jaloux. Il en est le type même pour ne pas dire la caricature: l'oeil à la serrure, par chambellan interposé, faisant manier aux autres la trique qu'il n'aurait sans doute pas la force de porter lui-même. Une fois l'amant parti il n'a plus de raison d'être. Il est trop borné pour qu'on puisse parler de son caractère. Sans existence psychologique, il n'est qu'une utilité, déclic un instant nécessaire pour déclencher l'aventure. Il représente pour le récit ce qu'est le démarreur pour la voiture et il ne sera plus utilisé par la suite.

Le lai d'*Eliduc* nous présente deux rois qui sont tous deux des personnages de second plan, ce qui ne les empêche pas d'offrir, aux rares moments où ils se montrent, quelques traits de caractère. Curieusement, le premier roi, en chassant de sa cour Eliduc nous fait faire la connaissance du second, qui, lui, accueille l'exilé. En effet Eliduc, tout comme Lanval, dévoué et fidèle vassal a été, lui aussi, victime de l'ingratitude de son roi. Ingratitude! Ce terme moral comporte déjà en lui-même un jugement sur cet autre roi de Petite Bretagne au service duquel se trouve Eliduc. Ce dernier envié et calomnié demande à son suzerain une procédure de justification. Cela sans résultat:

> Soventefeis requist le rei
> qu'il escundit de lui preïst . . .
> Mes li reis ne li respundi. (v. 48-49, 52)

Ce silence est éloquent et condamne durement celui qui se tait. Il montre dans ce dédain de l'explication ou même de la communication une hauteur et un orgueil que n'éclaire pas la raison. Car ce roi n'est ni intelligent ni bon. Il lui faut des revers, des châteaux perdus, des terres dévastées pour lui ouvrir tardivement l'esprit et peut-être le coeur: "Mut s'esteit sovent repentiz" (v. 557). En reconnaissant ses torts personnels il rend hommage à Eliduc et déclare l'avoir vengé par le châtiment de ses calomniateurs de naguère. Mais il reste tout de même dans l'appel pressant au secours qu'il adresse à Eliduc un sens trop précis de son droit et de son dû:

> Pur sun grant busuin le mandot
> E sumuneit e conjurot
> Par l'aïiance qu'il li fist
> Quant il l'umage de lui prist,
> Que s'en venist pur lui aidier
> Kar mut en aveit grant mestier. (v. 565-570)

Certes il commence son appel en évoquant sa détresse et il le termine en parlant de son très grand besoin. Mais dans l'intervalle on sent le suzerain autoritaire rappelant solennellement et avec force le vassal à ses devoirs, même si lui n'a pas respecté les siens. A ce moment le seigneur parle et l'homme encore une fois se tait. Tel est le premier roi d'Eliduc et il ne jouera plus de rôle dans la suite.

Le second roi accueille donc le malheureux Eliduc qui vient de traverser la Manche avec dix chevaliers pour lui offrir le service de ses armes. Ce roi sans avoir beaucoup plus de relief que le premier nous est du moins plus sympathique. D'abord pour le motif qui lui vaut dans la région d'Exeter l'hostilité déclarée du roi son voisin: le refus de lui donner sa fille en mariage. D'où la guerre avec ce dernier. La raison pour laquelle il n'a pas accordé sa fille à un roi son égal (v. 96-97) n'est pas mentionnée dans le lai. Mais du fait qu'il n'y avait pas mésalliance il faut chercher une explication en dehors du domaine social, donc sans doute dans le domaine psychologique. Ce roi dont la suite montrera les qualités humaines doit ne pas avoir voulu marier sa fille malgré elle. En tout cas on le voit, plus tard, la traiter avec égards et ne pas lui imposer sa volonté. Il souhaite qu'elle entre en relations avec Eliduc qu'il lui recommande chaleureusement[2] mais il ne va pas au-delà. A Eliduc il témoigne sa reconnaissance d'abord en lui accordant toute son affection[3] mais aussi de manière effective en faisant de lui le gardien de ses domaines.[4] Enfin il montrera que sa générosité est entièrement désintéressée. Même lorsque son territoire est complètement libéré et que, son ennemi étant devenu son prisonnier, il n'a plus aucun besoin d'Eliduc il continue à vouloir le garder auprès de lui. Son affection et sa reconnaissance éclatent dans ses offres comme ses promesses:

> Del suen li ad offert asez,
> La tierce part de s'herité
> E sun tresur abaundoné. (v. 628-630)

Il nous laisse le souvenir d'une nature sympathique et généreuse, mais c'est un souvenir éphémère.

Autre souvenir passager: celui du roi Marc dans *Le Chèvrefeuille*, brève histoire du rendez-vous d'amour que Tristant et Iseut se donnent à son insu. Pourtant, dans ce récit Marc a sa place. D'abord en tant que point de référence. On sait que ses déplacements officiels entrainent ceux d'Iseut et que là où on le trouvera on a bien des chances de rencontrer Iseut également. C'est un poteau indicateur très utile sur leur carte du Tendre.[5] Dans ces conditions le roi Marc, à première vue, ne prête pas à des remarques d'ordre psychologique. Pourtant, à deux reprises, il laisse entrevoir sa vie intérieure avec des sentiments susceptibles d'évolution:

> Li reis Marks esteit curuciez
> Vers Tristram sun nevu iriez;
> De sa tere le cungea
> Pur la reïne qu'il ama. (v. 11-14)

Ces vers sont intéressants moins parce qu'ils nous disent l'amour du roi pour Iseut mais parce qu'ils nous révèlent, qu'en exilant Tristan, Marc a cédé à la double poussée de la colère et de la peine. Par la-même nous devinons que ce mouvement peut n'être que passager. Effectivement la raison aidée par l'amour lui fera dépasser ce premier stade. D'ailleurs il l'a déjà franchi au moment où Iseut revoit Tristan et il en est même au stade du regret qui l'amènera facilement à la réconciliation.[6] C'est là tout ce que nous savons du roi Marc dans le lai du *Chèvrefeuille*. Mari aimant et faible il commence par céder à ses impulsions ou à subir des influences. Il lui faut un certain temps d'hésitation et de réflexion pour trouver une attitude personnelle équilibrée. Dans le cadre réduit d'un lai de 118 vers consacré à Tristan et Iseut il ne peut offrir que quelques minces traits de caractère.

Pour Arthur dans *Lanval* la situation est à la fois voisine et différente. Les critiques comme les lecteurs ont l'attention attirée et retenue à la fois par les trois personnages principaux du lai: Lanval, la reine Guenièvre et la fée anonyme, faite femme pour le temps du récit. Au roi Arthur on ne s'intéresse guère. Jean Rychner[7] expliquant minutieusement le procès de Lanval montre que le roi fait appliquer la coutume à laquelle on se réfère en pareil cas, notamment celle de Normandie, mais ne dit rien de la personne d'Arthur. Les derniers critiques restent également assez discrets à son sujet. Edgar Sienaert fait comprendre qu'Arthur organise bien le jugement mais il souligne aussi très justement son désir d'en finir plus tôt pour assurer sa tranquillité et celle de Guenièvre: "Soucieux de ne pas enfreindre la loi et tout en demeurant dans la stricte légalité, il n'en est pas moins surtout pressé de hâter la procédure pour des raisons de confort personnel pour lui et pour la reine."[8] Quant à Philippe Ménard, il fait judicieusement du roi "le porte parole de sa femme"[9] et il insiste avec raison sur la personnalité de la reine beaucoup plus forte que celle du roi. On ne peut que souscrire à ce jugement d'ensemble fortement étayé par les faits. Mais alors on se demande ce qui subsiste sur le plan psychologique de la personnalité d'Arthur. Car s'il est bien vrai que la fonction royale domine en lui (en particulier dans le procès) l'homme ne disparaît pas pour autant au cours du récit. Ne lisons-nous pas tout au début du lai:

> A Kardoel surjurnot li reis
> . . . Pur les Escoz e pur les Pis
> Ki destrueient le païs, . . .
> . . . Asez i duna riches duns. (v. 5, 7-8, 13)

On peut s'interroger légitimement à ce sujet: Son devoir lui permettait-il de rester insensible à la guerre que faisaient les Ecossais et les pictes dans le voisinage, tandis que lui-même oubliant de protéger ses sujets et leurs terres restait douilletement à l'abri dans son palais-refuge de Carlisle où il se distinguait par ses largesses à défaut de ses prouesses. Générosité relative donc parce qu'elle ne comporte pas d'efforts ou de risques personnels. Générosité irréfléchie aussi par l'oubli au milieu de ses distributions de toute nature de Lanval, un de ses plus fidèles sujets. Mais le destin va envoyer à ce dernier une double compensation, d'abord avec la fée qui lui donne son amour, puis avec Guenièvre qui lui offre le sien. Déjà pourvu il repousse la reine, qui, furieuse l'injurie grossièrement. Il riposte en lui jetant à la face qu'il est aimé par une femme exceptionnelle en tous points et dont les moindres servantes sont plus belles qu'elle-même, la reine. Violemment offensée elle se plaint au roi, prétendant que Lanval a voulu la séduire, la déshonorer et en outre l'a humiliée en assurant que les chambrières de sa dame lui étaient supérieures en beauté. A ces paroles le roi devient furieux et jure qu'il fera infliger à Lanval les pires châtiments: le bûcher ou la pendaison (v. 328) s'il ne se justifie pas. On remarquera qu'Arthur ne doute pas un instant de la révoltante accusation de la reine envers un vassal entièrement dévoué "ki tant aveit le rei servi" (v. 40). Pas une question à Guenièvre sur les circonstances de la rencontre avec Lanval ou sur les paroles exactes de ce dernier. Aucun esprit critique de la part du roi. Il lui emboîte immédiatement le pas et il va encore plus loin qu'elle dans la volonté du châtiment. Guenièvre, même déchaînée, voulait qu'il soit donné suite à sa plainte mais n'avait jamais demandé la mort de Lanval, ce que fait Arthur. Il est non seulement "porte parole" mais encore amplificateur. Les sentiments de Guenièvre s'exaspèrent en lui. Sans avoir réfléchi le moindre peu il se montre de plus en plus furieux contre Lanval et il n'a pour cela aucune raison nouvelle. S'il veut presser les débats du procès ce n'est pas pour faire appliquer la coutume et obtenir un jugement. C'est une première fois à cause de l'attente de la reine[11] et une seconde fois parce qu'elle est restée trop longtemps sans manger.[12] Ainsi, le sens de la justice d'Arthur est fonction de l'impatience ou de l'estomac de Guenièvre.

Que dire en définitive des aspects psychologiques du grand roi de la Table Ronde dans *Lanval*? On ne peut pas dissimuler que le bilan n'est guère positif. Arthur n'incarne pas le courage et il est plus attiré par les démonstrations grandioses de la générosité royale que par les dangers sanglants de la guerre. Il est inconstant dans son amitié et Lanval devient la victime de son ingratitude. Reste le mari, à propos duquel l'heureuse formule de Philippe Ménard mérite d'être citée: "La reine a beaucoup plus de relief que son époux."[13] Euphémisme généreux et subtil! Le roi Arthur a du relief dans toute la mesure où les ombres en ont. Car malgré l'ampleur sonore de ses parades royales il vit, sur le plan conjugal, dans l'ombre de Guenièvre. Ses colères et ses emportements ne sont pas spontanés. Ils suivent ceux de sa femme. Ce sont les colères et les emportements des faibles. Car Arthur, dans *Lanval* du moins, est un faible. Ses relations avec Guenièvre pourraient se résumer par le titre d'un roman de Pierre Louÿs, *La Femme et le pantin.*

Dans cette galerie de souverain les quatre rois qu'il nous reste à considérer ne manquent pas, eux, d'ampleur psychologique. Equitan d'abord. Marie de France le présente avec quelque solennité: "Sire des Nauns, justice e reis" (v. 12), c'est-à-dire Seigneur des Nauns,[14] juge souverain et roi. Malgré cette présentation on a tôt fait de découvrir qu'il sait fort bien se détacher de la pompe royale. On le voit par exemple partir à la chasse sans escorte ("priveement," v. 42), fait absolument exceptionnel, cela pour approcher la femme de son sénéchal. D'ailleurs peu à peu, le roi va faire place à l'homme. L'un des mérites de ce lai est précisément de montrer la parenté profonde qui unit tous les amants, qu'il agisse d'un mercenaire exilé comme Eliduc, d'un chevalier comme Guigemar, d'un roi comme Equitan. L'inquiétude douloureuse qui porte sur l'incertitude d'être aimé est leur part commune. Tous souffrent, se tourmentent et ne peuvent dormir. L'amour "suscite l'inquiétude et fait perdre la paix intérieure. Guigemar craint de déclarer ses sentiments, Equitan s'interroge douloureusement, Eliduc se sent partagé entre des aspirations contradictoires."[15] Influence du *Roman d'Enéas*, comme l'a pensé Ernest Hoeppfner? Peut-être. Mais surtout observation du coeur. En outre dans *Equitan* la naissance et la croissance de l'amour s'enrichissent de nuances particulières qui tiennent à la condition royale de l'amant. Aux inquiétudes morales s'ajoutent des inquiétudes sociales. Il n'a pas le droit d'aimer la femme de son sénéchal. Il le sait, il se le dit et un douloureux conflit éclate en lui:

> "Jeo quit que mei l'estuet amer.
> E si jo l'aim, jeo ferai mal:
> Ceo est la femme al seneschal;
> Garder li dei amur e fei
> Si cum jeo voil k'il face a mei." (v. 70-74)

Pourtant peu à peu, le roi recule devant l'homme. La chasse était sa première et seule passion en même temps qu'une de ses raisons d'être et voilà qu'il l'abandonne brusquement:

> Il est levez si vet chacier
> Mes tost se mist el repeirier. (v. 103-104)

Quand il se trouve devant la femme du sénéchal elle lui reproche son rang et son titre qui lui interdisent d'accéder à la vraie passion, celle qui naît d'échanges entre égaux. Et voici la conclusion de la femme qui se veut aimée: "Amur n'est pruz se n'est egals" (v. 137); donc, l'amour tient toute sa valeur de l'égalité. Autrement dit, la supériorité sociale du roi se transforme en infériorité. Il en prend conscience et est conduit au regret, presqu'à la honte d'être roi. Ainsi culpabilisé il va lui-même déposer son titre, se diminuer, renverser les rôles et se "vassaliser" devant sa vassale. Sa déclaration d'amour est un acte d'abdication:

> "Ma chiere dame a vus m'ustrei:
> Ne me tenez mie pur rei
> Mes pur vostre humme e vostre ami.
> Seürement vus jur e di
> Que jeo ferai vostre pleisir." (v. 169-173)

Le mot qui signe sa démission est lancé: "vostre humme," donc votre vassal. Le "pleisir," c'est-à-dire le pouvoir de décision est passé du côté de la femme et la promesse d'obéissance du côté de l'homme. Mais, est-ce vraiment une démission que celle qui conduit l'homme d'abord à l'égalité puis à la soumission en amour? Démission et régression sociales, oui, mais bien atténuées si elles sont consenties, comme c'est le cas dans ce lai.

Cependant on peut se demander si Equitan s'arrêtera à ce degré dans la descente. En exigeant un amant qui ne soit plus un roi la femme du sénéchal veut par là-même un homme libéré des interdits sociaux et moraux. Or, au cours de son monologue, lui-même s'était dit qu'il n'avait pas le droit d'épouser la femme de son sénéchal. Innocemment, je crois, en réservant son inconscient, il va maintenant révéler ce qu'il avait tout d'abord pensé pour lui seul.

> "Saciez de veir e si creez,
> Si vostre sire fust finez,
> Reïne e dame vus fereie." (v. 225-227)

L'interdit disparaîtrait donc en même temps que le sénéchal. Ce qui n'était probablement pour le roi qu'une hypothèse abstraite et intemporelle va aussitôt prendre corps dans l'esprit de la femme qui va en faire un projet à réaliser sans tarder (v. 233-34). A cette proposition de provoquer rapidement la mort du sénéchal non seulement le roi ne fait aucune objection mais encore il promet son aide. Et ce n'est pas docilité ou obéissance irréfléchie d'un homme aveuglé par l'amour. Il prend parfaitement conscience de sa culpabilité meurtrière puisqu'il ajoute:

> Ja cele rien ne li dirrat
> Que il ne face a son poeir
> Turt a folie ou a saveir. (v. 238-240)

Voici le meurtre prémédité et bientôt consommé. Ainsi Marie de France a très finement analysé les rapides étapes de la chute du roi qui passe irréversiblement de la démission sociale à la déchéance morale.

Le roi du *Deux amants* est sans doute une des créations les plus complexes de Marie. On peut parler fermement de création car l'apport de la narratrice est si important qu'il renouvelle entièrement le personnage. Il est bien vrai qu'il fait invinciblement penser au roi incestueux qui apparaît dans plusieurs contes anciens et notamment "dans le célèbre récit d'Appolonius de Tyr."[16] Il est juste aussi de dire qu'il a derrière lui toute une tradition littéraire dans laquelle la fille "fuit les assiduités de son père pour aller se marier dans un autre royaume."[17] Mais Marie a pris ses distances vis à vis de cette tradition tout en paraissant la respecter. Certes elle affirme que le roi ne pouvait se séparer de sa fille:

> Li reis n'aveit autre retur
> Pres de li esteit nuit e jur.
> Cumfortez fu par la meschine,
> Puis que perdue ot la reîne. (v. 29-32)

Cependant elle se garde bien de parler d'inceste et dit simplement que l'attitude du roi a prêté à des critiques sans suivre elle-même cette voie. Au contraire il semble même qu'elle fasse tout pour situer son attitude en dehors de l'interprétation incestueuse puisque dans son lai l'affection intense que le roi éprouve pour sa fille commence à partir du moment où le roi a perdu son épouse. Il est bien évident qu'il a constamment besoin de la présence, de la tendresse d'une femme et que sa fille lui apporte une indispensable consolation et compensation à la fois. Il opère après la perte de sa femme un transfert qui double son amour paternel. Il ne cesse de manifester pour sa fille une passion profonde tout au long du récit et cette passion devient pathéthique quand, à la mort de cette dernière il s'effondre de douleur et s'évanouit.

> Li reis chiet a tere paumez.
> Quant pot parler grant dol demeine. (v. 242-243)

Reste le "nuit e jur" qui est troublant. Evidemment il provoque les commentaires que l'on sait. Mais on peut constater qu'il est assez rare qu'un entourage royal soit bienveillant. Ni Lanval ni Eliduc, n'ont vu leurs services appréciés ou récompensés. D'autre part il ne faut pas oublier qu'au Moyen Age, même dans les familles royales, plusieurs membres de la famille couchaient dans une seule chambre. Le transfert d'amour du roi, le comportement malveillant de l'entourage, les conditions de la vie médiévale, tout en invitant à douter de la faute du roi, n'apportent pourtant pas la preuve de son innocence.

En revanche l'attitude de sa fille me paraît le disculper. Elle a pour son père la plus grande estime et cette estime lui dicte dans une large mesure le choix de l'homme qu'elle aura d'abord pour amant et qu'elle espère ensuite prendre pour mari:

> Pur ceo ke pruz fu e curteis
> E que mut le preisot li reis
> Li otria sa druërie. (v. 67-69)

Ce passage est important et ne doit laisser place à aucun doute: "sa valeur, ses vertus courtoises, la grande estime où le tenait le roi firent qu'elle accepta d'être son amie."[18] Premier point: les vertus courtoises ne comportent pas l'inceste. Second point: elle apprécie tellement le jugement de son père qu'elle en tient le plus grand compte avant de se choisir un amant. Pourrait-elle estimer autant son père et son jugement si ce père était incestueux et d'autre part pourrait-elle normalement à la fois avoir un amour incestueux et aimer un jeune homme voulant l'épouser? C'est un fait qu'elle aime son père au point de ne pas vouloir le quitter et le faire souffrir (v. 96), mais c'est un fait aussi qu'elle a un amant dont elle est bien décidée à faire son mari puisqu'elle lui dit nettement: "A votre retour dans ce pays vous me demanderez en mariage à votre père."[19] Or une jeune fille mentalement normale peut-elle vouloir pratiquer inceste et mariage, donc d'une part se soustraire aux contraintes morales et religieuses et d'autre part s'y soumettre? Il y a là une contradiction irréductible à moins que l'on admette que la jeune fille manque quelque peu d'équilibre. Or elle n'en manque absolument pas puisqu'elle met au point un plan extrêmement sensé et judicieux pour rendre son ami capable de gravir la pente de la montagne, condition exigée par le roi. Ainsi la contradiction tombe si l'on voit dans l'amante une jeune fille très attachée à un père devenu veuf et aussi une jeune femme décidée à épouser l'homme qu'elle aime. Tout devient normal et naturel, l'amour filial se conciliant parfaitement avec l'amour passion. Donc, si la jeune fille est disculpée de l'accusation d'inceste, le père l'est également. Pourtant il faut reconnaître qu'il est égoïste, possessif, abusif. Mais son portrait serait incomplet si l'on n'ajoutait pas qu'il est supérieurement intelligent. Il a bien compris que son opposition au mariage de sa fille le désignait aux plus vives critiques sur le plan moral comme le plan social[20] et qu'il serait en fin de compte obligé de céder. Il lui faut donc à tout prix une raison qui supprime les reproches de son entourage. Il va la chercher et la trouver en dehors des nécessités humaines. Celles-ci s'opposent à ce qu'il ne donne pas sa fille en mariage et qu'il la garde auprès de lui. Soit! Mais il y a des obligations et des lois devant lesquelles, de tout temps, les lois obligations et les lois humaines ont reculé, ce sont celles du destin. Et l'habileté du roi va précisément consister à faire surgir le destin dans un contexte qui au départ était purement humain. Ce n'est pas lui, dit-il, qui retarde le mariage de sa fille, mais le destin qui impose une condition:

> Sortit esteit e destiné,
> Desur le munt, fors la cité
> Entre ses braz la portereit
> Si que ne se reposereit. (v. 43-46)

Voilà d'un seul coup ses vassaux et les deux amants enfermés dans un même cercle magique qui met un terme aux demandes des premiers et oblige les seconds à tenter de vaincre un obstacle insurmontable. Seul le roi qui vient d'inventer le destin paraît bénéficiaire de l'opération. Mais le Destin, le vrai, ne se laisse pas mystifier. Il déjoue les calculs de ceux qui ont voulu se substituer à lui: d'abord le roi qui a imaginé la condition nécessaire au mariage, puis les deux amants qui par le recours au breuvage ont voulu échapper à leur destinée. Ainsi le roi des *Deux amants* a tenté d'enrôler le sort au service d'une passion possessive.

A dire vrai on éprouve pendant un certain temps quelque hésitation à faire entrer le père de Yonec dans le cortège des rois. En effet, il faut attendre le vers 519 d'un lai qui en comporte 558 pour lui voir attribuer ce titre: "De ceste tere ot esté reis" (v. 519). Toujours auparavant il est appelé chevalier[21] ou seigneur.[22] Cela se comprend d'ailleurs parfaitement puisque, pendant la plus grande partie du récit il n'a pas à se comporter en roi. Cepedant, comme il l'est en fait, on ne peut l'oublier dans cette galerie royale des *Lais*. L'aspect merveilleux[23] du roi n'a pas à être étudié dans cet article mais seulement son aspect humain. C'est donc simplement à l'homme aimant que nous aurons affaire. Malgré sa figure providentielle, puisqu'il survient immédiatement après une prière adressée à Dieu par l'héroïne malheureuse du récit, il se comporte, dans l'ensemble, comme les autres amants des lais. Amoureux fervent et passionné il promet d'être toujours fidèle:

> "Unkes femme fors vus n'amai
> Ne jamés autre n'amerai." (v. 129-130)

Guigemar (et ce ne serait pas le seul exemple) s'est lui aussi fermement engagé à n'avoir qu'un seul amour:

> "Ja n'eie jeo joie ne pes
> Quant vers nule autre avrai retur." (v. 554-555)

Ce n'est donc pas par l'ardeur d'un amour fidèle mais par deux points particuliers que dans *Yonec,* le roi se distingue des autres amants des lais. Tout d'abord il est le seul à être obligé de se soumettre à une condition préalable avant d'être accepté comme amant: prouver qu'il croit en Dieu. Il le fait volontiers et récite aussitôt un Credo quelque peu abrégé pour la circonstance (v. 149-154) mais il le complétera et demandera la communion (v. 161-162). Une double comédie où collaborent la simulation de la femme et le pouvoir magique du roi permet d'administrer le sacrement. Seconde particularité: sa fin tragique provoquée par la rupture du secret. En parfait amant courtois il avait demandé à son amie de ne jamais révéler leur amour. Elle a tenu parole mais la joie rayonnante de son visage a éveillé les soupçons du mari. Il a fait préparer un piège: des broches acérées où le roi est venu se blesser mortellement. D'ordinaire la fin du secret n'a pas des conséquences mortelles. Lanval a été malheureux mais a retrouvé sa dame. Découverts, les amants du *Laüstic* ont une séparation feutrée annoncée par la dame dans un mouchoir de brocart à l'amant résigné qui porteur de sa relique devient un discret pèlerin de l'amour. Rien de semblable ici. Amant providentiel, chrétien, surnaturel et pathétique tel est le roi dans *Yonec.* Le merveilleux est pour une fois vaincu par le terrestre et le roi-oiseau retrouve tragiquement sa dimension humaine.

Dernier roi, celui du *Bisclavret.* Nous le trouvons naturellement à la chasse mais sur la piste d'un loup-garou. Rencontre effrayante si l'on pense à tout ce que représente le loup-garou dans les croyances anciennes et même contemporaines de Marie. Pour mieux apprécier le comportement du roi il convient de laisser la narratrice faire la présentation de l'animal:

> Garvalf, ceo est beste salvage;
> Tant cum il este en cele rage
> Hummes devure, grant mal fait
> Es granz forez converse e vait. (v. 9-12)

C'est précisément ce qu'a dû se dire le roi en découvrant l'animal. Certainement, en un éclair, il a repensé aux histoires de loup-garou. Or ce sont toujours des récits "de dévastation, de carnage, de massacres de victimes innocentes. . . . Dans ces histoires dont le héros est un animal sanguinaire et meurtrier s'exprime la profonde peur qu'éprouvent les hommes devant les mystères et les cruautés de la vie sauvage."[24] Dans ces conditions, on s'attend à ce que, à la vue l'un de l'autre l'homme et l'animal jouent chacun leur rôle traditionnel où la violence leur sera commune dans l'attaque comme dans la défense. Or voilà qu'il n'y a ni attaque ni défense. Le loup-garou court vers le roi et non sur le roi. De plus il court à lui pour lui demander pitié ("quere merci," v. 146) et lui embrasse jambe et pied. Le roi est effrayé mais n'a pas de réaction instinctive de défense. Soudain, et c'est vraiment à souligner, le chasseur se tait en lui. Le cadre, la meute, l'entrainement, la fougue de la poursuite, tout le poussait à la violence. Or non seulement il ne s'y laisse pas aller mais il a la présence d'esprit d'essayer de comprendre l'incompréhensible. L'incompréhensible c'est le mystère de la bête sauvage devenue douce, pitoyable et ayant un comportement humain. Car c'est bien là le sens des paroles qu'il adresse à ses compagnons:

> "Ceste merveillë esgardez
> Cum ceste beste s'humilie!
> Ele a sen d'hume, merci crie." (v. 152-154)

Edgar Sienaert a donc tout à fait raison d'écrire: "Le roi, dès sa première rencontre avec le bisclavret dans la forêt a pressenti l'homme dans la bête."[25]

Mais pour rendre pleinement hommage au roi, il faut le suivre et l'étudier dans son attitude vis à vis de l'animal. Il devine, lui, une présence humaine dans la bête et il comprend que ses compagnons, eux, ne la devineront pas. Il sait qu'ils continueront sur leur lancée c'est-à-dire qu'ils frapperont l'animal. En se distinguant aussi nettement de son entourage il montre combien il est supérieur à tous en intelligence comme en bonte:

> "Chaciez mei tuz ces chiens ariere,
> Si gardez que hume ne la fiere!
> Ceste beste ad entente e sen." (v. 155-157)[26]

On aura remarqué à la fois le ton de commandement et la netteté des affirmations qui expriment son mépris si peu médiéval pour les chiens et mettent le loup-garou au même niveau mental que l'homme. Voilà qui explique le caractère absolument insolite de sa double décision: l'abandon de la chasse et la protection qu'il accorde au bisclavret. Il faut être un roi et un roi extraordinairement perspicace et écouté pour faire accepter à des chasseurs qu'ils laissent vivant un gibier que lui trouve intelligent et qu'en outre il va garder pour le protéger.

"Espleitiez-vus! Alum nus en!
A la beste durrai ma pes,
Kar jeo ne chacerai hui mes." (v. 158-60)

Son esprit et sa compréhension hors du commun, le roi les prouve encore en prenant du plaisir à vivre dans une atmosphère de merveilleux en compagnie d'un quadrupède qui participe de l'homme. Ce compagnonnage amical Roi-Bisclavret se poursuit donc grâce à la volonté et à l'amitié du premier extrêmement soucieux de ne pas le laisser manquer de quoi que ce soit: "Bien seit abrevez e peuz" (v. 174). Mais quoique vivant dans cette atmosphère de bonne compagnie Bisclavret conserve encore des caractères inquiétants. Il lui arrive parfois d'oublier qu'il est devenu un bon et brave chien doux et debonnaire (*deboneire,* v. 179) et d'avoir des remontées de sauvagerie. Mais par hasard en présence du mari de son ancienne femme il le saisit et il l'aurait mis à mal sans l'intervention du roi qui le menace d'un bâton (v. 202). Est-ce la fin de l'idylle et le retour à l'état d'affrontement naturel le loup-garou retrouvant ses crocs et l'homme-roi son bâton? Une seconde aventure le ferait croire: celle au cours de laquelle Bisclavret se trouvant devant son ancienne épouse est pris de fureur et lui arrache le nez. Tous les assistants menacent de tuer l'animal lorsqu'un chevalier de bon conseil rappelle au roi la douceur habituelle de Bisclavret à deux exceptions près. Il lui recommande alors de mettre la femme au supplice pour l'amener à des révélations. Et à ce moment même le roi donne une seconde preuve d'intelligence. Lui qui, au début avait fermement pris la situation en main en intégrant l'animal parmi les siens sans consulter quiconque accepte maintenant l'aide d'un subordonné pour tenter de mieux comprendre ce qui arrive. Cette aide, il sait l'admettre en dehors du "consilium" où ce serait pour lui un devoir. Il l'accepte à titre privé d'homme à homme. Et cette fois il montre autant de compréhension en suivant l'initiative d'autrui qu'en prenant au début sa propre décision en solitaire. Quand il apprend que la femme de Bisclavret a caché ses vêtements, le contraignant ainsi à rester dans la forêt, il reprend la situation en main. Il exige les vêtements disparus et les fait placer devant l'animal. Mais, ce n'est pas le bon moyen, lui fait remarquer son premier conseiller. Une nouvelle fois le roi est assez intelligent pour accepter la solution proposée: conduire Bisclavret dans son château et l'y laisser seul avec ses vêtements. Le roi alors, non seulement accepte mais encore l'emmène dans sa propre chambre où il le laisse, toutes portes fermées. Il revient après un certain temps accompagné de deux seigneurs:

En la chambre entrent tuit trei;
Sur le demeine lit al rei
Truevent dormant le chevalier. (v. 297-99)

Ce miracle est-il le fait du roi officiellement investi d'un pouvoir divin? Avons-nous affaire au roi thaumaturge que Roger Dragonetti pense pouvoir trouver, et légitimement, je crois, dans le Prologue des *Lais* où il voit dans le roi "une figure de Dieu," ce roi "en ki quoer tuz biens racine."[27] Dans *Bisclavret* il est bien vrai que le roi est "tout amour" et qu'il a fallu cet amour... pour sauver le Bisclavret de son aliénation fondamentale."[28] Mais peut-on attribuer au seul roi ce miracle et faire de lui l'instrument direct et officiel de la volonté divine. Je ne le pense pas car il ne faut pas oublier qu'à deux reprises il a agi sur les conseils d'un proche, d'abord en épargnant l'animal, ensuite en l'isolant avec ses vêtements. Mais il est bien vrai aussi qu'il est le principal instrument du salut de Bisclavret et véritablement son sauveur.

Au terme de ce récit il faut reconnaître, qu'il s'agit là d'un être singulier qui sait tourner le dos à son personnage de roi chasseur pour faire entrer résolument l'insolite et le merveilleux dans sa vie privée par l'adoption d'un loup-garou qu'il apprivoise. Union d'une bonté et d'une intelligence peu communes qui lui font refuser à Bisclavret l'animalité totale qu'imposaient cependant les apparences. Plus tard il fait preuve de la même compréhension généreuse en suivant et en accentuant les conseils qui permettront le miracle du retour à l'état humain. De l'homme dont il a pressenti la chute et la déchéance il a voulu la remontée et la résurrection. Chute, résurrection, voilà des termes qui évoquent le malheur de l'homme et le pouvoir de Dieu. Sans aller, puisqu'il n'agit pas seul, jusqu'à faire de lui un roi thaumaturge on peut croire que dans la pensée de Marie le roi du *Bisclavret* est une incarnation passagère mais éclatante de la puissance divine.

Marie de France dans la gamme des dix rois qu'elle fait intervenir dans douze lais a su introduire une étonnante variété. On peut sans grand effort y découvrir deux catégories: les personnages secondaires et les protagonistes. Mais encore faut-il reconnaître distinctions, nuances et degrés à l'intérieur de chaque groupe. Au niveau le plus bas: le vieux roi jaloux de *Guigemar,* personnage chiquenaude qui n'est là que pour lancer le récit. L'élan donné, il disparaît. Dans le même lai Hoël est destiné à montrer, tout au début un roi traditionnel, créateur d'atmosphère. C'est une image de première page. Les deux rois d'*Eliduc* jouent le rôle de promoteurs intermittents et n'offrent qu'une esquisse de psychologie extrêmement limitée. Quant à Marc, coincé entre deux héros de légende il présente, dans un conte très bref, une figure effacée. Arthur, lui, placé en apparence au premier plan est capable de faire illusion. Mais son violent conflit avec Lanval l'oblige à redevenir un homme et un mari. Il continue à prendre de nobles attitudes au cours du procès et on croirait qu'un esprit les dicte. En fait il n'obéit qu'à la coutume et surtout à la reine. Pour le comprendre il faut d'abord regarder Guenièvre et il n'apparaît plus alors que comme une très belle marionnette. Tels sont les six rois de *Guigemar, Eliduc, le Chèvrefeuille, Lanval.* Tantôt jalons ils balisent le récit, tantôt ils lui redonnent de l'élan ou lui font prendre un virage, mais jamais ils ne le conduisent ni le maîtrisent.

Dans le second groupe, les rois ont une envergure psychologique bien différente. Equitan se situe à première vue sur le plan du conte populaire où les préparatifs faits pour supprimer le rival se retournent en fin de compte contre l'instigatrice. Tel est pris qui croyait prendre. Mais en réalité il se hausse au niveau d'un personnage dramatique par le double conflit intérieur, social et humain, qui le tourmente et le déchire. Le roi des *Deux amants* doit sa profondeur à sa complexité. Après la perte de sa femme il transfère sur sa fille l'amour qu'il portait à la première. Il veut écarter les prétendants en plaçant les conditions qu'il fixe pour le mariage sous le contrôle du destin. Mais, pour avoir voulu mettre le destin dans son jeu il en devient lui-même le jouet. Avec l'introduction du destin, nous ne sommes pas encore dans un monde interférentiel mais nous le côtoyons. Un degré de plus et nous y parvenons en accédant au merveilleux que nous offre *Yonec.* Appelé par la prière éplorée d'une épouse malheureuse le roi du conte tombe du ciel sous la forme d'un grand oiseau. Redevenu seigneur il apporte l'amour humain et chrétien, prouvant que Dieu est amour et consolation. Mais son pouvoir surnaturel est bref, limité et sa fin tragiquement humaine. Quant au roi du *Bisclavret*, même s'il reste constamment homme, il est, des quatre rois importants des *Lais* celui qui me paraît le plus proche du Ciel. Ce roi chasseur abandonne soudain la chasse et adopte le loup-garou qu'il devait abattre. Bisclavret est un "révélateur." Il rend le roi à sa vraie nature qui comporte intelligence et bontè divines. Par lui s'opère le passage du merveilleux au divin. En rendant ses anciens vêtements d'homme à l'animal endormi il permet à la fois sa transfiguration et sa résurrection. Le roi du *Bisclavret* a des interférences avec Dieu.

Avignon

NOTES

[1]*Les Lais de Marie de France,* éd. Jean Rychner, 1e édition (Paris: Champion, 1966).

[2]"Entre cinq cenz nen ad meillur!" (v. 496).

[3]"Mut l'amat li reis e cheri" (v. 266).

[4]"De sa tere gardien en fist" (v. 270).

[5]A Tintagel deivent venir, / Li reis i veolt sa curt tenir, . . . / E la reïne i sera (v. 39-40, 43).

[6]Voici les paroles d'Iseut à Tristan, paroles qui expriment bien l'état d'esprit du roi Marc: "Puis li mustra cumfaitement / Del rei avrat acordement / E que mut li aveit pesé / De ceo qu'il l'ot si cungée" (v. 98-101).

[7]Jean Rychner et Paul Aebisher, *Le Lai de Lanval* (Genève, Paris, 1958), pp. 79-84.

[8]Edgar Sienaert, *Les Lais de Marie de France. Du conte merveilleux à la nouvelle psychologique* (Paris, 1978), p. 105.

[9]Philippe Ménard, *Les Lais de Marie de France* (Paris, 1979), p. 106.

[10]"Femmes et teres departi" (v. 17).

[11]"Pur la reïne kis atent" (v. 470).

[12]"La reïne s'en curuçot / Que trop lungement jeünot" (v. 545-6).

[13]Ménard, p. 106.

[14]On interprète Nauns tantôt comme habitants de Nantes et de sa région, tantôt comme nains.

[15]Ménard, p. 115.

[16]Ménard, p. 106.

[17]Sienaert, p. 111. Sur d'autres sources, voir E.J. Mickel, *Marie de France* (New York, 1974), pp. 85-86.

[18]*Les Lais de Marie de France*, traduits de l'ancien français par Pierre Jonin, 2e édition (Paris, 1978), p. 81.

[19]P. Jonin, p. 81-82.

[20]Effectivement il ne tient pas compte de l'intérêt dynastique impératif au Moyen Age. Cf. Sienaert: "En ne donnant pas sa fille en mariage, le roi empêche la perpétuation du lignage" (p. 110).

[21]v. 115, 119, 137, 187, 211, 285, 293, 343, 394, 414.

[22]v. 447.

[23]Cf. Sienaert, pp. 124-25; Ménard, pp. 154-57, 61.

[24]Ménard, p. 176.

[25]Sienaert, p. 92.

[26]Dans un article remarquable et fécond en idées comme en suggestions originales Roger Dragonetti commente ainsi ce passage: "Notons qu'aucun signe extérieur, sinon cet acte d'humilité ne pouvait faire soupçonner le 'sen' de la bête; c'est là, la merveille dont parle le roi. . . 'crier merci' serait alors l'acte essentiel par lequel le vrai savoir se montre." R. Dragonetti, *Le lai narratif de Marie de France: Recueil d'études offert à Bernard Gagnebin* (Lausanne, 1973), p. 40.

[27]Dragonetti, p. 36.

[28]Dragonetti, p. 40.

FORM, CONTEXT, AND DISJUNCTION

IN THE FABLIAU WORLD

Gregg F. Lacy

Despite the numerous contributions made by contemporary scholars to the study of the Old French fabliaux, much of what was or must have been funny in thirteenth-century France is hidden from us because of our ignorance of the social context of these short, often pseudo-moralizing, narrative poems in octosyllabic couplets. There exists even some doubt that humor was the only purpose of all those tales we today call "fabliaux": Carter Revard has proposed in a recent paper that some pre-Chaucerian fabliaux (especially the earlier ones clearly identified with sermon anecdote literature) intended to promote a more redemptive value than humor.[1] Therefore, the fabliaux scholar should pursue any possibility in order to bring to light late medieval social as well as aesthetic contextual elements which may have affected fabliau thematic inspiration or compositional technique. As humor and context are intrinsically related, any such knowledge can only add to our understanding of the humorous intentions of these authors. Furthermore, words or events which are *implausible* within a commonly known or understood context can also create laughter. Today we recognize the pun, the ethnic joke, the scatological story as examples of this phenomenon. This paper will explore the hypothesis that many fabliau poets purposefully placed improbable situations or actions in common contexts for a humorous purpose.

To begin, we can clearly demonstrate that, Revard's probably accurate observation notwithstanding, many fabliaux were first and foremost intended to amuse:

> Mos sans vilonnie
> Vous veil recorder,
> Afin qu'en s'en rie,
> D'un franc Savetier. . . .[2]

> Ai abasies granz tançons,
> Car, quant aucuns dit les risées
> Les forts tançons sont obliées.
> (Dou Povre Mercier, MR II, 114, vv. 8-9)

Yet, many of these obviously comic stories indeed appear to be touched by an atmosphere of seriousness, illustrating their points with short moral glosses, *sententiae*, or proverbs. Some authors go so far as to enhance the "credibility" of their often fantastic themes by insisting on their "truthfulness":

Se fabliaus puet veritez estre,
Dont avint il, ce dist mon mestre,
D'uns vilains à Bailluel manoit.
    (Du Vilain de Bailluel, MR IV, 212, vv. 1-3)

Un example vous en dirai,
Si vrai que ja n'en mentirai,
Ainsi c'on me conta pour voir.
    (Le Sentier battu, MR III, 247, vv. 13-15)

En lieu de fable vos dirai
Un voir. . . .
    (Li Dis de le Vescie a prestre, MR III, 106, vv. 1-2)

Several scholars have commented on this apparent ambiguity of the purpose of the fabliaux: although the name "fabliau" was frequently and consciously used to designate the genre, these poets also called their works *fable, exemple, proverbe,* and *aventure.* Did a clear idea of genre not exist, or are we strictly dealing with thirteenth-century tongue-in-cheek humor?

In *The Humor of the Fabliaux* edited by Thomas D. Cooke and Benjamin Honeycutt (which collection I believe to be among the more enlightening of recent studies on the fabliaux), a number of articles underline this incongruous aspect of the fabliau.[3] Jürgen Beyer illustrates how fabliaux cloak their coarseness with didactic form as they emerge from oral tradition into a written version.[4] Benjamin Honeycutt describes various styles and roles in several so-called "courtly" fabliaux, the shifts of which he calls "the nuclei of the ironic humor in these stories."[5] Norris J. Lacy uses "De Celle qui se fist foutre sur la fosse de son mari" (MR III, 118) to illustrate how "the humor of the fabliau is consistently based on an incongruity" and how the "work depends on the opposition of illusion and reality and on that of expectation and resolution."[6] An intentionally comic theme placed within the context of the serious didactic and religious motifs of "De Brunain, la vache au prestre" (MR I, 132), Howard Helsinger argues, can be seen as a humorous contradiction of the Pauline precept against too much literal-mindedness.[7] Helsinger further elucidates how the portrayal of the partridge as a "notoriously lecherous" bird intensifies the comic effect of "Le Dit des perdriz" (MR I, 188), while our understanding of the conventional image of the "Good Shepherd" creates an explanatory context for "Du Bouchier d'Abevile" (MR III, 227) (pp. 95-96, 98-100). These scholars seem to agree that the fabliaux, as a genre, often create an illusionary world, based upon the incongruity of an exaggerated or unpredicted action or expectation within a context which would normally evoke another action or expectation.

Even in fabliau style, we are struck by the degree of incongruity present. Much issues from the liberty which scholastic theory permitted by the late twelfth and early thirteenth centuries. For example, no longer did language alone determine stylistic level. Geoffroi de Vinsauf shows us in his *Documentum* that instead of styles determining characters (a classical phenomenon), styles were determined *by* the characters one dealt with. When one treated high-born persons in the late Middle Ages, the style then *became* grandly eloquent; when dealing with lowly persons, the style *became* low.[8] The social and hence stylistic incongruity of the fabliaux is frequently illustrated: "De Berengier au lonc cul" (MR IV, 57) portrays a wife who makes fun of her inept, would-be-knight husband (high character) by humiliating him (low style) without being recognized; in Jean de Condé's "Le Sentier batu" (MR III, 247), the courtly positions of the two main protagonists (high characters) do not disguise the crudeness of the jokes they tell (low style). The misplacement of stylistic levels, as well as the discrepancy of associated theme and imagery, demonstrate an enormous degree of literary freedom. But the evolution of stylistic freedom alone in the thirteenth century does not explain the widespread popularity of the use and appreciation of stylistic incongruity.

In order to gain perspective, let us turn to another domain, medieval architecture, to examine the creative process and specifically the interrelationship of form, context, and meaning.[9] Richard Krautheimer describes medieval church architecture, despite its great variety of forms, as referential: the shape of the parts refers back to or recalls a specific context which has content or meaning. For example, churches all over Europe had attempted to capture the significance of the Church of the Holy Sepulchre in Jerusalem. Yet, by the late Middle Ages, the buildings vary "surprisingly from each other; they are also astonishingly different from the prototype which they mean to follow."[10] Krautheimer recognizes this lack of literal resemblance as "a well-known phenomenon" in all medieval visual communication (p. 120). Each referential part conveys a separate significance transmitted from the original. Although any original whole meaning is sacrificed, a new creation with a new meaning is thereby generated: "The parts which have been selected in these 'copies' stand in a relation to one another which in no way recalls their former association with the model. Their original coherence has been discarded. . . . This procedure of breaking up the original into single parts and of reshuffling these also made it possible to enrich the copy by adding to it elements quite foreign to the original" (p. 125). Each single reference to a previous context, when reorganized into a new work, reflects a new and contemporary context with a new purpose.

If we can accept the giant leap from visual to verbal creativity, Krautheimer's observation helps shed light upon fabliau references to previous forms. These humorous stories are in no way *exempla, fables, dits, proverbes,* or *aventures.* But by purposefully adding these bits and pieces familiar from another form, the author consciously creates a new one. In other words, placed in a new context these older static elements communicate a new changed purpose.

Ervin Panofsky reinforces Krautheimer's theory of the relationship of the static to the changing: "In history as well as in physics time is a function of space, and the very definition of a period as a phase marked by a 'change of direction' implies continuity as well as dissociation."[11] Referring specifically to the dissociation of early Renaissance art from its classical origins. Panofsky calls this phenomenon the "principle of disjunction": "Wherever in the high and later Middle Ages a work of art borrows its form from a classical model, this form is almost invariably invested with a non-classical, normally Christian, significance; wherever in the high and later Middle Ages a work of art borrows its theme from classical poetry, legend, history or mythology, this theme is quite invariably presented in a non-classical, normally contemporary, form" (p. 84). Panofsky, like Krautheimer, recognized the widespread applicability of this observation: "the 'principle of disjunction' applies almost without exception, or only with such exception as can be accounted for by special circumstances" (p. 85). As human experience knowingly or unknowingly leaves behind one context and accepts a new one, the essence of form can be imitated, but the original essence of meaning is necessarily altered. Although error can create many discrepancies over a period of time, the "'principle of disjunction'. . . cannot be accounted for by the accidents of transmission alone. It would seem to express a fundamental tendency or idiosyncracy of the high-medieval mind. . ." (p. 106).

The fabliaux, of course, evoke a less grandiose interest than does early Renaissance art, but nevertheless, the principle of disjunction may be seen to operate in them as well. In order to appreciate better its role in fabliau humor, let us examine references to various contexts in one fabliau, *De Guillaume au faucon* (MR II, 92). William, a young squire who shows little enthusiasm for becoming a knight, languishes with love for the castellan's lady. During an absence of his lord to attend a tournament, William gathers enough courage to describe to the lady his own personal feelings towards her, but in very general, non-personal terms. He asks her for advice to a fictitious forlorn lover. She suggests that his lover suffer no longer, but tell the beloved of his secret anguish. William then admits to her that he is indeed that lover and she the beloved. Outraged, the lady threatens to tell all to her husband. As he feels betrayed, William in turn threatens to die by fasting unless she returns his love. The castellan returns, enquiring about William's illness. The lady begins her accusation, but at the last moment changes her language, substituting for William's desire for her his desire for one of the castellan's falcons. William's master, moved by the apparent simplicity of his request, grants the falcon, and unknowingly, his now willing lady.

De Guillaume au faucon contains several thematic motifs which remind us of different twelfth-century narrative forms. As in many a *lai*, both William and the anonymous lady are of the highest physical as well as social order:

> Jadis estoit .I. damoiseax
> Qui molt estoit cointes et beax;
> Li vallez ot à non Guillaumes.
> Cerchier péust-on .XX. réalmes
> Ainz c'on péust trover si gent,
> Et s'estoit molt de haute gent.
> (vv. 5-10)

Yet, as in many twelfth-century romances, both have a fault: William "n'estoit mie chevaliers" (v. 11), and he shows no real promise of becoming one in the near future: "Li vallez n'avoit nul talent / D'avoir armes hastivement" (vv. 17-18). The noble lady's "molt grant pechié" (v. 43) is to refuse to recognize William's torment. Furthermore, their relationship contains elements of the kind of love portrayed by the twelfth-century troubadours. True love or *fin'amors* in the poetry of Marcabru, for example, requires "Jois, Sofrirs et Mezura."[12] William's lack of discretion and *mesure* invites the lady's reaction. She, however, is the one who recognizes the need for discretion, refusing to tell her husband what had happened during his absence. On the other hand, William now behaves as a lover should: "l'amant courtois ne vit dans la gaieté et la joie, mais dans la souffrance et dans l'angoisse."[13] Her joy, in giving in to William, is to join him in this physical anguish:

> Amors li a gité .I. dart;
> Ele en doit bien avoir sa part.
> Froidir li fait et eschauffer;
> Sovent li fait color muer.
> (vv. 589-92)

These various motifs, easily recognizable by a thirteenth-century audience as common to their heritage, nevertheless lack the coherence of their original forms.

We know that the context has changed, in part because of the use of the word "fabliau" in many of these tales. Robert Harrison traces the word to the French translation of the twelfth-century *Disciplina Clericalis*, where it means a special kind of *exemplum*, "a tale of adultery in which the lady extricates herself from a contretemps by duping her husband."[14] Adultery had taken on a higher significance in the didactic metaphors of these twelfth-century sermon anecdotes, as it portrayed a preference for *cupiditas* over *caritas*.[15] But by the thirteenth century a "fabliau" had lost most of this truly didactic intention, despite such vestiges as inappropriate proverbs, *sententiae*, and the now comic pseudo-moralizing glosses. Sexual imagery now evolved from popular sources, although the Church continued to use the metaphors effectively in other contexts. In order to appreciate the falcon image in *De Guillaume au faucon*, for example, we can turn to a twelfth-century bestiary which tells us that "Accipiter the Hawk. . . is an avid bird at seizing upon others whence it is called Accipter, *i. e.,* Raptor—the ravisher, the thief."[16] A thirteenth-century book of hours as well as a fourteenth-century psalter use the falcon in marginalia in a context which clearly reflects a common knowledge of the falcon's sexual connotations in a popular milieu.[17] The use of the falcon in *Guillaume* thus provides an appropriate humorous allusion which is based upon the obviously purposeful mixture of meanings.

Ernst Curtius calls such stylistic mixtures in Latin texts the "collocation of jest and earnest," the popularity of which he attributes to Ovid.[18] Since most of the educated in the later Middle Ages were still exposed to the Latin scholastic method, it is possible that the effect of stylistic disjunction also played a role in vernacular humor. The author of *De Guillaume au faucon* displays clearly an awareness of the impact of such mixtures. The nobility of the three principal characters suggests high style to an audience, and perhaps the pretention of a serious work. *Amplificatio* is used to underscore the neoplatonic beauty of the lady: one-tenth of the tale describes her perfections. The introductory lines "Jadis estoit uns damoiseaux / Qui molt estoit cointes et beax" (vv. 5-6) suggest to the audience a story situated in a lofty, distant, even imaginary place, not "down here" in the so-called "real world." The consistency with which the author maintains the tone of a serious work ingeniously prepares the granting of the falcon (and simultaneously the wife) to William, a surprise ending based upon literal, popular metaphoric and linguistic meanings. The poet, obviously conscious of the possible effect of this kind of disjunction, has used it effectively to provoke laughter.

With the help of perspectives borrowed from the art historians Krautheimer and Panofsky, we have re-examined the issue of the relationship of form to meaning. In architecture, according to Krautheimer, medieval form implied content. The intent of the creator became immediately clear through the form chosen. Panofsky extends this concept by considering the impact of time upon this form-meaning relationship: with one point of contact with the past (or tradition) and another with the ever-changing present, the sense of continuity mixes with the feeling of opposition, depriving form of its "realness." When this idea is applied to literature, one may observe the creation of an imaginary world, such as found in the fabliaux. Through an investigation of *De Guillaume au faucon* we have tried to explore this relationship, in order to help us establish a method for answering the author-audience questions of who, why, and how.

The fabliau poets wrote to please an audience, and needed to rely on familiar *sens* as well as *matière*: the courtly tradition, erotic imagery taken out of its didactic context, and a purposeful mixture of styles, signaled a relationship to a new context, to the real world which surrounded this contemporary public. The borrowed material may have provided an indirect way of viewing this world, and of softening its harshness through laughter. *De Guillaume au faucon*, one of the better examples of fabliaux because of its careful development and good timing, recognizes and takes advantage of the accepted use of disjunct motifs, images and stylistic techniques. The author has attached these elements to the contemporary milieu, providing perfect openings for irony, parody, puns, and comic tension. Even though we do not know exactly for whom fabliaux were composed, the broad use of a variety of disjunct signs suggests that the popularity of these tales was due in part to their appreciation by various social groups. These audiences and the author shared a common knowledge— they understood that the distance established by these inappropriate references permitted an escape from the reality of life. For a brief moment all members of the social spectrum could step back from their daily existence, look into a far-off mirror, and laugh, if only for a brief moment, at themselves.[19]

North Dakota State University

NOTES

[1]"Fabliaux as Moral Tales: Some Pre-Chaucerian Instances," Fifteenth International Congress on Medieval Studies, Western Michigan University, 1-4 May 1980.

[2]"Du Prestre qui fu mis au lardier," *Recueil général et complet des fabliaux des XIIIe et XIVe siècles*, Anatole de Montaiglon and Gaston Raynaud, eds. (1872; rpt. New York: Burt Franklin, n.d.), II, 24, vv. 1-4; hereafter these volumes will be referred to by the traditional MR plus volume and page.

[3]Thomas D. Cooke and Benjamin L. Honeycutt, *The Humor of the Fabliaux: A Collection of Critical Essays* (Columbia: University of Missouri Press, 1974).

[4]"The Morality of the Amoral," in Cooke and Honeycutt, pp. 15-42.

[5]"The Knight and his World," in Cooke and Honeycutt, p. 76.

[6]"Types of Esthetic Distance in the Fabliaux," in Cooke and Honeycutt, p. 116.

[7]"Pearls in the Swill: Comic Allegory in the French Fabliaux," in Cooke and Honeycutt, p. 94.

[8]Edmond Faral, *Les Arts poétiques du XIIIe siècle* (Paris: Champion, 1923), p. 87 (my paraphrase).

[9]I owe a great debt of gratitude for these observations to Stephen G. Nichols, Jr. and the members of his National Endowment for the Humanities Summer Seminar, Dartmouth College, June-August 1975.

[10]Richard Krautheimer, *Studies in Early Christian, Medieval, and Renaissance Art* (New York: New York University Press, 1969), p. 117.

[11]*Renaissance and Renascences in Western Art,* 2nd ed. (Stockholm: Almquist and Wiksell, 1965), p. 3.

[12]Moshé Lazar, *Amour courtois et fin'amors dans la littérature du XIIe siècle* (Paris: Klincksieck, 1964), p. 79.

[13]Lazar, p. 79.

[14]*Gallic Salt: Eighteen Fabliaux Translated from the Old French* (Berkeley: University of California Press, 1974), p. 8.

[15]For additional detail on this topic, see my article "Augustinian Imagery and Fabliau 'Obscenity'," *Studies on the Seven Sages of Rome and Other Essays in Medieval Literature*, H. Niedzielski, H. R. Runte, W. L. Hendrickson, eds. (Honolulu: Educational Research Associates, 1978), pp. 219-28.

[16]T. H. White, ed., *The Bestiary: A Book of Beast Being a Translation from a Latin Bestiary of the Twelfth Century* (New York: Putnam, 1954), pp. 138-39.

[17]D. W. Robertson, Jr., *A Preface to Chaucer: Studies in Medieval Perspectives* (Princeton: Princeton University Press, 1962), pllates 9 and 64.

[18]*European Literature and the Latin Middle Ages*, Willard R. Trask, trans. (Princeton: Princeton University Press, 1967), p. 419.

[19]A version of this paper was first presented at the Fifteenth International Congress on Medieval Studies, Western Michigan University, 1-4 May 1980.

THE SCRIBE AND MINIATURIST AS READER

Hans R. Runte

In calling for an " 'anthropology' of medieval narrative," one of Professor Craig's former students recently demonstrated the desirability of "total recuperation of medieval texts as cultural phenomena."[1] Such an approach would combine established critical "tools, concepts and methodologies" with those of "structural anthropology, linguistics, historiography [and] semiotics" (188). If it can be assumed that this canon of ancillary disciplines was not meant to be exhaustive, one further set of "recovery procedures" (188), gleaned largely from the field of art history, may perhaps be added. It would indeed appear that the process of "production of meaning" (12) in a given text and the "intimacy" (11) between that text and its reader-viewers can often be reconstructed to an unexpected extent and in an exemplary fashion by means of visual analyses.

The visual imparting of meaning to a text and the striving for visual appeal fall into the domains of scribe and miniaturist: "Le copiste réservait dans le manuscrit certaines pages ou certaines parties de pages pour recevoir des peintures, et c'est seulement après l'achèvement de ce premier travail que l'enlumineur pouvait commencer le sien."[2] Illustrated manuscripts may thus be expected to contain a wealth of precious information about how contemporaries understood, and related to, the texts they read, produced and caused others to read. For in "laying out" his assignment, the above-mentioned *copiste* could not but impose his view of the text on what he was doing with it,[3] just as the *enlumineur* was likely to impose his.[4]

In order to demonstrate how visual structuring by the scribe and pictorial interpretation by the artist can add to the understanding of the total medieval reality of a literary work, a test text had to be found. That scribe and artist are indeed, as it were, the first interpreters of their copies can be shown most conveniently by examining the *Roman des sept sages de Rome.* As a frame narrative, this text has the methodological advantage of having confronted scribe and artist with a time-honored[5] and essentially unalterable narrative structure against which both traditional and innovative structural and interpretative attempts by the craftsmen-as-exegetes can be measured. What, then, is the visual evidence presented by the *Sept Sages,* and what does this evidence suggest for a modern reconstruction of the medieval meaning of the work?

Most medieval readers of the *Sept Sages*, including many a scribe,[6] took the work for nothing else than what it had and has been supposed to be for centuries: a collection of originally unrelated stories held together by the tight frame of a week-long debate in which the Roman emperor's second wife attempts to prove that her temporarily dumb-struck stepson has set out to overthrow his father whom the seven sages try to convince of women's wickedness. Few miniaturists and even fewer scribes escaped the structural dangers and interpretative limitations of this literary undertaking. In a first group of six[7] of the thirteen manuscripts under discussion, only a single miniature at the very beginning of the text was deemed artistically necessary or materially possible. It presents without exception an innocuous stock scene showing the emperor committing his young son to the seven sages' educational care.[8]

None of the people involved in the production of these manuscripts seems to have been interested in alleviating the congeneric repetitiveness of the frame plot or in exploiting the potentially dynamic tensions which hold frame and embedded stories together.

The scribes' range of potential visual presentation has been considerably widened in a second group of manuscripts (B, B^1, Ha) in which there was the possibility of truly structuring and interpreting the text pictorially with a *number* of illustrations.[9] In this group it is possible for the first time to observe how scribes and artists conceived of the text as a whole. The pictorial evidence proves that they were mainly concerned with holding the discrete pieces of the tale collection together by dealing exclusively with, and thus underlining the importance of, the frame. MS. B^1, for example, sequentializes the text by presenting each of the seven sages as he arrives on his appointed day at the imperial palace to counter the empress's *exemplum* with a story of his own. The resulting narrative bias against the visually non-existent empress has been corrected in MS. *Ha*, which adds to the depictions of the sages six drawings of the stepmother and thus preserves on the pictorial level[10] the text's confrontational nature and structure from which stems its most basic narrative dynamism. MS. *B* could have been illustrated in the same manner but for unknown reasons was assigned only four miniatures: an introductory one (see note 8) and one each for the empress's first and last story and her stepson's long-awaited summation: "Ci commence la dame son conte du petit pinel qui essorba le grant pin" (fol. 3ª, *arbor*), "Comment le fils a l'empereour de Romme conte a son pere le conte de celui qui son enfant geta en la mer" (fol. 15ᵈ, *vaticinium*), "Comment la male marrastre conte un conte pour sa destruction" (fol. 16ᵉ⁻ᶠ, *noverca*).[11]

While far from being perfect, MSS. B^1 and *Ha* make it nevertheless possible to get a glimpse of the medieval rationale for structuring the *Sept*

Sages the way they do. By featuring only the seven sages and thus drawing attention to their stories, MS. B^1 propounds a rather narrow-minded interpretation of the text as an antifeminist diatribe.[12] The impact of the intended -message would be jeopardized or nullified by visually pointing to the aggressive empress whose stories put the aging sages on the defensive. A similar interpretation through visual structuring may incidentally be gleaned from the pictorial omission of empress's stories 3 (*aper*) and 7 (*senescalcus*) in MSS. *V* and *G* which reduce the illustrations of alleged filial insurgence from seven to five, while retaining all seven illustrations of the blatant, feminine evil expounded by the sages.

MS. *Ha* suggests in a rudimentary way that there may be more to the *Sept Sages* than single-minded antifeminism.[13] By giving the empress and her stories equal space, MS. *Ha* raises questions of political conduct and educational methodology also pointed to in some of the other manuscripts.[14] In addition to rëechoing a few of the characteristics of a *Fürstenspiegel*, and despite its artistic imperfection (see note 10), MS. *Ha* also proposes an almost perfect and logical structuration: one miniature for each of the empress's and the sages' seven stories, plus possibly an additional one at the beginning of the text and a sixteenth to accompany the son's tale.[15]

Such is in fact the scheme adopted in MSS. *V*, B^2 and *G* of a third group of manuscripts. The scribes have struck a satisfactory balance between the opposing forces of antifeminist diatribe and *Bildungsroman* which hold the frame together, and then have left it to the artists to deal, in the blank spaces, with a structural and interpretative problem of another kind.[16] The manuscripts of the second group, especially MSS. B^1 and *Ha*, considerably undercut the obviousness and value of the points they make by neglecting to incorporate into their frame design the lessons of the fifteen embedded stories. In fact, none of the craftsmen referred to in the preceding paragraphs understood that in a text which ultimately recounts its own birth and survival, structural frame and embedded-story content ensure each other's existence and meaning in the sense that the text *is* only as long as the empress and the sages continue to speak.[17] They have been unable to solve the double-edged problem of how to render pictorially the strict textual structure without becoming as monotonously repetitive as the text (B^1, *Ha*), and of how to do justice to the turbulent content without jeopardizing the very stability of the frame by abandoning it to the stories.[18]

It is in MSS. *V*, B^2 and *G* that the problem is addressed directly. By attempting to deal creatively with the mechanistic frame/content dichotomy, the scribes and especially the artists responsible for the execution of these copies propose a contemporary, long-since neglected yet still valid interpretation of the frame narrative. They see it not as a rectilinear stringing-together of a series of stories, but as a dynamically contrapuntal and complex composition in which the bipolar frame, instead of having been superimposed artificially on the text, has become an integral part of the embedded-story content.

In order to arrive at a balanced view of the *Sept Sages*, it was necessary to avoid the structuro-pictorial excesses of MSS. B^1 and *Ha* on the one hand, and of MS. E^1 on the other, and to find a satisfactory compromise. With the naturalness of true ingenuity, the artist of MS. *V* was the first to solve this problem, at least in part, by formulating the basics of a visual principle of simultaneity.[19] Having completed one six-part and two single miniatures devoted to the introductory portion of the text, the artist had to fill twelve blank spaces distributed throughout the main textual body. Among the nine illustrations which depict embedded-story content,[20] four deserve special attention. In stories 1 and 5 the empress is shown in conversation with the emperor before whom are being cut down the exemplary old tree (fol. 3^d, *arbor*) and the no less exemplary old father (fol. 5^f, *gaza*). Correspondingly, in stories 10 and 12 the emperor listens to one of his sages who points to the imminent killing of the misled bird (fol. 10^a, *avis*) and the widow's hanging of her husband's body (fol. 11^d, *vidua*). According to the idea of pictorial simultaneity, empress and sages, as frame narratees turned story narrators, here step out of the frame and meet their own, frame-invading narratees half-way in four miniatures which thus illustrate neither the structure nor the *exempla* of the *Sept Sages*, but both.

A similar artistic concept governed the illustrator of MS. B^2. In all of the fourteen pertinent miniatures,[21] the artist has taken care to represent both story tellers and story protagonists. However, while in MS. *V* tree and ax-swinging gardener have invaded the imperial palace (*arbor*) and emperor and sage have stepped out under the gallows (*vidua*), MS. B^2, being careful to fuse but not to confuse, shows in the left half of each miniature the emperor sitting either on his throne when addressed by a sage, or on his bed when entertained by the empress, and in the right half a full cast of characters playing out the respective story. As a variant of visual simultaneity, this method of juxtaposition may well improve the results obtained in MS. *V*, but also risks separating, albeit within the same miniature, one visual component from the other. How then can the two sides of the miniature be brought into a mutually signifying, but differentiating relationship?

Recognizing that certain artistic practices, current by the time the youngest manuscript was being completed in the late 1460's,[22] are particularly suited to the *Sept Sages*, the miniaturist of MS. *G* was able to compromise between simultaneity and juxtaposition by both insisting on and overcoming the visual frame/content opposition.[23] This paradoxical procedure of "perspection" calls first for a visible divider between the palace as place of narration, and the narrated locale. A palace wall goes therefore up in the center of the miniature. But then this wall is pierced, opened up and reduced to the mere casings of a large door-window which literally frames the exterior story scene and guides the reader's view from the palace's interior to the outside. Here at last a perfect balance has been found between the antithetical structural elements of the *Sept Sages*. Each of the ten miniatures in question reflects, as in a microcosm, the global textual struggle between frame and content. This has been made possible by the permeable demarcation line which differentiates between frame and content illustrations and at the same time permits visual communication between the violent exterior[24] shown in the latter and the apparently sedate palatial interior depicted in the former. Such communication is established by persons who enter (fol. 2^b) or leave (fol. 3^b) the palace through the mediatory door-window, by exaggeratedly elongated index fingers with which narrators point through or toward it (fol. 3^d, 6^c, 10^a, 12^c, 13^d), and by cross-identification of characters: the beheaded father (*gaza*), the publicly chastised husband (*puteus*), and the gold-drinking Crassus (*Virgilius*) all exhibit the emperor's facial features, while it is none other than the empress who is being blood-let in *tentamina*. A more nearly perfect demonstration of the frame structuring the stories and the stories interpreting the frame is hardly imaginable. From it the *Sept Sages* emerge as much more than a traditional indictment of womankind. They are a political treatise on the use, abuse, usurpation and handing over of imperial power. The empress may well be an untrustworthy, ambitious and plotting stepmother, but her stories nevertheless contain serious warnings against an aging, indecisive and ineffectual ruler who has fallen under the sway of both his sages and his wife. By cutting the emperor down to size and by rehabilitating the empress's role, MS. *G* has escaped the *Sept Sages*' traditional stereotype and condensed its meaning to echo many a medieval educational *miroir:*

> Sint ergo . . . consiliarii tui quinque [sic][25] in comprehensione operum tuorum . . . Tempta ergo in anima tua eorum voluntates . . . et declina ab eorum consiliis in eo quod contrariantur voluntati tue . . . Quando ergo congregas eos pro aliquo consilio dando in tua presencia, non immisceas aliud consilium cum eis, andias ergo in quo conveniunt. Si ergo festinanter respondent et concordant cito, resiste eis tunc in hoc et ostende eis contrarium . . . Et ego dico tibi quod judicium imitatur corpus; quando ergo debilitatur corpus debilitatur judicium.[26]

> Sor totes choses vos gardez
> Que jai en serf ne vos fiez;
> Maint grant maul en sont avenu
> Et maint proudome confondu.
> . . .
> Princes qui malvais homme croit,
> Ne dites jai que proudons soit.[27]

One of the masters responsible for this reinterpretation and restructuring is relatively well known, while the identity of the second gives rise to some tantalizing speculation.

MS. *G* was completed by scribe Michel Gonnot in 1466. Cedric E. Pickford has shown[28] that Michel Gonnot did not work for Jean II, Duke of Bourbon, as Thorpe and Joseph Palermo believed,[29] but for Jacques d'Armagnac, Duke of Nemours. This puts the *Sept Sages*, represented by MS. *G* and possibly by its likely model MS. *V*, into the sphere of a fifteenth-century bibliophile of some renown.[30] Pickford also rejects (259) Bradley's identification of Michel Gonnot as a scribe-illuminator.[31] Indeed, not only would Gonnot's considerable scribal output seem to have left him little time for illustrating, but Jacques d'Armagnac also employed, besides Gonnot and four other known scribes, illumination specialists. Léopold Delisle conjectured, for example, that Jacques' copy of Josephus's *Antiquités juives* (Paris B. N. f. fr. 247) was partly illustrated by Jean Foucquet.[32] The same Delisle, following Antoine Thomas,[33] also placed Evrard d'Espinques in the service of Jacques d'Armagnac (ibid.). Evrard illustrated the Chantilly *Tristan* written by Gilles Gassien, one of Jacques' scribes, and he illustrated Jean du Mas' copy of the *Livre des propriétés des choses* mentioned above (note 22). The pictorial similarities between the *Livre* (see fols. 101ᵛ, 104, 120ᵛ, 187, 361ᵛ) and MS. *G* are so striking (the miniature on fol. 361ᵛ seems the very mirror image of *puteus* in MS. *G*, fol. 7ᶜ) that associating Evrard d'Espinques with both Jacques d'Armagnac and Jean du Mas would be no more speculative than Pickford's suggestion attributing the art work in MS. *G* to Guillaume Oléry (258-59).[34] Until the two texts are studied more closely than is possible here, perhaps François Avril's cautious admission that Jacques d'Armagnac and Jean du Mas "auraient pu employer les mêmes artistes"[35] may be taken to strengthen the supposition that Evrard d'Espinques illustrated MS. *G*.

The illuminated manuscripts of the *Sept Sages* reveal much about their reception throughout the Middle Ages. Even the mono-miniature copies summarily referred to above reflect to a certain degree their socio-cultural status, at least on a superficial, esthetico-material level. Not only are they associated scribally with such well-known authors as Wace (G^2, Y^1) or Robert de Borron (Q), but their popularity and importance, usually deduced from the number of surviving versions and manuscripts,[36] can also be judged by the artistry and craftsmanship bestowed to them and the volumes in which they appear. MS. Q, for example, was perhaps illustrated by Richard de Verdun, son-in-law of Maître Honoré from the Rue Erembourg-de-Brie (Boutebrie) in Paris. Its treatment of light and shadow, of gestures, detailed hands and rounded faces, and of the proportions of heads to bodies makes it "l'un des monuments les plus importants de la peinture du Nord de la France dans la seconde moitié du XIIIe siècle."[37] MS. G^2, the famous "Grand Recueil La Clayette" written between 1270 and 1275 in the Ile-de-France region, deserves a brief mention for its extraordinary musicological importance.[38] And MS. E, from Flanders, sums up late thirteenth and early fourteenth-century Flemish illustrating in its quintuple Gothic arches, its numerous, rigorously vertical vestimentary folds, its treatment of hands and round-chinned faces, and its use of carmine and green.[39]

Similar observations could be made for the multi-miniature copies of the *Sept Sages*.[40] More importantly, however, these seven copies hold the answers to more properly literary questions about how scribes and artists, as the only traceable and reconstructable representatives of the medieval "general reader," understood the text. The foregoing essay has tried to demonstrate that the *Sept Sages* were not unanimously considered to be simply a traditional tale collection as intellectually uninspired and artistically unchallenging as the innumerable *Narrationes*, *Sermones*, *Exempla*, *Sommes*, *Etats*, *Evangiles*, *Controverses*, *Enseignements* and *Miroirs* of that and later ages, and that modern attempts to explain the *Sept Sages'* popularity and literary significance through the intricate interplay of their structural components receive most authoritative justification and proof from contemporaries such as Michel Gonnot and perhaps Evrard d'Espinques.

The test case of the *Sept Sages* has shown which role the visual arts can play in the "recuperation of medieval texts as cultural phenomena." It points directly to the need for close cooperation between literary critics and art historians who together may wish to consider infinitely more controversial works and, for example, enrich the modern debate about Chrétien de Troyes' narrative structuring by a medieval argument based on the study of the illustrated copies of his works.

Dalhousie University

NOTES

[1]D. Maddox, *Structure and Sacring: The Systematic Kingdom in Chrétien's Erec et Enide* (Lexington, 1978), p. 188.

[2]H. Martin, *Les Miniaturistes français* (Paris, 1906), p. 13.

[3]"Copiste" and scribe are used here to describe in simplified terms a potentially complex production process. It is indeed not inconceivable, though almost impossible to document, that organization of miniature spacing is based on authorial recommendations. More often, it is not the scribe but his superior and/or workshop master who designates miniature space. Finally, visual lay-outs may simply reproduce the visual structuring found in the parent copy.

[4]References to the artist are meant to include the production roles played possibly by the author and more frequently by the master miniaturist and/or workshop head. In assessing the original artistic interpretation of a given text, it must be borne in mind that artists often work according to instructions and sketches not their own: see note 16 and L. Delisle, *Le Cab. des mss. de la Bibl. Imp.* (Paris, 1868), I, 491; J. H. Middleton, *Illuminated Mss. in Class. and Med. Times* (Cambridge, 1892), pp. 239-56; S. Berger and P. Durrieu, *Mém. de la Soc. Nat. des Antiquaires de France*, 53 (1893), 1-30; Martin, *Miniaturistes*, pp. 99-115; id., *Les Peintres de mss. et la miniature en France* (Paris, [1927]), pp. 23-24; E. G. Millar, *An Illuminated Ms. of* La Somme le Roy (Oxford, 1953), pp. 49-51; J. Porcher, *Jean Lebègue: Les Histoires que l'on peut raisonnablement faire sur les livres de Salluste* (Paris, 1962), pp. 9-14.

[5]See, for example, G. Paris, *Les Contes orientaux dans la litt. fr. du moyen âge* (Paris, 1875), pp. 8-12; T. Todorov, *La Grammaire du Décaméron* (The Hague, 1968).

[6]There are seven extant French versions of the work. The version discussed here is the influential and as yet unedited Version A which has been transmitted in thirty extant mss.; thirteen of these are illustrated (see *Scriptorium*, 15 [1961], 194, 199-200, 387-88, and 16 [1962], 160, 201, 204-5):

Q	Paris, B.N. f. fr. 95 (*c.* 1280)
R	1421 (late 13th cent.)
G^2	nouv. acq. fr. 13521 (late 13th cent.)
Y^1	Ars. 3516 (1268 A.D.)
Y	Florence, Bibl. Laur. Ashb. 49 (14th cent.)
E	Brussels, Bibl. roy. 9433 (*c.* 1330)
B	9245 (*c.* 1330)
B^1	10171 (1293 A.D.)
Ha	London, Brit. Mus. Harley 3860 (early 14th cent.)

E^1 Saint-Etienne, Bibl. mun. 109 (late 15th cent.)
V Paris, B.N. f. fr. 22548 (late 13th cent.)
B^2 Brussels, Bibl. roy. 11190 (*c.* 1370)
G Paris, B.N. f. fr. 93 (1466 A.D.)

[7]They are: 1. MS. *R*; 2. MS. Y^1, described in L.-J.-N. Monmerqué and F. Michel, *Lai d'Ignaurès* (Paris, 1832), pp. 35-41; 3. MS. *Y*, see L. Thorpe, *Le Roman de Laurin* (Cambridge, 1950), pp. 31-33; 4.-6. MSS. *Q, G^2* and *E*, see notes 37-39.

[8]The same introductory stock scene is featured in MSS. B^1, *G* and *V* of the multi-miniature group of manuscripts. MSS. E^1 and B^2 break the presentation scene into two and three separate miniatures respectively. In MS. Y^1 the space provided was never filled.

[9]The art work in MS. *B* has been described by A. Bayot, *Cat. des mss. fr. de la Bibl. roy. de Belgique* (s.1., s.d.), pp. 57-60; G. Doutrepont, *La Litt. fr. à la cour des ducs de Bourgogne* (Paris, 1909), pp. 18, 134; C. Gaspar and F. Lyna, *Les Principaux Mss. à peintures de la Bibl. roy. de Belgique* (Paris, 1937-47), I, 275-82; Thorpe, *Laurin*, pp. 24-28. For MS. B^1 see Bayot, p. 85; J. Van den Gheyn, *Cat. des mss. de la Bibl. roy. de Belgique* (Bruxelles, 1905), V. 12-13; L.-F. Flutre, *Les Mss. des Faits des Romains* (Paris, 1932), pp. 30-31; Gaspar and Lyna, *Manuscrits*, I, 124-26. And for MS. *Ha* see H. L. D. Ward, *Cat. of Romances* (London, 1893), II, 199-206.

[10]The rather unattractive pen-and-ink drawings are an artistic afterthought as the scribe's failure to provide appropriate spaces has forced the emperor and the empress into the margins.

[11]Five mss. of Version A contain more than the usual fifteen embedded stories. MSS. *B* and E^1 add *noverca* after the fifteenth story; MSS. *Q* and Cambridge, Univ. Libr. Gg. VI. 28 insert *filia* between *vidua* and *inclusa* and add *noverca* as a seventeenth story; MS. Y^1 replaces *Rome* by *filia* and also adds *noverca* at the end.

[12]See R. M. Lumiansky, *Tulane Studies in English*, 7 (1957), 5-16.

[13]For a well-balanced and innovative interpretation of the European *Seven Sages* cycle, see J. Jaunzems, *Studies on the Seven Sages of Rome... Dedicated to the Memory of Jean Misrahi* (Honolulu, 1978), pp. 43-62.

[14]See M.P. Cosman, *The Education of the Hero in Arthurian Romance* (Chapel Hill, 1965-66), pp. 147-52.

[15]Such a fifteenth and sixteenth illustration has been realized in MS. *Ha*; MSS. *G* and B^2 also include a final miniature showing the burning of the empress.

[16]The scribes may also have tried to deal with the problem themselves: "Le chef d'atelier a sur la table devant lui le volume à illustrer qu'on lui a livré tout écrit, en cahiers volants. Il regarde les places blanches destinées à recevoir les images. Le libraire lui a donné pour modèle un manuscrit orné déjà de miniatures qu'il ne s'agit que de reproduire; ou bien le copiste a écrit dans la marge, en caractères minuscules, quelques notes indiquant brièvement, en face de chaque place blanche, la scène que le miniaturiste devra représenter. *Quand le chef d'atelier a bien compris ce qu'il a à faire*, il exécute le dessin à l'endroit même où il doit être: plus souvent encore il se contente d'esquisser au crayon sur la marge une légère ébauche du sujet. Ce premier travail achevé, on procède à la préparation des couleurs" (Martin, *Peintres*, pp. 23-24; my italics). See also note 4 above.

[17]V. Roloff, "Motiv und Motivation des Schweigens in der Rahmenerzählung des *Roman des sept sages*," in his *Reden und Schweigen: Zur Tradition eines mittelalterlichen Themas in der französischen Literatur* (München, 1973), pp. 78-85; H. R. Runte, "*Temps du récit* vs. *temps de l'histoire* in the *Seven Sages of Rome* Prose Cycle: A Structural Examination of a Medieval *roman à tiroirs*," Thirteenth Conference on Medieval Studies, Medieval Institute, Western Michigan Univ. (Kalamazoo, 1978).

[18]MS. E^1 falls into this extreme; it sweeps away all structural pretensions and creates visual chaos by inundating the text with a possible total of 51 illustrations of which 44 have survived. On the other hand, MS. E^1 provides most of the visual comment on the introductory part of the *Sept Sages*, from the presentation of the emperor's son to his imprisonment. On MS. E^1 see J.-B. Galley, *Cat. de la Bibl. de la ville de Saint-Etienne* (Saint-Etienne, 1885), p. 209; Ministère de l'Instruction publ. et des Beaux-Arts, *Cat. gén. des mss. des bibl. publ. de France* (Paris, 1893), XXI, 241, 266-67.

[19]MS. *V* has been described by Thorpe, *Laurin*, pp. 10-14; see also Thorp, *Le Roman de Laurin . . . : Text of MS. B.N. f. fr. 22548* (Cambridge, [1960]).

[20]Stories 8 (*tentamina*), 11 (*sapientes*) and 14 (*inclusa*) are illustrated with frame motifs.

[21]See Gaspar and Lyna, *Manuscrits*, I, 416-18.

[22]MS. *G* presents a number of remarkable pictorial similarities with, among others, Jean du Mas' copy of Jean Corbichon's translation of Barthélemy's *Livre des propriétés des choses* (Paris, B.N. Rés. 9140); with the *Trésor des histoires ou trésor de sapience* (Paris, Ars. 5077) which in turn, according to Martin (*La Miniature fr. du XIIIe au XVe s.* [Paris and Bruxelles, 1923], pp. 80, 104), resembles the *Heures du Maréchal de Boucicaut* (Paris, B.N. 1941); and with the *Roman de Renaud de Montaubon* (Paris, Ars. 5072) which Loyset Lyedet illuminated for Philippe le Bon in 1467.—On the *Livre*, see H. Omont, *Cat. gén. des mss. fr.: Ancien Suppl. fr.* (Paris,

1895), I, 313; see also below.—On the *Heures*, see Durrieu, *Le Maître des Heures du Maréchal de Boucicaut* (Paris, 1906), p. 22.—On the scribe and miniaturist of MS. *G*, see below.

[23]Descriptions of MS. *G* are summarized in Thorpe, *Laurin*, pp. 33-36; see also K. Chesney, *Medium Aevum*, 21 (1952), 80-82.

[24]Most of the embedded-story content of the *Sept Sages* conveys an impression of violence which threatens to blow apart the well-ordered and predictable debate, from the felling of a tree (*arbor: E^1, V, B^2, G*) to a father attempting to drown his son (*vaticinium: E^1*).

[25]See however further on in the text quoted: "Si forte non occurrant tibi quinque bajuli qui tibi placeant sint saltem tres et non minus, quia maximum bonum proveniet ex hoc, scilicet, ex tribus, quia nisi tertius esset nichil penitus nosceretur. Quia primum super quod fundate sunt omnes res est trinitas, et per quinarium mediantur, et per septenarium perficiuntur" (pp. 139-40).

[26]R. Steele, ed., *Secretum Secretorum*, vol. V of *Opera hactenus inedita Rogeri Baconi* (Oxford, 1920), pp. 135-36.

[27]J. H. Fox, *Robert de Blois: Son Œuvre didactique et narrative* (Paris, [1948]), pp. 112-13; see also J. Ulrich, *Die didactischen und religiösen Dichtungen Robert's von Blois* (Berlin, 1895), p. 34; Ch.-V. Langlois, *La Vie en France au moyen âge* (Paris, 1926), pp. 190, 192: "Méfiez-vous des 'losenjors,' des flatteurs et des traîtes. C'est le pire venin du monde." On *Fürstenspiegel* in general see J. Röder, *Das Fürstenbild in den mittelalterlichen Fürstenspiegeln auf französischem Boden* (Münster, 1933).

[28]In *Medieval Miscellany Presented to Eugène Vinaver* (Manchester, 1965), pp. 245-62.

[29]Thorpe, *Laurin*, p. 36; Palermo, *Le Roman de Cassidorus* (Paris, 1963), I, pp. XXXV-XXXVI.

[30]Delisle, *Cabinet*, I, 86-91; B. de Mandrot, *Revue historique*, 43 (1890), 274-316 and 44 (1890), 241-312; Delisle, *Bibl. de l'Ecole des Chartes*, 66 (1905), 255-60; A. Thomas, *Journal des Savants*, NS 4 (1906), 633-44; Ch. Samaran, *Journal des Savants* (1966), 66-77.

[31]J. W. Bradley, *A Dictionary of Miniaturists, Illuminators, Calligraphers and Copyists* (London, 1888), II, 52-53.

[32]*Journal des Savants*, NS 1 (1903), 265-75.

[33]*Comptes rendus des séances de l'Acad. des Inscr. et Belles-Lettres*, 23 (1895), 74-78. On Evrard d'Espinques, see A. Bosvieux, *Mém. de la Soc. des sciences nat. et arch. de la Creuse* (1863), 14; P. de Cessac, *Mém. . . . de la Creuse,* 6 (1887-90), 60-63; L. Guibert, *Ce qu'on sait de l'enlumineur Evrard d'Espinques* (Guéret and Limoges, 1895).

[34]See F. Lecoy, *Romania*, 90 (1969), 559-62.

[35]Oral communication, Spring 1979.

[36]See, for example, K. Campbell, *The Seven Sages of Rome* (Boston, 1906), p. xvii.

[37]J. Porcher, *Les Mss. à peintures du XIIIe au XVIe s.* (Paris, 1955), p. 32. See also G. G. Vitzthun, *Die Pariser Miniaturmalerei* (Leipzig, 1907), pp. 144-45; R. S. and L. H. Loomis, *Arthurian Legends in Medieval Art* (New York, 1938); Porcher, *L'Enluminure fr.* (Paris, 1959), pp. 47-48; M. A. Stones, *The Illustration of the French Prose Lancelot*, Diss. Univ. of London, 1970; id., in C. Kleinhenz, *Medieval Mss. and Textual Criticism* (Chapel Hill, 1976), pp. 91 ff. and nn. 28-29.

[38]For bibliography of descriptions, see J. Brakelmann, *Jahrbuch f. rom. u. engl. Lit.*, 11 (1870), 102-03; M. Roques, *Romania*, 75 (1954), 431; Bibl. Nat., *Nouv. Acq. fr. 1946-1957* (Paris, 1967), p. 45.

[39]Gaspar and Lyna, *Manuscrits*, I, 310-12; Thorpe, *Laurin*, pp. 28-31; G. Dogaer and M. Debae, *La Librairie de Philippe le Bon: Exposition* (Bruxelles, 1967), p. 98 and Planche 4.

[40]In MS. Brussels, Bibl. roy. 10168-10172, the *Sept Sages* (B^1) are preceded by *Li Fait des Roumains* and *L'Histoire des empereurs de Rome;* they are followed by the *Histoire d'Alexandre* in MS. Brussels, Bibl. roy. 11190-11195 (B^2). MS. *Ha* also contains Grosseteste's *Articuli Fidei Christianae.*

COURTLINESS AND COMEDY IN *AUCASSIN ET NICOLETTE*

Norris J. Lacy

It was Molière, in *La Critique de l'Ecole des femmes*, who insisted that comedy is no less difficult to write than tragedy. It is also true, I think, that comedy is often more difficult to write *about* than is tragedy. The comic impulse is complex and elusive, and all too often the critic errs by reducing comedy to a formula, that is, by oversimplifying it. That tendency is all the more common when the object of study is a work like *Aucassin et Nicolette,* a short, direct, apparently simple and naive poem, which is nonetheless characterized by a subtle comic structure involving an overlay of several types of humor and parody.[1]

This latter term—parody—has become a commonplace of *Aucassin et Nicolette* criticism, and like most commonplaces, this one demands re-examination. Courtly poetry, from its inception, possessed the potential for self-parody; the germ was always there. The lyric resisted such self-parody (in most cases) because the context of courtly love was entirely consonant with its sentiments. In other words, a courtly lover at a court that accepted courtly love is virtually immune to parody. But transposed to an uncourtly, incompatible context, *courtoisie* easily assumes parodic contours.

Aucassin et Nicolette indisputably contains parody, but it is parody of a particular nature, entirely unlike that of a Colin Muset, for example. Colin retains all the forms and formulas of courtly love but replaces their traditional object by another; he lavishes affection not on a lady but on cakes, capons, and pliant patrons.[2] Aucassin, on the other hand, keeps the formulas *and* their traditional object, but he does so within a society to which *courtoisie* is foreign. Thus, the primary design of the poem seems to me less the authorial parody of courtly love than the author's presentation of a character in love not only with Nicolette but also, perhaps, with the notion of courtly love. Aucassin is a kind of Quixote in reverse, clinging tenaciously to his romantic pretensions and distinguishing himself not by compulsive activity but by his obsessive inactivity. Like Quixote, he simply has the misfortune to have been born in a time or place when the values he holds are not espoused by those around him. Thus, although I refer to the poem's parody, it is to be understood to be related closely to comedy of manners and character, presenting as it does the inevitable collision of a thoroughly "courtly" lover with a most uncourtly world. And because the parody depends on our recognition of courtly theme and formula, it is also, of course, a comedy of language. Consequently, we cannot reduce the comedy of the poem to formulaic terms, except by resorting to very general (and consequently inadequate) descriptions: contrast, incompatibility, incongruity, etc.

Inversion is a technique that critics detect throughout the poem, from stylistic transformations in particular passages to the thematic inversion that makes Torelore a *mundus inversus,* a topsy-turvy world. Most critics have contended as well that the poem is characterized, in a more general sense, by an inversion of "usual" courtly roles. Nicolette proves herself active, resourceful, and strongwilled, whereas Aucassin is essentially passive and weak. She acts, while he reacts. She repeatedly takes matters into her own hands, while Aucassin sighs and weeps about his cruel fate. But to say that typical roles are thus altered is to do very little more than oversimplify the diversity of courtly literature. Enide, Lunete, at times Isolde, and other women in other texts play active, resourceful roles as well. And if Aucassin's love-sickness is comical, so must be that of numerous other characters or authors. In fact, insistence on the poem's courtly inversions may blind us to many "uninverted" excesses in the work. While Aucassin's weeping and sighing may strike us as immoderate and "unmasculine," his behavior in fact conforms to much of thirteenth-century courtly doctrine. It is admittedly exaggerated, but not entirely atypical. We may recall, for example, that the God of Love in Guillaume de Lorris' *Roman de la Rose* advises the true lover to bestow his every thought on his beloved, to suffer and sigh from his love.[3] In other words, the *Rose* counsels behavior that is essentially that of Aucassin. And however extreme and amusing we may find his insistence that he can neither act nor live without Nicolette, his sentiments are scarcely more immoderate in their expression of romantic agony than are numerous lyrics which are, by all measures, quite serious. Blondel de Nesle, to offer a single example, writes words that could have come from Aucassin's mouth:

> Tant aim et vueill et desir,
> que ne puis ailleurs penser;
> si me fait Amours languir
> et seur mon voloir chanter.
> Tant l'ai amee et servie,
> que la mort ai desservie,
> s'a ce me convient faillir
> que tant me fait desirrer.[4]

Moreover, if Aucassin permits love to inhibit rather than inspire him, he has a clear model in Chrétien de Troyes's Erec. Thus, in terms of its roles, themes, and conventions, this poem is scarcely less "typically courtly" than are a good many of the texts it is presumed to parody.

Whether we consider the roles to be inverted or exaggerated (or both), we must recognize that they are considerably more complex than either term suggests. As we know, Aucassin long resists going into battle, and once there he forgets to fight. When captured, however, he indulges in a kind of logic somewhat peculiar to this poem, but nonetheless unassailable: if they cut off his head, he will never see Nicolette again.[5] The necessity of keeping his head (literally) in order to see Nicolette spurs him to action; he defeats his enemy, takes the Court Bougars de Valence prisoner, and thus ends the war that has lasted a full twenty years. Thus, while love had earlier inhibited action, it ironically and in convoluted fashion does inspire Aucassin in this episode to conform to another courtly convention, whereby love inspires the lover to act and enables him to perform extraordinary feats. In other words, this poem fulfills courtly expectations, but it does so in its own particular way.

This example indicates how comedy arises out of Aucassin's complex motivation and actions; it suggests moreover that such comedy may be related to a basic contradiction within the courtly code: there is an implicit discrepancy between the dictum that the lover thinks only of his beloved (and sighs, weeps, and pines for her), and the notion that love inspires him to commit marvelous acts. These are not irreconcilable, of course, but they maintain an uncomfortable tension: one impulse is essentially introverted, self-centered, perhaps passive; the other is extroverted, altruistic, and active. Comedy in *Aucassin et Nicolette* derives not only from the exaggeration of both, but also from their simultaneous development, which emphasizes (as in the battle scene) the convoluted logic that leads Aucassin to act in spite of his explicit desire not to do so. In fact, there is frequently, in this work, an ironic dislocation of result from motivation, and this phenomenon underlies much of the poem's essential humor. As I have already noted, it would be erroneous to suggest that the work does not satisfy courtly expectations or resolve courtly situations; on the contrary, it does exactly that, but it does so in unorthodox fashion. The lovers repeatedly find each other largely by accident; Aucassin achieves military victory after refusing to fight. Conventional situations achieve conventional resolutions, but in unusual ways.

This dissociation of result from intention is illustrated, for example, by the scene in which Aucassin leaves his father's house during a *feste* (which is intended to cheer him but which depresses him instead). At a guest's urging, he rides in the forest, and this virtually unmotivated act leads him to be reunited with Nicolette. Much that happens in the work happens, in fact, by accident rather than by design—except of course that such "accidents" are part of the author's ironic design. For we can have no serious doubt that fate will unite the couple, regardless of what they are or do. And in such a system, a prime target for the poet's comedic urge will inevitably be the characters' actions and responses within a destiny largely beyond their control.

Nicolette and Aucassin differ in this regard, of course. In general, he simply declines to act, or does so only when he has no alternative. He responds to confinement with resignation and tears, while Nicolette escapes from her prison. And after their final separation, it is she who sets out to find him. She is thus considerably more resourceful than Aucassin, but both times it is fate that guides her and dictates her success in finding, indeed in almost stumbling upon, her beloved.

But while Aucassin and Nicolette differ in many ways, they also have much in common, and the two of them are frequently contrasted to other characters. In fact, a good deal of the humor of the poem derives not from the simple exaggeration of courtly style or convention, but from the juxtaposition of incompatible styles or, frequently, from emphasis on the primary characters' rigid adherence to their *courtoisie* in the face of situations that reasonably demand flexibility and change.

Comedy results, sometimes in a rather elementary way, from inappropriate speech. In one episode, for instance, Aucassin (forever the love-stricken noble youth) speaks to a cowherd in allegorical terms incomprehensible to the latter, who takes his mention of a hunting dog literally and berates him for grieving over a *cien puant* (xxiv, 43)—an unwitting and thoroughly unflattering reference to Nicolette. Aucassin is ridiculous here because of the discrepancy between his speech and the reasonable demands imposed by the situation; the cowherd serves to deflate his allegorical rhetoric. Similarly, the watchman (xv) praises Nicolette in refined, courtly terms and then abruptly shifts to a direct and unadorned style more consonant with his purpose (Vance, p. 47). At least *he* can adapt to circumstances, an ability not shared by Aucassin. The hero remains thoroughly lost in his own love-smitten world, in spite of the developing realities around him. The text abounds in examples of this, but one of the most striking and comical instances—involving both of the lovers—occurs when they speak together through a crack in the dungeon wall (of course, Nicolette, having escaped, is outside, while the resigned Aucassin weeps within). They engage in a spirited debate over men's and women's relative capacities for love. The discussion is amusing in its own right, but as usual, comedy arises less from content than from context. Nicolette is being sought by guards intent on capturing or killing her, but the lovers' preoccupation with their *courtoisie* effaces other considerations. Their debate is proper material for a court of love or for an interior monologue or even for a discussion between Yvain and Laudine or Lancelot and Guenevere. It might be exaggerated in any event, but it is comical here because it is entirely inappropriate in its context. The comedy of the scene and the implied criticism of the lovers' courtliness are due primarily to their rigidity, to their inability to save courtly debates for the castle or the chamber, and to their failure to react to physical danger in realistic and practical fashion.

Thus far, I have mentioned content and context, but not the form of the poem. As the preceding discussions have suggested, the comedy of the work does not remain uniform throughout; the comic techniques—and consequently the kinds of humor—vary from one passage to another. Herein lies much of the work's complexity. Torelore does not function as does the poem's beginning; certain parts of the work are broadly humorous, while others appear largely devoid of comic intent. In this regard, we should note that the very form of the *chante-fable* bears a significant relation to its parodic and comic function; that is, the alternation of prose and verse sections is far more than a historical curiosity—far more, also, than an indication of the poem's dramatic intention or method of presentation. The form of the work cannot be ignored in any consideration of its tone and character.

Eugene Vance notes that only noble characters are permitted within the confines of the verse portions.[6] Those passages are thus the repository of noble language and sentiments, of a harking back to a pure and unfettered *courtoisie*—or at least a pretense thereof. It is notable, in this regard, that the comic or parodic content of the work is communicated almost entirely by the prose sections. This contention is supported by an experiment doen recently with a group of students: a "naive reading" of the verse portions of the work, without the prose, yielded little or no evidence or parody.[7] It is true that some portions of the verse are lyrically effusive and rhetorically excessive, but— onec again—they become comical when re-established in the narrative context, in situations in which they are inappropriate. Parody's vehicle, at least in this work, is prose. The primary explanation for this is related to the referentiality of the language.

Literature has been defined as language referring to itself. That is, literary discourse is distinguishable from non-literary by its degree of reflexive reference. Literary discourse is not only the vehicle of expression but also the thing being expressed, whereas non-literary language is intended to remain largely transparent while referring to something outside itself.[8] Of particular significance for *Aucassin et Nicolette* is the fact that there is an innate difference in the level of referentiality of prose and verse. Prose tends by its nature to be expansive and referential, directing attention beyond itself. In other words, it signifies. Verse is more self-contained and contractive, referring more to itself than to something outside itself.[9] If it signifies, it is also, to a large extent, the signified—a system of internal references, a poetic construct possessing its own esthetic value.

Both tradition and the nature of verse confer on the lyric sections of *Aucassin et Nicolette* the capacity to sustain exaggeration without becoming ridiculous.[10] The lexical content of the work also merits attention in this regard. Simone Monsonégo, following a computer-assisted study of the text, has noted a preponderance of nouns and adjectives in the verse, and of verbs in the prose.[11] This is hardly surprising, since the prose is heavily narrative, while the verse consists mostly of meditations and evocative developments of Aucassin's amorous agony. But the implications of this revelation are significant. Benveniste defines a verb as ". . . l'élément indispensable à la constitution d'un énoncé assertif fini," and he adds that "une assertion finie, du fait même qu'elle est assertion, implique référence de l'énoncé à un ordre différent, qui est l'ordre de la réalité."[12] In other words, the lexical content of the work supports the contentions made here about referentiality. The verse, with comparatively few verbs, makes relatively less reference to reality, including—presumably—the external literary reality of the courtly system that is the target of parody and the object of humor. But the prose, verbal in character, creates situations in which reality (whether of the world or of the courtly text) provides an effective context for comedy.

*		*		*

Why is Aucassin's refusal to fight amusing when Erec's is not? What this question illustrates is that comedy derives less from theme than from style, tone, and the relation of any given episode to the meaning and intention of the entire work. It suggests moreover that comedy, parody, humor are far too complex to be encompassed by a formula (such as "role reversal," for instance). *Aucassin et Nicolette* is courtly parody; it is sophisticated comedy; it is also an enduring and endearing story. The comic structure of the work cannot be defined simply; there is undoubtedly parody of courtly situations or works, but it is certainly not a simple parody of courtly manners that inverts roles and overturns conventions to create a humorous tale. There is humor ranging from a refined comedy of language to the broad burlesque of the Torelore episode. And, finally, the tension between lyric and parodic/narrative permits the poet to avoid caricature and to present the characters both as marvelous comic creations and, remarkably, as young lovers who, despite their atypical behavior and Aucassin's frequent buffoonery, engage and keep our sympathy.

University of Kansas

NOTES

[1] I do not intend this paragraph as a condemnation of specific critics. There are numerous important studies of *Aucassin et Nicolette*, among which we might note especially Barbara Nelson Sargent, "Parody in *Aucassin et Nicolette:* Some Further Considerations," *French Review*, 43, No. 4 (March 1970), 597-605; Omer Jodogne, "La Parodie et le pastiche dans *Aucassin et Nicolette*," *Cahiers de l'Association Internationale des Etudes Françaises,* No. 12 (June 1960), 53-65; Eugene Vance, "The Word at Heart: *Aucassin et Nicolette* as a Medieval Comedy of Language," *Yale French Studies,* No. 45 (1970), 33-51; Nathaniel B. Smith, "The Uncourtliness of Nicolette," in *Voices of Conscience,* ed. Raymond Cormier (Philadelphia: Temple Univ. Press, 1977), pp. 169-182.

[2] For example, "Ma bele douce amie / la rose est espanie / . . . / Vos serez bien servie / de crasse oe rostie"; quoted from Carla Cremonesi, *Lirica francese del medio evo* (Milan: Cisalpino, 1955), pp. 152-3.

[3] Vss. 2221 ff., esp. 2263-6.

[4] Cremonesi, p. 103.

[5] *Aucassin et Nicolette,* ed. Mario Roques (Paris: Champion, 1969), x, 17-22.

[6] P. 41. The only exceptions are the narrator and the shepherd (when the latter is playing at being noble).

[7] In a course in Old French, University of Kansas, Fall 1978. If the verse sections do carry any parodic intent or effect, it is primarily by the influence of the prose. This montage effect, this "spilling-over," this influence of context on text may cause us to read:

> Douce amie, flors de lis,
> biax alers et biax venirs
> biax jouers et biax bordirs . . .

as parody, but there is nothing *in the passage itself* to suggest anything other than the repetitious daydreams and perhaps sensual fantasies of Aucassin.

[8] As Terence Hawkes notes (in *Structuralism and Semiotics* [Berkeley: Univ. of California Press, 1977], p. 64), "No word is *ever* really a mere proxy for a denoted object." Hawkes quotes Jakobson's contention that ". . . words and their arrangement, their meaning, their outward and inward form acquire weight and value of their own."

[9]My discussion of the character of verse must be taken as a large oversimplification; quite obviously, the standard narrative verse of medieval romance or perhaps of a Voltaire poem approaches the status of prose.

[10]Robert Harden, in "*Aucassin et Nicolette* as Parody," *SP*, 63 (1966), 1-9, sees the seven-syllable line in the poem as a parodic departure from the traditional octosyllable; I think we might, with equal justification, see it as an attempt to move further away from the standard narrative form (the octosyllable) and thereby to reduce further the referentiality of the verse sections.

[11]In *Etude stylo-statistique du vocabulaire des vers et de la prose dans la chantefable "Aucassin et Nicolette"* (Paris: Klincksieck, 1966).

[12]Emile Benveniste, *Problèmes de linguistique générale* (Paris: Gallimard, 1966), p. 155.

USES OF RHETORIC IN MEDIEVAL FRENCH DRAMA

Alan E. Knight

Late medieval drama was a marriage of mime and rhetoric. By mime, I refer to the representation of a dramatic action, of which there were two types in the fifteenth and early sixteenth centuries. The one, consisting of biblical plays, saints' lives, and the like, was the imitation of a historical action and had the function of keeping a significant past alive and relevant to late medieval society. The other, consisting of morality plays and farces, was the representation of an invented or fictional action and had the function of providing examples of behavior for the spectators to imitate or avoid. Rhetoric, conjoined with mime, served parallel memorial and exemplary functions. The rhetoric of the historical plays bound the spectators into a community of belief with a common heritage, while that of the fictional plays exhorted them to act in conformity with community standards for the common good. Because of the importance of rhetoric in the composition and production of medieval plays, I would like to examine briefly a few of its uses in both the historical and fictional genres. We shall look particularly at sermon rhetoric and levels of style.

James J. Murphy in his *Rhetoric in the Middle Ages* has shown that the medieval art of preaching differed from classical oratory in that the latter attempted to persuade by presenting arguments based on logic and probability, while the former attempted to persuade by presenting a religious truth.[1] In the one case the hearer could make an intellectual choice based on the arguments; in the other case he had to make a moral choice based on the common perception of good and evil. The art of preaching was a branch of rhetoric that was raised to a high level in the Middle Ages and that exerted a strong influence in many domains of medieval life and art. There were no doubt close ties between homiletic practice and the development of medieval drama, but that would be a full-length study in itself. Once fully developed, the historical plays, which we usually call mystery plays, bore a greater resemblance to religious rituals than to sermons in that they were often performed as acts of petition or thanksgiving. But just as sermons were usually preached in conjunction with religious rituals, so were they preached in association with the mystery plays. It is this incorporation of complete sermons into the mystery plays that we shall consider here.

The fact that writers of historical or mystery plays were steeped in the sermon rhetoric of their day becomes immediately apparent on examining the sermons included in the plays. There were two ways of incorporating sermons into the plays: they could be preached directly to the audience by a Prologue figure or they could be preached within the action of the play by one character to other characters. In either case the sermons followed the generally accepted outline of a sermon as taught by medieval rhetoricians. This consisted of four or five basic parts such as Prologue, Theme, Division, Proof, and Amplification, but the structure could be greatly elaborated should the occasion require it. The rhetoric of the sermon was develoed in the late twelfth and early thirteenth centuries. Except for minor variations, the theory of preaching remained virtually unchanged from that time until the Renaissance. Here, for example, are the six parts of the artistic or university sermon as outlined by Thomas of Salisbury in the early thirteenth century:

1. Opening prayer for divine aid.
2. Protheme, or introduction of theme.
3. Theme, or statement of a scriptural quotation.
4. Division, or statement of parts of the theme.
5. Development of the members named in the division.
6. Conclusion.[2]

Over two hundred years later Jean Michel followed an almost identical pattern for the sermon that serves as Prologue to his *Mystère de la Passion.* [3] Michel's sermon opens with an introductory statement of the biblical quotation to be used as the theme: *Verbum caro factum est.* There follows the prayer, which in the mystery plays usually took the form of a public recitation of the *Ave Maria.* Next is the protheme with a statement of how the preacher intends to treat it. This latter amounts to a preliminary or minor division. Before the major theme and division, however, there is the conventional disclaimer in regard to possible theological errors in the dramatic text. The preacher then restates the theme and divides it into four parts corresponding to each of the four Latin words. Each part is developed and amplified with biblical and theological proofs. There is no conclusion, but the play begins immediately with another sermon, that of John the Baptist.[4]

The dramatic distinction between the sermon of the Prologue and that of John the Baptist should be made clear. In the first case a preacher addresses the audience directly with a sermon that, while part of the play, is not part of the historical action being represented. In the second case a dramatic character is reenacting the delivery of a sermon from biblical history. This presents us with an interesting theoretical problem that sheds some light on the nature of the medieval theater in general. As we know, there are two levels of discourse in dramatic language. At one level the playwright is speaking to the public (*discours rapporteur*), while at the other level one character is speaking to another (*discours rapporté*).[5] This theoretical structure, which may be applied to modern plays as well as to most medieval plays without difficulty, becomes problematic when applied to the sermons preached within the dramatic action of the mystery plays. In medieval productions of these plays certain characters were required on occasion to preach to large crowds of people. One thinks of Christ, for example, preaching his sermon on the mount to a great multitude. In Gréban's version of this scene Simon is amazed by the size of the throng:

> Oncques si grant collection
> de peuple je ne veis ensemble
> que je voy icy, ce me semble.[6]

In this and similar cases, however, no extra actors were brought into the theater just to play the part of the listeners. Instead, it was the people attending the plays who provided the crowds necessary for the sermons. Thus, when Simon gestured toward the multitude in a medieval production of Gréban's *Passion*, the spectators were momentarily transformed into characters of the play, bringing the two levels of discourse into convergence.

We see here something of the communal character of medieval drama. The Prologue sermons fostered a sense of community among the spectators by reiterating a shared set of beliefs; but the sermons preached within the dramatic action enabled the spectators to relive their common heritage by actually participating in the re-creation of important historical events. Thus the converging of the two levels of discourse signals a parallel convergence of drama and real life. Indeed, the two were not always clearly separable in late medieval society, where events important in the life of the community were, as a matter of course, transformed into spectacle.

The morality play, lacking the historical dimension of the mystery play, is an allegorical fiction related in structure and function to the *exemplum*. As such, it may be viewed as an extension of the sermon, because the use of *exempla* was considered in medieval sermon rhetoric to be one of the standard means of amplification.[7] Willem Noomen has described the *Jeu d'Adam* as a "prédication par personnages,"[8] but there is even more justification for so designating the morality plays. They fit perfectly Robert of Basevorn's definition of preaching as "the persuasion of the multitude . . . to worthy conduct."[9]

One of the problems the medieval preacher had to deal with was how to speak to a mixed audience of both learned and unlearned people. In the early thirteenth century Alexander of Ashby suggested that the preacher would do well "sometimes to present a charming allegory and sometimes to tell a pleasant story (*exemplum*), so that the learned may savor the profundity of the allegory while the humble may profit from the lightness of the story."[10] The late medieval morality play solved the same problem in a similar way by combining erudite allegory presented in long, learned, didactic speeches with fast, hard-hitting action. Alexander also suggested that the preacher be no "less vehement in his commendation of virtue than he is in the reprehension of vices."[10] This too was a technique of the morality play. There were elegant presentations of the static virtues for the learned to savor, interspersed with the fascinating activities of the vices, which served to warn the unlearned. These same ideas were echoed some three centuries later in the *Instructif de la seconde rethoricque*, which was published in the *Jardin de plaisance* (1501). To write morality plays the author advises:

> Item on les doit decorer
> De belles collocutions;
> Icelles aussi honnorer
> De belles demonstracions,
> Rethoricques ornacions;
> Et qu'ilz soient auctorisees
> Par deues diffinicions
> Affin que mieulx soient prisees.
>
> Item que l'on blasme et desprise
> Les vices fort en general
> Sans ce qu'on particularise
> Sur aucun suppost parcial
> En cas infame especial;
> L'on doit donc les vertus priser
> Et des vices dire le mal,
> Puis les vertus auctoriser.[11]

The alternation between long speeches and rapid action is a characteristic of the morality play that makes sense only when we have understood the rhetorical underpinnings of the genre. We must not expect a dramatic action in the usual sense of a closely linked chain of events leading to a dénouement. Instead, the morality play is an allegory of a moral progress through a series of states of mind or stages in life. In reading the morality plays we must sensitize ourselves to the rhetoric of the constant repetitions and the verbal prolixity so that we may understand them, not as impeding the flow of the action, but as enhancing the moral states at the heart of the action.

There seems to be a law in the medieval drama that the greater the importance of a character in the social or religious hierarchies, the more the verbal discourse relating to that character takes precedence over physical action. Scenes representing heaven, for example, are almost completely static in terms of physical movement. Here, addresses to the diety surround God with a nimbus of honorific formulae in verbal imitation of the winged cherubim that were thought to encircle his throne. The language of such scenes is extremely formal and ceremonial, and is written in the most elevated style that the playwrights of the time could command. This style may be illustrated by a short passage from the morality of *L'Homme Juste de l'Homme Mondain*, where an angel addresses God in the following way:

> Souverain dieu, puissant roy des roys glorieux, remply de toute amour et bonté et sur tous victorieux, ton nom soit glorifié et benoist. Hault et excellent plasmateur, tousjours voyons et congnoissons la bonne amour et grant desir que tu as eu et encores as de jour en jour a la povre nature humaine.[12]

This type of language is not limited to angels, of course; every other character in paradise speaks to God in much the same way. Obviously the language of everyday life would not be suitable for such discourse. The angel here speaks in a highly formal Latinate style; but no less formal is the speech of God himself. Having just created the souls of Homme Juste and Homme Mondain, God says of his work:

> Par ma puissance incomparable et infinie et pour la tressinguliere amour, ardante dilection et faveur que de long temps j'ay eu, que encores j'ay et tousjours incessamment j'auray a la povre nature humaine, j'ay bien voulu creer a mon ymaige et divine semblance deux ames immortelles. (fol. c. ii. rᵒ)

Such formulae, which are perhaps even more impressive in prose than in verse, are used constantly in the long paradise scenes. By contrast, the scenes of debauchery involving Homme Mondain are spoken in a low style resembling that of the farces. On his way to Malle Fin, for example, Homme Mondain plays a game of cards with Tromperie (fols. r.i to r.iii), the style of which is worthy of the tavern scenes in Jean Bodel's *Jeu de St. Nicolas*. The hell scenes in this play are filled with vulgar and abusive language expressive of the eternal conflict in that domain. All scenes written in the low style are also characterized by a great deal of physical action. There are many other rhetorical styles in the morality plays. Lyrical styles, for example, are often put into the mouths of the vices. In *L'Homme Pecheur*, Luxury makes a striking entrance with a speech that combines lyric form with fearful context:

> Par moy, Luxure,
> Par ma morsure
> Je courray seure
> D'estoc, de taille.
> Mainte censure
> Par moy s'asseure,
> C'est chose seure,
> C'est ma vitaille.
> Mon advanture
> Convaint nature
> Qui desnature
> Toute rayson.
> Car ma facture
> Et mourriture
> Est pourriture
> Toute saison.[13]

Subtle uses of rhetorical styles can convey meanings not contained in the words themselves. In *Le Gouvert d'Humanité*,[14] for example, the main character, Humanité, speaks in a middle or non-elevated style that has both pastoral and urban overtones. By contrast, the three vices, Peché, Temptation, and Luxure, introduce themselves in high-style speeches that are filled with Latinate words as well as biblical, mythological, and historical allusions. Here, for example, is the beginning of the speech that Tempation makes on entrance:

> Je suys filz du grand roy Plutho
> De la nation cerbericque,
> Le germain de dame Aletho
> Et la deesse Arsericque. (120-24)

All three vice figures enter the dramatic action with a great deal of bluster, proclaiming their own importance in set pieces that should probably be viewed as parodies of the high style. After the introduction, however, their speech descends to a middle or low style as they interact with Humanité in their efforts to lead him astray. Later in the play there is a scene in which Humanité, contemplating a skull, delivers a soliloquy on death. The Latinate vocabulary of the first part of his meditation recalls the elevated style of the introductory speeches of the vices:

> O folle beaulté transitoire,
> Qu'esse que de monde la gloire?
>   Ce n'est que abuz,

> Laberint, infernal paludz,
>   Puys plutonicque,
> O mort, ou n'a nulle replicque,
> O mort terrible et inique
>   Que tout abas,
> Tu faict cesser plaisirs, esbas,
> Tu faict a plusieurs dire: helas! (553-62)

But when he thinks of the eyes, mouth, and nose that once belonged to the skull, he adopts a familiar style that evokes their simple pleasures:

> Ou sont les baisers tant honnestes,
> Ou est la grace des fillettes? . . .
> O pouvre nez, villain et sale,
> Qu'as odoré en mainte sale
>   Fleurs et bouquetz! (584-89)

One is forcefully reminded of Hamlet's contemplation of Yorick's skull: "Here hung those lips . . . Where be your gibes now?" (V, 1). But there are obviously differences here. Humanité is on the point of repenting his sins, and Remort de Conscience has given him the skull to speed his repentance. When, as readers of the play, we visualize the scene, we see Humanité looking at a skull and meditating on death, much as we would see Hamlet doing. But if, at the same time, we listen carefully to the rhetorical style, then we perceive another dimension in the scene. The skull itself becomes a character—the character Death, who, in the voice of Humanité, makes his high-style speech upon entrance and then drops to the lower, familiar style of the *ubi sunt* theme.

We can see, then that the morality play is more than just a metaphor or allegory of the moral world; it is also a rhetorical model of that world. The court of heaven is portrayed in the sublimity of the high style, human society in the naturalness of the middle style, and hell in the comic exaggeration of the low style. Only the earlier and longer morality plays, however, portray the moral universe in its full scope. The later plays tend to deal with more limited and specific moral problems—the raising of children, for example. Nevertheless, we have seen that the longer plays combine the rhetorical levels of style with an exemplary story representing the moral progress of an individual. Just as the mystery plays enabled the medieval spectators to see their place in the history of the world, so the full scope morality plays enabled them to see their place in the moral universe. To medieval rhetoric is due much of the credit for bringing these worlds into being.

Pennsylvania State University

NOTES

[1]James J. Murphy, *Rhetoric in the Middle Ages* (Berkeley, University of California Press, 1974), pp. 276-77.

[2]Murphy, p. 325.

[3]Jean Michel, *Le Mystère de la Passion*, ed. Omer Jodogne (Gembloux: J. Duculot, 1959), ll. 1-888.

[4]John the Baptist actually preaches two sermons at the beginning of the play. The first occupies ll. 889-1172; the second, ll. 1548-710.

[5]Anne Ubersfeld, *Lire le théâtre* (Paris: Editions Sociales, 1977), p. 254.

[6]Arnoul Gréban, *Le Mystère de la Passion*, ed. Omer Jodogne (Brussels: Palais des Académies, 1965), ll. 12794-96.

[7]Murphy, p. 341.

[8]Willem Noomen, "Le *Jeu d'Adam*, étude descriptive et analytique," *Romania, 89 (1968), 189.*

[9]Murphy, p. 345. This is Murphy's paraphrase.

[10]Alexander of Ashby, *De modo praedicandi.* Quoted by Murphy, p. 313.

[11]Eugénie Droz and A. Piaget, *Le Jardin de plaisance et fleur de rhétorique,* vol. 1, facsimile edn. (Paris: Firmin Didot, 1910), fol. c. ii. r°.

[12]Simon Bougouin, *L'Homme Juste et l'Homme Mondain* (Paris: Anthoine Verard, 1508), fol. c. iii. r°. The copy of this play consulted is in the Bibliothèque Nationale, Rés. Yf. 125.

[13]*L'Homme Pecheur* (Paris: Le Petit Laurens for Guillaume Eustace, n.d. [early 16th c.[), fol. c. i. r°. The copy consulted is in the Bibliothèque Nationale, Rés. Yf. 27.

[14]Jean d'Abondance, *Le Gouvert d'Humanité*, ed. Paul Aebischer, *Bibliothèque d'Humanisme et Renaissance*, 24 (1962), 282-338.

THE SAINT AND THE DEVIL:

CHRISTOLOGICAL AND DIABOLOGICAL TYPOLOGY IN

FIFTEENTH CENTURY PROVENÇAL DRAMA

Moshé Lazar

Parallel to the cosmogonical battle between Christ and Antichrist in visionary literature and to the dramatic confrontation between Notre Dame and Satan in legend and on the stage,[1] the permanent struggle between Everyman and his Vices, as an ever-lasting *psychomachia*, represents in poetry and in drama the more familiar and more immediate experience of Good and Evil. In this latter category we ought to distinguish two main varieties: the traditional allegories, both in art and drama, narrating the conflict between the Vices and the Virtues[2] on one hand, the numerous plays and artworks illustrating the lives of Saints besieged by the Devil and his agents on the other. The emissaries of Satan might be represented by diabolized human beings (Herod, Nero, Pilate, Jew, etc.) and/or by diabolized personifications (*Pride, Heresy, Lechery, War, Sloth,* etc.), and thus constitute an elaborate *diabological typology* in absolute contrast with *christological typology.*[3] Plays about Saints were close to the hearts of medieval audiences because they exemplified the story of an Everyman becoming a Christian Hero after successfully fighting and defeating the Devil and his agents. Among the plays and artworks dealing with the confrontation between *Saints/Virtues* and *Devils/Vices*, those about Saint Anthony are the most emblematic and also the most dramatic.

Among the few medieval Provençal plays which have survived (hardly amounting to a dozen), some seven are concerned with the lives of Saints and were written and performed in the latter half of the 15th century in the alpine region of Briançon. In each case, the story is that of a Saint who, with the help of Heaven, overcomes hell-inspired trials and tribulations and enters Paradise, to the frustration and dismay of the devils. Mirroring the development of their French counterparts, these plays are not mere imitations, in regard to the place and functions they attribute to the devils; on the contrary, their authors have increased and enriched the diabological typology. In addition to the stock-type devils such as the coward, the braggart, the petty thug, the whining complainer, etc.,—all to be found in contemporary or earlier French plays—there is a very definite association of the various devils with the Seven Deadly Sins. The influence of allegorical drama, which was developing in the second half of the 15th century, is most noticeable in the Saint Anthony play, where the Saint is tempted by the Seven Deadly Sins. But the anonymous author has avoided the total abstraction of the *Jeu des sept péchès mortels et des sept vertus*[4] by having the sins represented by specific devils (e.g., the actor playing the role of Lucifer also plays the role of Pride, Mamonas plays Avarice, etc.). In the *Saint Peter and Saint Paul* play, for example, the association is particularly emphasized by the unique device of a hell-bound character's last testament: specific parts of the body, which are related to clearly defined sins, are willed to specific devils (e.g., the head, seat of pride, is left to Lucifer).

The study presented here, in a somewhat summary way, aims to illustrate the evolution and development of the diabological typology in Provençal drama through three of its plays about Saints: the *Istoria Petri et Pauli,* the *Mystère de Saint Eustache*, and the *Mystère de Sant Anthoni de Viennès*, all published almost a century ago by Paul Guillaume.[5]

The *Mystère de Saint Eustache* is the shortest of the three (2, 850 lines, out of which 250 relate to Devils and *diableries*). The story dramatizes the glorious life of the Roman general Placidus, a Christian convert who was martyred around the year 118. The play faithfully retells the legend: the general, out hunting one day, sees between the antlers of a stag the image of Christ, who exhorts him to convert. Changing his name to Eustache, the general is baptized along with his family. Having lost his possessions and his post, the general flees to Egypt where he loses his wife and children. Fifteen years later, after many hardships and tribulations, he is brought back to Rome and reinstated by Trajan, commands a victorious army against the king of Turkey and finds his wife and children. But then, refusing to participate in pagan celebrations honoring Apollo, Eustache and his family are thrown to the lions (who exhibit the same tameness as Daniel's lions) and finally die in a white-hot bronze monster. Their souls are taken to Paradise by the angels.

The christological typology is very clearly presented through the image of Christ between the antlers of the stag, the reminiscence of Job's situation and that of Daniel. The christological axis *Job-Daniel-Martyr* will be paralleled by the diabological one: *Satan-Devils-Beasts* (although less developped here than in the two other plays). The first appearance of the devils on stage is the familiar *Consilium diaboli*[6](vv. 710-835); the scene occurs shortly after Eustache's baptism, as the devils get together to decide what should be done about the situation. Infernus, one of the most important devils (his role being the one Satan usually has in other mysteries), laments Eustache's desertion from their pagan realm which is dwindling daily because of the Christian converts. Satan, assuming here the role generally played by Lucifer, is chained to his throne and presides the infernal Council. Astaroth eagerly suggests that they all work spreading evil on earth and not waste time in useless deliberations. But, it is Satan (the traditional Satan, not Lucifer) whose advice is most respected, and Infernus asks him to teach the others his subtle art of temptation. The prince of Hell then lapses into a short reminiscence of the good old days before having been chained (*"Davant que fassoc encheyna"*), boasting of his triumphs over Adam and Eve, and how he made Cain kill Abel. He then advises that they diligently destroy the consciences of those who are to die, for if they fall into sin, they cannot lift themselves up again. Leviatam's opinion is asked and he answers (in the typical manner of the *miles gloriosus*) that they should go and confront Christ himself and kill him. Infernus, both wiser and scared, tries to dissuade him from this impossible project. Leviatam loudly asserts his pride and courage: he is not afraid of Jesus, he will beat him up and then, when he's not looking, he will get him from behind. This speech of the *braggart devil*, a *diabolus gloriosus*, is very often part of Satan's role, particularly when Satan and Lucifer play different parts (the latter being chained to his throne, the former assuming his role as field commander of all the devils). Upon the advice of other devils it is decided that Eustache will be tormented and made to suffer "until he becomes another Job on earth" (*Tant que ung autre Job sio en terro*). The scene closes with the terrible lament of a poor soul, Anima, imprisoned forever in Hell: "I am the soul which cannot die/Though I have long desired to die" (*L'armo soy, que non po murir/De murir longoment ay desira*; vv. 828-29).

The devils next appear carrying out their plans to kill Eustache's children (vv. 1165-1320). The diabolized beasts Leo and Lupus have been designated to perform the task, but are prevented by some good peasants, and go whimpering off to Hell, explaining to Infernus that they tried their best, but *"custodit parvullos Dominus"*! Balsabut, who is in charge of the operations on earth, calls to Hell for reinforcements; Infernus sends Astaroth, who, despite Balsabut's confidence, has doubts about the outcome of their mission.

The next scene with devils (excepting the brief appearance of Balsabut who takes Trajan off to Hell upon the latter's death) is at the end of the play, following Eustache's death and ascension to Paradise. It is the familiar *diablerie*, a scene more grotesque and hilarious than terrifying and didactic, in which the devils express their frustration and despair. Balsabut and Astaroth, in this case, are the scapegoats, and all the blame is put on them. In a scene closely resembling a meeting of gangsters, henchman Infernus asks the boss Satan what to do; Satan orders that the two who muffed the job be given a hellish punishment. The two villains, Balsabut and Astaroth, vainly try to defend themselves, blaming the supernatural powers of King Jesus. Infernus orders the other devils, who are itching for a fight, to go ahead and give those "dyables fals" a lesson they will never forget. The two scream for pity as their fellow devils joyfully beat them up. Infernus then expresses his confidence that the soldiers of Hell will do better in the future.

Both purposes of the play, to teach and to entertain, are very well served by its opening *consilium diaboli* and its closing *diablerie*, by opposing Satan and Christ, Infernus and Eustache, the diabolized beasts and the innocent peasants, and by presenting the sad lament of a soul in Hell as a counterpoint to Eustache's blessed soul in paradise.

A more elaborate structure will be found in the *Istoria Petri et Pauli* (a play to be performed in two days, its text having 6,135 lines of which some 660 relate to the devils), whose direct source of inspiration, rather than the *Acta Apostolorum*, was probably the 15th century French *Martyre de saint Pierre et saint Paul* (a much shorter play of 840 lines).[7] The original story had already been considerably elaborated and changed before the composition of the Provençal play, but never before was the typological confrontation between God and Satan, or rather between their representatives Peter and Simon the Magician, so clearly outlined within the framework of the story of the apostles Peter and Paul. Simon the Magician has become as important a character as Peter, if not more so (and certainly more than Paul). In fact, Peter's main role has become combatting Simon.

The play opens in Jerusalem where the two rivals perform various miracles, thus enacting the opposition Christ-Antichrist and presenting right at the opening of the play how important and central the christological and diabological typology is to the structure and significance of this drama. From Jerusalem to Antioch and from there to Rome, the roads of Simon the Magician and Peter intersect: the former achieving considerable popular success before being defeated and confounded by the latter. These ups and downs of Simon are mere prefigurations of his final downfall from his attempted ascension. In the meanwhile, Simon is cordially received and held in high esteem by Nero (a typical incarnation of a diabolized human being). The first day's action ends at the height of Simon's success, with Nero adoring him as a God (owing to a well simulated death and resurrection scene). Peter is summoned to appear before the emperor for a special *disputation* with Simon. As expected, Peter wins by succeeding in bringing back to life a young man; Simon, having failed, leaves Rome but is soon brought back by the bored Nero. The final encounter between the two rivals of the univeral *disputatio* takes place in the symbolic and emblematic scene of Simon's attempt to ascend to heaven and his deadly fall: Simon the Magician, as Lucifer and Antichrist, is defeated by Peter the Apostle, servant of God and Christ.

The second half of the play treats the conversions and miracles performed by Peter and Paul, Peter's attempt to leave Rome and his vision of Christ, the persecution of the two apostles and their martyrdom. The story ends with the death of Nero and his prefect Agripa.

Simon the Magician is always presented in the play as a close relative of the devils; he has the power to invoke them at will and does so three times. There is also a very clear association of him with Antichrist, as he claims repeatedly to be the son of God and the promised Messiah: "I am the prophet and Messiah / of whom Isaiah spoke . . . / I am the son of God Almighty . . ." *(Iou siouc propheto et Messias / De qual parlo Ysayas / . . . Filh siouc de Diou ominpotent)*. Later, to Nero, he proclaims "*sum lux, veritas et vita*" and promises eternal life to those who believe in him. His simulated death-and-resurrection scene is both the parody and the typological negative reproduction of Christ's Passion. The legend of Antichrist and the story of Simon the Magician, which are quite distinct in Apocryphal and Apocalyptic texts, are perfectly superimposed in the dramatic treatment of the Provençal play.

The devils appear in only one scene during the first day of the play (vv. 245-350), a fact which enhances the importance of the satanic role assumed by Simon the Magician. The devils are invoked by Simon when he finds himself confounded by Peter in Jerusalem. At his call, all hell breaks loose: Lucifer, the Supreme Master of Hell, urges his servants· to assist their friend Simon. The scene that follows is the typical *consilium diaboli*; the various devils introduce themselves and boast of their particular talents: Belial teaches men to play cards and dice and to practice usury; Tartarus causes men to swear and to fight with one another; Asmodeus inspires evil thoughts and makes people think ill of the good; Cerberus is the watchdog of Hell. It is finally decided that Satan, Lucifer's right-hand devil, and Belsebuc (very often Satan's companion) should go to earth to help Simon in his difficulties with the troublesome Peter.

The devils are next invoked early in the second part of the play: when, before Nero and his court, Simon calls forth infernal dogs to devour Peter. The apostle, however, suspecting something of the sort, has taken the precaution of hiding consecrated bread under his robes; and, upon seeing the bread, the dogs flee (they are later turned against Simon himself). Belsebuc appears shortly thereafter to try to help Simon ressucitate the child, but he is chased away by Peter. Devils appear briefly again (vv. 3,530ff.) to support the attempted flight of Simon. A *diablerie* follows (vv. 3,560-3,650): Satan reports the death of Simon the Magician to his master Lucifer, and all the devils rejoice while preparations are being made for the torture of this new addition to Hell. He will be plunged in boiling lead, wear great iron chains, be roasted and cooked, and have serpents crowning his head. It is part of the devils' nature and functions to rejoice in the downfall of one of their fellows or one of their diabolical agents on earth. It is the devil's desire to win for Hell new souls of innocent and good people, but when these are not in easy reach, the soul of a "poor devil" will have to serve them as well. This scene prefigures in the play the fate of Nero and his prefect Agripa.

The next project of the devils is to insure that Nero will be theirs; for this purpose, Satan and some of his companions are sent to earth (vv. 5,710-5,745). Before Nero kills himself and is carried off to Hell, he confesses his crimes in a most unusual and poignant speech ("I don't know a more inhuman man", etc.; vv. 5,815ff.). He then wills parts of his body to the various devils: his head is donated to Lucifer (*"como plus especial"*); his lustful body to Asmodeus; eyes, mouth and nose to Mamonas; stomach to Berit and all the remaining devils. The rejoicing is great among the devils who prepare to welcome and torture Nero. Special emphasis is also put on the culinary aspects of the devil's feast: worm-meat, sauces and soups of toads, serpents, etc.

As Cerberus welcomes Nero to his new palace of eternal torment, Satan and Belsebuc are already plotting the fall of Agripa. Despairing at Nero's death, Agripa makes an elaborate confession of his sins, placing heavy emphasis on lust and lechery; he had always held a grudge against Peter for converting his concubines (a humorous scene takes place in the first day where, to his fury, the new converts refuse to fulfill his carnal desires). He then makes his will, similar to that of Nero but far more elaborate. In this very original scene, the various parts of the body are associated with specific sins and are donated to devils directly related to those sins. There seems to be also a definite correlation with the Seven Deadly Sins, and their order in the text corresponds to the degree of their importance. The correlation between the Seven Deadly Sins and specific devils and the association of certain parts of the body with particular sins were part of a well-established tradition in visionary literature and in iconography, and in popular sermons such as those of Vincent Ferrer:[8]

> "Nos inveniemus in Sacra Scriptura *septem demones qui temptant de septem peccatis mortalibus* . . . Primus est *Leviathan* qui temptat de

superbia . . . Secundus est *Asmodeus* qui temptat de *luxuria . . .* Tertius qui temptat de *invidia* dicitur *Beelzebub . . .* Quartus qui temptat de *gula* dicitur *Beelfegor . . .* Quintus qui temptat de *ira* et facit durare corda dicitur *Baalberith . . .* Sextus qui temptat de *accidia* dicitur *Astaroth . . .* Septimus qui temptat de *avaricia* dicitur *Mammona . . .*

The variations of the hierarchy and attributes of the seven devils and their corresponding Seven Deadly Sins are minimal, as can be seen in the Saint Anthony play which we analyze below.[9]

In Agripa's testament, the head which raised itself in pride (*"s'es eleva en arguel"*) is willed to Lucifer; the eyes, full of lusty regards, go to Astaroth; precious objects he adored are donated to Mammonas; his evil-speaking mouth and serpent-like tongue are given to Belsebuc; his ears, which took pleasure in listening to malice, go to Belial; his heart, accustomed to evil thoughts, is willed to Hasmodeus; arms and legs and bowels are given to Tartarus; and, finally, *"tant quant y a de vitualho"* (all the remaining victuals) are offered to Cerberus (evidently representing here gluttony). The order of appearance of the Seven Deadly Sins is therefore: Superbia, Luxuria, Avaritia, Invidia, Ira, Accidia, Gula. In Nero's testament the order was: Superbia, Luxuria, Avaritia, Gula, Invidia, Accidia, Ira. The three sins of Pride, Lust and Covetousness are generally considered the most important and constitute the opening group of devils-sins in scenes of temptations, tortures in Hell and often in deviltries; the variations in the groupings of sins and devils occur mostly among the other four deadly sins.

The last appearance of the devils in the *Istoria Pauli et Petri* occurs evidently in the final *diablerie*, similar to the one following Nero's death and, before that, the death of Simon the Magician. The first day of the play is dominated by Simon the Magician (incarnating Lucifer and Antichrist), the second day by Nero (the diabolized human being) and his double Agripa. The diabological typology is perfectly organized and powerfully enacted in this play. It seems evident from various stage indications that the visual aspects and the theatricalities of its performance must have enhanced both the didactic and the spectacular scenes of the story. For example, no effort was spared in staging Simon the Magician's attempt to ascend to heaven and his terrifying act of rebellion, followed by his downfall. The actor, playing the role of Simon, while standing high on a tower, was replaced at a certain moment by a dummy resembling Simon and suspended in the air, as though flying, attached to some light colored ropes, held up by walking devils who would suddenly drop Simon after the appropriate suspense was created in the audience. "Hic habeat corpus fictum, ad simultitudinam Simonis, cum corona in capite, et volet per aerea (sic)." It was, as it is today in the movies, the breathtaking stunt.

The *Mystère de Sant Anthoni de Viennès*[10] is a play of 3,966 lines (or of about 4,500 lines if one counts those added to the text at some later performance than the first known one of 1503), but unlike the two preceding plays it reserves about one third of its dialogues and probably half of its performance time to the devils and their deviltries (about 1,290 lines). Some twenty-five roles, out of about eighty required by the play, are given to devils and to the Seven Deadly Sins. It should be noted that, when more than eight devils are being used (Lucifer and the seven principal ones), new names are being created (as in the case in this play), some allegorical and some grotesque, such as Discordio, Otracudanso, Diodamors, Farfara,[11] Danaton, Farfais, Basinnet, and even names associated with typologically demonized characters from pagan and Jewish history, such as Olophernus and Mordechays.[12]

The story of the play is relatively simple. Anthony renounces the world and, despite the protests of his family, gives all his belongings to the poor and withdraws to the desert; he is admitted to an abbey and, after withstanding numerous temptations and torments of both the flesh and the spirit, dies and is brought by singing angels to Paradise. The play closes with the supreme confrontation between Satan and the archangel Michael, the victory of the latter corresponding to the triumph of Anthony over Satan's emissaries. It is also, in the framework of the allegorical *psychomachia*, the victory of the Virtues (each and all of them embodied in Anthony) over the Vices (each and all of them incarnated by Satan). Because the temptations and the torments are so central to this story, the contrast between the christological and the diabological worlds is more sharply drawn here than in other plays about saints and devils.

The organization of this individual and cosmogonical struggle is clearly presented in a series of alternating sequences between the emissaries of heaven and the agents of Hell, preceding and following an extensive part of the dramatic text (about 1,600 lines) which retells essentially the life of Anthony as it was transmitted through the *Vita sancti Anthonii*. *Sequence I*: Anthony in his family; a sermon on renouncing the world and Anthony's desire to do so; council of angels, attended by the Virgin Mary, and God's intervention (about 550 lines). *Sequence II*: Council of the devils, attended by Satan, and presided by Lucifer (about 530 lines). *Sequence III*: Anthony's saintly life and his admission to the abbey (some 1,600 lines). *Sequence IV*: Temptations and torments of the seven deadly sins (about 300 lines). *Sequence V*: Encounter between Saint Paul and Saint Anthony (some 100 lines). *Sequence VI*: Further tortures of Anthony by the demons (some 80 lines). *Sequence VII:* Death of Saint Paul and his burial by Anthony (some 100 lines). *Sequence VIII:* Supreme offensive of the demons against Anthony (about 200 lines). *Sequence IX:* God and angels assist Anthony in his agonizing battle, in his *imitation of Christ* (some 150 lines). *Sequence X:* Saint Anthony's death and the emblematic confrontation between Satan and archangel Michael (about 100 lines). As the structure of the play clearly shows, the stage is conceived as an arena for the presentation of both an individual *psychomachia* and a cosmogonical struggle. The Council of the angels at the close of Sequence I and the Council of the devils of Sequence II are at the beginning of the play like a prefiguration of the ultimate confrontation of Sequence X.

As in the two preceding plays, the first appearance of the devils is in the *consilium diaboli* scene. The devils introduce themselves and their particular talents in this extremely long and amusing scene. Each of them claims to be the most important, the most powerful, the most seductive. Lucifer, having a hard time dealing with all these braggart soldiers, agrees with each one. The strongest rivalry is between the braggart Outracudanso and Satan, the latter being considered as the *"capitani general"* (Supreme Commander of Hell). It should be noted here that archangel Michael, in this play, is given the title of *"general capitany de paradis"* (Supreme Commander of Paradise).

Later, in this same sequence, the devils are already associated with the Seven Deadly Sins: Mamona is the *"moneyer"* (banker) who rules mankind with gold and silver; Diodamors dominates the people by instilling in them the desires of the flesh; Bausabuc is in charge of all the good food in Hell (as there is already the devil Arsanat who is in charge of the kitchen, either there is a confusion here, or Hell has two cooks, Bausabuc holding the role of *Chef*!); Astarot teaches men from his *"libro de chercho-mal"* (Book on Quest of Evil) the art of denying God; Beric rules the world through envy; Laviato claims to possess the art of keeping people in sin, or in despair, not allowing them to confess (thus representing *accidia*). Other devils, associated with all kinds of non-deadly sins or minor vices, are then introduced as a gallery of comic characters: Farfara is the big talker, all words and no action, who complains of his being unjustly excluded from the mission; Danaton is a great traveller; Belial is the intellectual master of the seven arts and, most especially, of the art of disputation; Farfais is the master of trickery; Basinnet knows all games and has charge of the devils' entertainment.

The significance of this sequence of devils becomes more clear in the temptation scene that follows (vv. 2,784-3,072): the order of sins treated is almost exactly the same. Arguel (Pride) is played by Lucifer and, in light of the stage indication, Avaricio (Avarice) was probably played by Mamonas, Luxurio (Lust) by Diodamors, Iro (Anger) by Astarot, Golo (Gluttony) by Bausabuc, Envidio (Envy) by Beric, and Pereso (Sloth) by Laviato.

The scene takes place in the woods, where Anthony has retreated by orders of God (through his archangel Gabriel). As the saint prays to resist temptation, the seven sins present themselves. Resplendent Argeuil exhorts Anthony to return to the world, offering him honor and riches; Anthony politely refuses and asks to be left alone. Feigning pity, Avaricio calls Anthony a poor, simple creature and suggests that he would be better off were he to join a religious order; Anthony thanks him for his concern, but is resolved to stay; Avaricio then asks him to accept a bag of money. Luxurio arrives as a beautiful woman (although rare, Diodamors—"god of love"—could be a female devil) and claims to be a young noble woman who has searched for him all over to give him her love. She is described as *"belo e gracioso / et principalement amoyroso / Blancho coma la flor de lys."* She then proceeds to display her body in a kind of striptease scene: *"Regardo lo meo corsage / lo qual est beos per avantage; / et si voles veyre mas mamellas / que sont tant graciosas et bellas / ya los vos mostrarey"* (Look at my body / which is exceptionally beautiful; / and if you want to see my breasts / which are beautiful and attractive / I will immediately show them to you). Anthony, this time, is quite disturbed: *"Helas! Qui la poyro suportar? / Non pas yo, se Dio m'aju."* (Alas! Who can resist such temptation? / Not me, so help me God); lust is stronger than the other sins and, in despair, Anthony orders the woman to leave—in the name of Christ! Iro presents himself and, asking Anthony why he squandered all his goods, concludes that Anthony must have been cheated; he offers to help him recover his belongings and assist him in taking revenge. Anthony, polite again, refuses. Golo arrives next, bringing food and wine; he warns Anthony that unless he accepts he will die soon from all this fasting; and that, moreover, he will never reach heaven by fasting. Anthony sends him away, while Envidio enters: he promises a lordship to Anthony. His exit marks the entry of the last sin, Pereso, who impresses Anthony by his disguise as a poor and humble man; the temptor says that he, too, renounced all worldly goods but became convinced that it was all in vain; he exhorts Anthony to return to the world before it is too late. This last temptation overcome, Anthony calls out in despair and God comes to his rescue.

Sequence VIII, in which the devils descend with fury and rage upon the saint, threatening to pull off his fingernails and toenails, to yank out his teeth and break his neck, and finally lifting him up in the air to carry him off to Hell,—this sequence, if translated visually, resembles very closely Martin Schongauer's famous engraving of the Temptation of Anthony by nine zoomorphic and anthropomorphic creatures (dating from the 1470's), which influenced other artists and, especially, Hieronymus Bosch's treatment of the similar theme (Temptation of Saint Anthony, Lisbon triptych).

The didactic and burlesque function of the devils is easily recognized in each of the three plays. Moreover, despite important differences of treatment, there is a basic structure common to the three in their organization of the standard devil scenes which are derived from the French mysteries. First, the Council of Devils which takes place in Hell: the various devils introduce themselves, complain that their realm is dwindling, decide that certain devils ought to be sent on earth to capture new souls. Next, the devils appear on earth trying (and mostly failing) to carry out their plans: in *Saint Eustache*, they try to kill Eustache's children; in *Petri et Pauli*, they help Simon the Magician in his attempt to kill Peter (by means of ferocious dogs) and in his attempt to ressucitate the child and, finally, in his attempt to fly; in *Saint Anthony*, they appear in the form of the seven deadly sins to tempt the saint. Finally, there is a scene of physical violence in which the devils beat or torture each other or a soul they have obtained: in *Saint Eustache*, Balsabuc and Astarot, blamed for the failure of the mission, are beaten by the other devils; in *Petri et Pauli*, the only play in which the devils enjoy some real measure of success, tortures are prepared and the devils welcome three souls of diabolized creatures, those of Simon the Magician, Nero and Agripa, to the infernal torments; in *Saint Anthony*, Satan, the scapegoat for all the devils' failures, is beaten by his fellow demons.

Of the three, the *Mystère de Saint Eustache* seems the most typical of medieval mysteries dramatizing the lives of saints. Both the *Mystère de Sant Anthoni*, by virtue of the considerable place given to the temptations and the individual characters of the devils, and the *Istoria Petri et Pauli*, for its treatment of the diabolical trinity Simon-Nero-Agripa in addition to the devils, demonstrate a greater originality in their dramatization of the problem of evil. The play *Istoria Petri et Pauli* is, in fact, permeated by the problem to such an extent that the best character portrayals are, if not of the devils themselves, certainly of those closely related to them. And these latter, less burlesque than the devils, resemble the animalized and demonized human beings of Hieronymus Bosch, whose works were contemporary with some of these Provençal plays.

University of Southern California

NOTES

[1] See our study "Satan and Notre Dame: Characters in a Popular Scenario," in *A Medieval French Miscellany*, ed. Norris Lacy (Lawrence, Kansas, 1972), pp. 1-14.

[2] See, in particular, A. Katzenellenbogen, *The Allegories of the Virtues and Vices in Medieval Art* (New York: Norton, 1964); M.W.Bloomfield, *The Seven Deadly Sins* (East Lansing: Michigan State Univ. Press, 1952, rpt. 1967).

[3] See our article "Les Diables: Serviteurs et Bouffons," in *Trétaux* (Bulletin de la Société Internationale pour l'Etude du Théâtre Médiéval, 1978, I, 2), pp. 51-69.

[4] Edited by G. Cohen, in *Mystères et Moralités du manuscrit 617 de Chantilly* (Paris: Champion, 1920).

[5] P. Guillaume (ed.), *Le Mystère de Saint Eustache* (Extrait de la *Revue des Langues Romanes,* 3e série, T. VII-VIII, Paris, 1883); *Le Mystère de Sant Anthoni de Viennès* (Paris, 1884); *Istoria Petri et Pauli* (Paris, 1887).

[6] A scene already fully developed in the first major vernacular play *Jeu d'Adam.*

[7] Edited by A. Jubinal, in *Mystères inédits du quinzième siècle*, 2 vols. (Paris: Téchener, 1837).

[8] As quoted by E. Roy, *Le Mystère de la Passion en France du XIVe au XVIe siècle* (Dijon: Damidot Frères, 1904), p. 427, note. We underline.

[9] A detailed presentation of the devils' roles in various French and Provençal plays and their association with the Seven Deadly Sins is given in our introduction to *Le Jugement Dernier* (*Lo Jutgamen General*), *drame provençal du XVe siècle* (Paris: Klincksieck, 1971), pp. 19-32.

[10] We will present a full analysis of the Saint Anthony theme in literature and art in the introduction to a new critical edition of this Provençal play.

[11] In the Italian version of the Theophilus legend, *Il miracolo di Teofilo*, one of Satan's emissaries is called *Farfalletto* or *Farfarello*, whose talent consists in making people sleep and dream. See our article "L'enfer et les diables dans le théâtre médiéval italien," in *Studi di Filologia Romanza* [offerti a Silvio Pellegrini] (Padova: Liviana Editrice, 1971), p. 242.

[12] Mordechay, name of Esther's uncle, was not an uncommon first name among the Jews of Southern France, mainly concentrated in the area of Avignon, Isle-sur-Sorgue and Carpentras.

FROM FABLIAU TO FARCE: A CASE STUDY*

Christopher Pinet

Critics of fifteenth and sixteenth century French farce have frequently stated that farce and *fabliau* share the same spirit.[1] They also point out that farces become popular at the very moment when *fabliaux* cease to be written (Petit de Julleville, p. 55). Indeed, both are written in octosyllabic verse and they share many of the same subjects: shrewish wives, hidden lovers, cuckolded husbands and debauched priests and monks. Some farces actually dramatize specific *fabliau* themes, as in the case of the *Cuvier*, the *Chaudronnier, Le Poulier à six personnages* and *Le Testament Pathelin* (Petit de Julleville, pp. 55-56). Louis Petit de Julleville sums up the general similarity as follows: "Le fabliau raconte vivement dans un rythme court et dans un style aisé, une aventure plaisante; la farce s'empare du même fait, et, dans le même style et la même mesure, elle met en dialogue et en scène ce que le fabliau avait raconté" (pp. 54-55). In spite of so many similarities, Petit de Julleville maintains that farce is an independent genre because the subjects are usually different and he concludes of farce: ". . . elle est néanmoins tout à fait indépendante et dispose d'un fonds comique en grande partie originale et propre à elle" (p. 56).

We can understand better Petit de Julleville's uncertainty about the degree of influence that *fabliau* exercised on farce by considering the differences between the two, something he did not elaborate: for example, the *fabliaux* present many variations on the theme of courtly love, including parodies of it while farces rarely make courtly love the central theme and are not usually given to parody.[2] The *fabliaux* often depict class oppositions,[3] something rare in farce where artisans and the "menu peuple" predominate; thus, there are no knights in farce and few aristocrats. In addition to these differences in theme and subject matter, the *fabliaux* and farces may have been destined for different audiences, at least in their original versions. The *fabliaux* were to be read aloud for the entertainment of aristocrats and the upper bourgeoisie whereas the audience for farce was wider and included urban tradesmen and the "menu peuple" (Many of the farces were performed in the marketplace at Carnival time). Jean Rychner has demonstrated that the "contes en vers", as the *fabliaux* have sometimes been called, could be adapted to suit lower class listeners (In the second half of the sixteenth century farces were adapted and played at court), but the greater stylistic sophistication in the original version of each of the *fabliaux* studied by Rychner points to an audience that was aristocratic.[4]

Two critics have attempted to resolve the question of influence by considering the form of *fabliau* and farce: Per Nykrog believes that a *fabliau* could have been presented so as to resemble a farce: ". . . il n'est pas improbable qu'un fabliau vivement dialogué, récité par un jongleur doué d'un talent dramatique, ait pu ressembler à une petite farce."[5] Grace Frank, on the other hand, thinks that farce may very well have developed when a professional writer, perhaps a *trouvère*, presented his narrative *par personnages*. Professor Frank puts it this way:

> . . .when such narratives were reworked so that their dialogued portions might be spoken by a group of persons, whether jongleurs or members of some *puy*, guild or other society, each impersonating a character, and when their descriptive portions might be replaced by mimetic action or suitable *mise en scène*, then they were presented *par personnages* and another type of entertainment resulted which we call drama.[6]

As Professor Frank says, the key element in the shift from *fabliau* to farce is the added dimension of the "stage" and two or more actors, or what Wayne Booth describes as the difference between "telling" and "showing".[7] However, her assertion would be strengthened by some examples of this shift in order to show precisely how the two genres may differ. By scrutinizing the process of change it will be seen that the end product deviates considerably from its source and that, contrary to Nykrog's view, the comedy works quite differently. A comparative analysis will also clarify how the farce author transforms his source to fit not only dramatic necessity but also to reflect the particular concerns and contexts of his own age.

First, it would be helpful to consider two *fabliaux*: Jean de Conde's *Des Braies le priestre*[8] (113 lines) and a longer version entitled *Des Braies au cordelier*[9] (360 lines), and finally the farce *Frère guillebert*[10] (530 lines) which, according to Hellman and O'Gorman, is based on the earlier *fabliaux*.[11] These texts are apt for several reasons: first, the theme of the breeches is common to all three; second, they treat a subject which was popular in both farce and *fabliau*, that is, a love triangle involving a member of the clergy; and finally, all three incorporate dialogue, although the farce author employs it differently from the authors of the *fabliaux*. Specifically, I will consider the texts from the point of view of language and audience (narrative and dialogue as narrative versus dialogue as drama), topicality, characterization, and visual humor.

It is not clear which of the *fabliaux* was written first, but *Des Braies le priestre* is the shorter version. The narrator starts, as is often the case in *fabliaux*, by saying that he has heard many amusing tales; in this case of how priests have shamed men by sleeping with their wives and that he has a new one to tell based on a true story. He then introduces the characters and the essential elements as follows:

> Il avoit à unne cité,
> N'a mie lonc tamps, .l. boucier;
> Sa femme eut .l. priestre plus cier
> De lui, car mius faisoit sen gré
> Quant à li parloit à secré.
> Li bouciers, qui mot n'en savoit,
> Ens ou markiet aler devoit
> O compaignons de sen mestier:
> D'argent çou qu'il en eust mestier
> Quist pour mouvoir à l'endemain,
> Quil dsit qu'il voloit aler main.
> Sa femme fist savoir au priestre
> K'en pais poroit avoec lui iestre.
> Li priestres qui le couvoita,
> Dou boucier le meute gaita;
> Celle qui haioit son signour
> Le fist mouvoir devant le jour.
> Quant de sa maison fu issus,
> Li priestres, qui n'e [s] t mie ensus,
> S'est ou lit la dame couciés. (*MR*, VI, 257-58)

As Jean Rychner[12] says in a discussion of the differences between the two *fabliaux*, Jean de Condé uses a strict minimum of narration to introduce the characters and the plot: we learn almost nothing of the personalities or motives of the three but only that the butcher's wife prefers the priest, presumably because he makes love better, that the butcher knows nothing of the affair, that the priest strongly desires the butcher's wife and that she cannot stand her husband; finally, that as soon as the butcher has left, the priest, who has been waiting, gets a signal from the wife and hops into bed with her. In *Des Braies au cordelier*, on the other hand, there is from the outset a much greater emphasis on detail and development of personality traits, which give this *fabliau* a quite different tone and emphasis from Condé's: first, the story is given a setting, Orléans; second, the woman is identified as a "bourgeoise"; finally, she is presented as a shrewd woman who is capable of any necessary ruse in order to have affairs without being caught. At the same time, however, we are never told her husband's specific trade. The result of these differences is that the "bourgeoise" becomes the main focus of interest in the second *fabliau* because she is given a psychological dimension which the woman of

Condé's *fabliau* does not possess (nor do the other characters for that matter). Beyond this difference, however, there is another which distinguishes *Des Braies au cordelier* from *Des Braies le priestre*; this is the courtly element which Rychner alludes to but does not elaborate. This dimension of the *fabliau* becomes clear in the lines introducing the "bourgeoise":

> Il avint, si com j'oi dire,
> C'uns clers amoit une borgoise
> Qui mout estoit sage et cortoise;
> Mout savoit d'enging et d'aguet:
> A feme, qui tel mestier fait
> Et qui veut amer par amors,
> Couvient savoir guenches et tors,
> Et enging por soi garantie;
> Bien couvient que saiche mentir,
> Tele eure est, por couvrir sa honte.
> La borjoise dont ge vos conte
> Fu bien de ce mestier aprise,
> Comme cele qu'amors ot mise
> Et bien enlacie en ses laz.   (*MR*, III, 275)

The adjective "cortoise", the phrases "Et qui veut amer par amors" and the lines "Comme cele qu'amors ot mise" and "Et bien enlacie en ses laz" all point to the courtly theme and a burlesque of it if not a later reworking of Condé's version. This is also true of the line "C'un clers amoit une borjoise" which contrasts with "Li priestres qui le couvoita" of the Condé *fabliau*. In fact, *Des Braies le priestre* does not use the word "love" at all, but rather the expression "eut .l. priestre plus cier" when describing the woman's desire. If two *fabliaux* with the same basic theme can make such divergent uses of a tale, what happens in a sixteenth-century farce based on them?

The farce *Frère Guillebert* takes another approach to the theme of the love triangle: Whereas Condé took twenty-seven lines to get the butcher out of the house and the priest into bed with the man's wife and *Des Braies au cordelier* takes eighty-eight lines (most of which are devoted to a presentation of the wife's guile), Frère Guillebert presents himself to the audience in seventy-two emphatic lines as a formidable seducer of women of all ages: "doulces fillettes", "dames mariées" and "vieilles ésponnées". In fact, as one might deduce from the title, this farce, at least initially, is less about a love triangle involving a monk than about this particular monk who comes to represent all debauched monks: This is made clear in Frère Guillebert's opening lines in a macaronic Latin which everyone understood:

Foullando in calibistris,
Intravit per boucham ventris
Bidauldus, purgando renes.
Noble assistence, retenez
Ces mots pleins de devotion;
C'est touchant l'incarnation
De l'ymage de la brayette,
Qui entre, corps, aureille et teste,
Au precieulx ventre des dames: (*ATF*, I, 305)

The author[13] satirizes the clergy by juxtaposing the words "devotion" and "incarnation" with the illicit sexual act proposed by Brother Guillebert. The shift from "braies" (breeches) of the *fabliaux* to "brayette" ("cod piece") makes the image ("ymage") much more strikingly visual and points to the author's concern for the staging of the play and the verbal cues necessary for a complementary "body language" of movement and gesture. In fact, Brother Guillebert's opening lines serve as a curtain raiser to the play; he is "warming up" the audience.

After giving "practical" advice to young girls and married women (single girls should be careful not to get pregnant), advice which always ends with the refrain "Foullando in calibistris", Brother Guillebert goes one step further in a style which closely resembles the "cri" of a sixteenth-century tradesman selling his wares:

Je vous recommande à mon prosne
Tous nos frères de robe grise.
Je vous promectz c'est belle aumosne
Que faire bien à gens d'esglise.
Grans pardons a, je vous advise,
A leur prester boucham ventris,
Foullando in calibistris. (*ATF*, I, 306-7)

The suggestion that sexual favors could be bartered for indulgences is a clear swipe at the Catholic Church and the practice of selling indulgences and reflects the concerns of the Reformation.[14] The fact that the play was printed in Rouen would seem to support this contention since Protestantism was particularly strong there.[15] Thus, from the outset, the farce departs in several important ways from the earlier *fabliaux*: the purely descriptive nature of Condé's tale and the emphasis on the "bourgeoise" as a schemer in a courtly burlesque (*Des Braies au cordelier*) are abandoned for direct and pointed satire of monks (especially the Franciscans; "robe grise") and the Church reflecting the religious tensions of the period.

The scene following Brother Guillebert's monologue presents several further departures from the earlier *fabliaux* while introducing a new character, the "commere". The "commere" in her discussion with the wife sets the stage for the entrance of the other characters; especially Brother Guillebert, since he has not yet been linked to any specific woman (in the *fabliaux* an illicit relationship between monk/priest and wife was established from the outset. The conversation between the woman and her crony helps to strengthen the illusion that the dramatist is "showing" rather than "telling". Thus the drama seems to be unfolding before our eyes, an illusion which adds to the potential for suspense and dramatic tension:

> La Femme
> Dieu vous gàrd, ma commère
> Agnès
> Et vous doint santé et soulas.

> La Commère
> Ha, ma commère, bien venez.

> La Femme
> Dieu vous gard, ma commère
> Agnès.

> La Commère
> Que maigre et pale devenez;
> Qu'avez-vous, ma commère,
> hélas?

> La Femme
> Dieu vous gard, ma commère,
> Agnès,
> Et vous doint santé et soulas.
> Que cent foys morte me
> souhaitte.

> La Commère
> Et pourquoy?

> La Femme
> D'estre mise ès lacz
> D'un vieillart et ainsi subjette.
> De jour et nuict je vous
> souhette;

Mais de poindre c'est peu ou point.
Quel plaisir à une fillette,
A qui le gentil tetin point! (*ATF*, I, 307-08)

All that Condé told us was the butcher's wife preferred a priest. In *Des Braies au cordelier* the woman prefers a monk, but *Frère Guillebert* presents a new theme: a young woman married to an old man who is unsatisfactory in bed (this kind of marriage was the object of ridicule at carnival time and in "charivaris"[16]). By furnishing the young woman with an acceptable motive for seeking a lover, the author takes a less cynical stance towards women than the two *fabliaux* and the focus of the play shifts to the other characters, as the subsequent dialogue makes clear. The "laz" of courtly love have become the "lacz" (prison) of a marriage to an old and possessive husband.

After the young wife has told how unhappy she has been in trying to consummate her marriage (without saying what she is going to do about it), her friend gives her advice which prompts her to seek a lover:

La Commère
Il vous fault ung amy gaillard
Pour supplier à l'escripture.
Dieu n'entend point, aussi
nature,
Que jeunes dames ayent
souffrette.
Mais cerchez une creature
Qui ayt la langue un poy
segrette.

La Femme
Il est bien vray; quant on
en quette,
On est regardé de travers;
Mais, quoy qu'on jase ou
barbette,
Je jouray de bref à l'envers.
Doibit mon beau corps
pourrir en vers
Sans voir ce que faisoit ma
mère?
Vienne, fust-il moyne ou
convers,
Je luy presteray mon
aumoyre. (*ATF*, I, 308-09)

Not only does the "commère" change the meaning of the Bible and of God's intentions in order to persuade the young woman, much as Brother Guillebert misuses religious words to justify his intentions, but the woman herself is easily convinced and says that she will accept anyone, even a monk or a convert ("convers" may be a reference to someone newly converted to Protestantism or a manual worker in a monastery; Cotgrave defines a "convers" as "one that has turned to the Faith"). Perhaps more important is the play on "con" and the use of "aumoyre", "little box" which also had the religious connotation of the place "wherein the sacrament is kept" (cf. Cotgrave).

A few lines later Brother Guillebert makes his entrance. However, he does not jump immediately into bed with the young woman (*fabliaux* go straight to the point; farce draws out the denouement), but instead has to convince her to accept him as her lover much as her friend had to convince her to seek a lover in the previous scene. He does this by assuring her that no one will find out about their affair since this seems to be her greatest fear. It is only at this point that she gives him a rendezvous for the following morning. As though to confirm the fact that the author of the farce is more interested in building dramatic tension through a series of scenes leading to a comic climax than in simply recounting an amusing anecdote, the next scene presents a direct confrontation between the old husband and his young wife. She tells him openly that she is unhappy with him and too young for him. After he protests that he does the best he can, she convinces him to go out to the market the following morning so that she can be alone with Brother Guillebert. But what happens next is a far cry from what takes place in the *fabliaux*. In *Des Braies le priestre* the departure of the husband is followed by the arrival of the priest:

> Quant de se maison fu issus,
> Li priestres, qui n'e [s] t mie ensus,
> S'est ou lit la dame couciés   (*MR*, VI, 258)

Although the husband returns unexpectedly (his wife had made him leave earlier than necessary) and ends up sharing the bed with his wife and the priest: "Li priestres se gisoit à diestre/Et ses maris devers seniestre" (*MR*, VI, 258), he leaves a second time without realizing what has happened! It is only when he arrives at the market that his friends point out to him that he is wearing the priest's breeches (the purse he takes from the breeches bears the priest's seal) and that he has been cuckolded (he had put on the priest's breeches by mistake when he left the second time). *Des Braies au cordelier* gives a slightly different version of the story and describes in some detail the wife's cunning and her lovemaking with the priest: "La dame sot mout de renart;/Engigneuse fu de toz tors." (*MR*, III, 283)

The author of *Frère Guillebert*, on the other hand, takes the departure and arrival scenes and expands them into a long series of comings and goings, near discoveries, asides and monologues worthy of Molière. These scenes illustrate best how the author of farce adapts the *fabliaux* in order to achieve the maximum dramatic and visual effect on his sixteenth century audience. For example, just before the husband leaves, we see Brother Guillebert singing a *rondeau* with great bravado as he prepares to join the old man's wife:

> Hé, gentil tetin,
> Que tant tu me tiens en l'oreille
> Pour une qui s'appareille,
> Ung vray chef-d'oeuvre de nature,
> Mon corps veulx mettre à l'avanture;
> A les sangler pour la pareille
> Mon corps et membres j'appareille,
> N'escondire pas créature
> Pour une, et ce.
>   Si son mary dort ou veille,
> Mais que accès j'aye à la figure,
> Je veulx que l'on me defigure
> Se point un grain je m'esmerveille
> Pour une. (*ATF*, I, 313)

Just as the wife probably had her face powdered with flour to emphasize her paleness in the opening scene, Brother Guillebert's words suggest that he is making up in front of the audience; his primping making him the object of great laughter. This is only a taste of what is in store once the husband leaves; in fact, every possible visual effect is explored in this, the longest scene of the play. The opening exchange between the wife and Brother Guillebert tips us off to what is to follow:

> Frère Guillebert
> Hola, hay, je viens bien à
> point.

> La Femme
> Oy; devestes chausses et
> pourpoint.
> Et aprochez; la place est
> chaulde.

> Frère Guillebert
> (se despouille)
> Au moins y a-il point de
> fraulde?
> Je crains la touche, sur mon
> ame:
>
> La Femme
> Pas n'estes digne d'avoir dame,
> Puisque vous etes si paoureux.
> (*ATF*, I, 314)

Not only do we get to see Brother Guillebert undress, but we learn something of his suspicious and cowardly nature. Even the wife is put off by him, a total departure from the *fabliaux*. The very next lines are those of the husband who, unlike the husbands in the *fabliaux*, returns home before he has ever reached the market or seen his friends, ostensibly because he has forgotten his purse. Brother Guillebert panics and wishes aloud that he had never made a play for the wife:

> Que c'est vostre homme, vertu bieu.
> Helas, je suis bien malheureux;
> Le dyable m'a faict amoureux,
> Je croy, ce n'a pas esté Dieu.   (*ATF*, I, 314)

Once he has sensed danger, he quickly changes his earlier boastful tone and admits that his "love" for the woman was the devil's work, a form of public confession. The wife then insists that he must hide, but Brother Guillebert is petrified ("le cul me tremble") and asks whether or not her husband would kill him if he found him there. The wife does not assuage his fears when she responds:

> Jamais pire homme je ne vis,
> Et si crains bien vostre instrument.
>
> Frère Guillebert
> Le dyable ayt part au hochement
> Et a toute la cauqueson.
> Accoustre seray en oyson;
> Je n'auray plus au cul aue plume.   (*ATF*, I, 315)

The realization that he may be castrated (a punishment to fit the crime) throws Brother Guillebert into further panic and he probably accompanies his exclamation, "Ha, Pater noster et Ave!", by repeatedly crossing himself in a number of places. The suggestion that he will probably be castrated by an irate husband if discovered radically transforms the *fabliaux* by stressing both the sinful nature of what the monk is trying to do and the punishment to be meted out. The comparison to a young goose is reminiscent of the slaughter of geese at carnival time. More important, the author has created a hilarious scene where the comedy is a function of whether or not the search for the purse may inadvertently uncover the terrified monk. The next development shows this, for after the wife convinces Brother Guillebert to hide under a chest, he says:

> Or ca donc, puisque le cas s'offre,
> Me voicy bouté à l'acul.
> Et covrez-moi un poy le col;
> Je sens bien le vent qui me frappe.
> A'une foys du danger je escape,
> S'on m'y ra, je seray asseuré. (ATF, I, 316)

Once again the frightened monk is shown in an unfavorable light; it is easy to imagine the delight of the spectators as the wife tries to cover his "col" (could this be a play on "cul"?) before her husband sees him.

After hiding Brother Guillebert, the woman lets her husband in and the "search" is on. While husband and wife discuss what has become of the purse, Brother Guillebert carries on frequent asides with the audience. Of the eight asides, one is a forty-one line monologue in which Brother Guillebert makes up a will with many sexual allusions including the suggestion that after he is dead his breeches will be capable of giving pleasure to young women (In *Des Braies au cordelier* they were a sign of fertility). Each section of the will is followed by the refrain, "Frère Guillebert, te fault-il mourir?" One of the other noteworthy aspects of the scene is the dual role of the wife who serves both as a nominal ally of the monk and as a catalyst for the comedy of discovery. For example, she not only mocks the monk's fear, but she also increases the chances that he will be discovered by her husband since she knows full well that he is hidden under the chest:

> L'Homme
> Ne suis-je point bien fortuné?
> J'avois oublié mon bissac.
>
> Frère Guillebert
> A ce coup je suis a bazac;
> Je suis, par Dieu, couché
> dessus.

> Et sainct Fremin et puis Jesus,
> C'est faict, helas! du povre
> outil;
> Vray Dieu, il estoit si gentil,
> Et si gentement encresté.
>
> La Femme
> Je vous l'avois hier apresté
> Sur ce coffre, avant que
> coucher.   (*AFT*, I, 316-17)

When her husband actually goes over to the chest, his wife tells him that the purse is not there, but in the meantime Brother Guillebert has let out more howls about his fears of castration in an aside. And it is the wife who implies that the purse might be there. A further bit of visual play occurs when the husband, probably holding his nose, complains of the stench in the room. Brother Guillebert justifies the scatological reference by explaining the power of fear to the audience! This comedy of fear ends with a prayer in Latin by Brother Guillebert who asks out loud (he is on his knees) whether or not he can gain anything by praying and identifying himself to the husband by showing his tonsure. Finally, the husband mistakes Guillebert's breeches for his purse as he is leaving; the farce rejoins the outline of the *fabliaux* as monk and wife discover the husband's mistake and Guillebert decides to leave in a hurry saying: "Mes mains me serviront de brayette."

For all intents and purposes this scene furnishes the comic climax of the play, but the lines which follow are noteworthy because they depart so drastically from the perspective of the *fabliaux*. *Des Braies le priestre* told of a husband so stupid that he deserves to be cuckolded; if there is a moral, it is that "Priestre(s) sont trop rade de rains". *Des Braies au cordelier* also tells of a husband who is stupid and a cuckold largely because his wife is so cunning: "Bien s'est la borgoise chevie;/Mout a bien son plait afiné". In *Frère* Guillebert, however, things are more complicated. The satire of the monk is fierce in spite of the accompanying laughter. References already cited as well allusions to "papars" and "papelards" and criticism of the sale of relics make it clear that this play was a part of the religious debates of the Reformation. And Brother Guillebert does not succeed in cuckolding the husband; he is every bit as ridiculous as the husband. The wife, on the other hand, has regrets about her actions:

> Helas, et suis-je bien meffaicte?
> N'est-ce point bien icy malheur?

En amours je n'euz jamais eur. (*ATF*, I, 321)
Las, je ne sçay que deviendray:

She narrowly escapes a beating by her husband who is finally convinced by the "commère" that Saint Francis' breeches were present only to help his wife conceive. Thus, all three main characters receive a kind of object lesson, but as is often the case in farce, the play ends on a humorous note with Brother Guillebert asking everyone to kneel and pray:

> . . .boutez-vous tous à genoulx,
> Affin que le sainct prie pour
> nous,
> Et se vous fault baiser tous
> trois
> Les brayes de monsieur sainct
> Françoys;
> Vous aurez l'alaine plus doulce.

> La Femme
> Baillez m'en une bonne touche,
> Puisqu'en ay eu si grant
> doulceur.

> Frère Guillebert
> C'est tres bien fait, ma bonne
> seur,
> Car c'est un fort beau reliquère.
> (*ATF*, I, 327)

What I have tried to show is that it is not enough to say that *fabliaux* are recited by a *fableor* and farces based on *fabliaux* are performed by actors who simply divide up the lines and/or dialogued portions of the *fabliau*. The suggestion that a *fabliau* is merely an unenacted farce is a gross oversimplification. The styles are quite different, primarily because farces are conceived for the stage and *fabliaux* are not. This means that the author of a farce may take considerable liberties with the *fabliau* he uses as his source. In the case of *Frère Guillebert* this involved substantive changes in plot, sequence of events, language, characters and characterization, topic, and finally, purpose. The fact that *Frère Guillebert* is conceived for the stage enables the author to explore and amplify fully references by one character to the physical appearance of another, to complement words with gestures (often repeated for maximum comic effect), to introduce "asides" to the audience and to emphasize the physical interaction (pratfalls and the like) of the characters in ways uncommon to *fabliau.* *Fabliau* calls on the imagination of the listener to create a mental image of what is happening; farce paints a three-dimensional picture. And since farce highlights the interaction between characters, these characters use much more colloquial language than that of *fabliau*: this includes exclamations, popular *cris*, refrains and topical songs. This results in the feeling of greater intimacy; the immediacy of the marketplace where the spectators are treated as participants (cf. the asides of Brother Guillebert). This popular appeal is also reflected in the topicality of criticisms aimed at the sale of indulgences and relics which goes beyond the commonplace anti-clerical stance of the *fabliaux.*

The humor of *fabliau* and *farce*, then, is really very different and what farce "shows" and *fabliau* "tells" is as much a function of time and of place as of genre.

Montana State University

NOTES

*This article was presented in a different form at a special session on *farce* and *fabliau* held at the December 1975 Convention of the Modern Language Association.

[1]Louis Petit de Julleville, *La Comédie et les moeurs en France au Moyen Age* (Paris: L. Cerf, 1886), p. 54; Barbara Bowen, *Les Caractéristiques essentielles de la farce française et leur survivance dans les années 1550-1620* (Urbana: University of Illinois Press, 1964), p. 4. Subsequent references to Petit de Julleville are given in the text.

[2]See Michel Rousse "L'Allégorie dans la farce de *La Pipée*" *CAIEF* (1976), pp. 37-50 and Jean-Ch. Payen "Un théâtre nostalgique: *La Pipée*, farce courtoise," *Romania* 98 (1977), 220-245, for discussion of courtly elements in farce.

[3]Robert Harrison, *Gallic Salt* (Berkeley: University of California Press, 1974), pp. 8-9.

[4]Ibid, pp. 5, 10.

[5]Per Nykrog, *Les Fabliaux: Etude d'histoire littéraire et de stylistique médiévale*, Diss. Aarhus 1957 (Copenhagen: Munksgaard, 1957), p. 17.

[6]Grace Frank, *Medieval French Drama* (Oxford: Clarendon Press, 1954), pp. 213-214.

[7]These terms are drawn from Wayne C. Booth, *The Rhetoric of Fiction* (Chicago: University of Chicago Press, 1961), pp. 3-20.

[8]All references to *Des Braies le priestre* are from Anatole de Montaiglon and Gaston Raynaud, eds., *Recueil général et complet des fabliaux des XIIIe et XIVe siècles*, 6 vols. (1872-1890; rpt. New York: Burt Franklin), VI, 257-60. This collection is subsequently referred to as *MR*.

[9]All references to *Des Braies au cordelier* are from *MR*, III, 275-287.

[10]All references to *Frère Guillebert* are from *Ancien Théâtre François* also known as *Collection des ouvrages dramatiques les plus remarquables depuis les Mystères jusqu'à Corneille*, 10 vols. (Paris: P. Jannet, 1854-57), I, 305-27.

[11]Robert Hellman and Richard O'Gorman, eds. and trans., *Fabliaux: Ribald Tales from the Old French* (New York: Thomas Y. Crowell Company, 1965), p. 104. The Condé *fabliau* is from the fourteenth century.

[12]Jean Rychner, *Contribution à l'étude des fabliaux: Variantes, remaniements, dégradations*, 2 vols. (Geneva: Droz, 1960), pp. 32-36.

[13]The play is signed "Du jeune clergié de Meulleurs". I have not been able to discover his identity.

[14]For an extended discussion of the relation of farce to the Reformation see my article, "Monks, Priests and Cuckolds: French Farce and Criticism of the Church from 1500-1560," *Stanford French Review* (1980); see also Jean Delumeau's "Les mentalités religieuses saisies à travers les farces, les sotties et les sermons joyeux (XVe-XVIes)," *Actes du 99e Congrès National des Sociétés Savantes*, Besançon, 1974, Section de philologie et d'histoire jusqu'à 1610, I (B.N., 1977), 181-195.

[15]Raymond Lebègue, "La Vie dramatique à Rouen," *Bulletin Philologique et Historique du Comité des Travaux Historiques et Scientifiques* (1955-56), p. 402. I am grateful to Professor Alan Knight for calling my attention to this article.

[16]See Natalie Davis, *Society and Culture in Early Modern France* (Stanford University Press, 1975), pp. 97-151 for a discussion of *charivari* and carnival.

MICHELET ON RABELAIS

John R. Williams

> Quel homme et qu'était-il? Demandez
> plutôt ce qu'il n'était pas. Homme de
> toute étude, de tout art, de toute langue, le
> véritable *Pan-ourgos*, agent universel dans
> les sciences et dans les affaires, qui fut
> tout et fut propre à tout, qui contint le
> génie du siècle et le déborde à chaque
> instant.
>
> —Michelet, *Histoire de France*

The Romantics may be said to have initiated the modern discovery of the authentic Rabelais beneath the seemingly uncomprehending judgments of the seventeenth and eighteenth centuries.

During the sixteenth century, Rabelais had, of course, been highly regarded; the universality of his mind and the almost unlimited freedom of his thought and language were believed to reflect the age.[1] But in the seventeenth century artistic taste underwent a reversal. Profound changes in the realm of literary criticism and in the freedom of writers took place, culminating in 1690 in La Bruyère's celebrated attack on Rabelais in *Les Caractères*.[2] Although Rabelais was not without his followers during the century (notably La Fontaine, Saint-Evremond, and the *Libertins*), the classical spirit with its uniform rules governing taste did not permit an appreciation of Gallic humor and linguistic invention. The eighteenth century continued a period of disfavor and worse: in order to make Rabelais accessible linguistically and morally to the reading public, he was expurgated and his language modernized; moreover, commentaries were usually uninformed. Voltaire represented the majority opinion when, in the *Lettres philosophiques*, he found him unintelligible, impertinent, and full of foolishness. The nineteenth century maintained in its early stages the literary prejudices of the eighteenth. This could only be expected of such neo-classic critics as La Harpe and Lemercier. With the Romantic movement, however, the tone begins to change. Professional critics were still often uncomprehending or moralistic (e.g. Saint-Marc Girardin, Philarète Chasles, and, despite some of the best pages written on Rabelais, even Saint-Beuve), but Nodier as early as 1810 began to view Rabelais in a number of articles as a universal genius. Chateaubriand echoed this in 1836 in his famous *Essai sur la littérature anglaise* when he ranked Rabelais among the *génies-mères* of humanity, alongside Shakespeare, Homer, and Dante. The

Romantic poets were equally enthusiastic (although not necessarily well-informed): Gautier, Hugo, and Vigny left positive judgments (Lamartine, for moral reasons, was a dissenter). This breach in the wall between Rabelais and his readers was a first step toward emancipating him from the tenets of neoclassicism. It made possible the more critically detached studies of Rabelais that the positivistic spirit of the late nineteenth century eventually fostered and which continue to this day.

For the Romantic historian Jules Michelet (1798-1874), writing in the middle of the nineteenth century, Rabelais offered what he presumed to be the most complete portrait of French society during the Renaissance. And no historian offers a more original synthesis of Rabelais than he. Before tracing his confrontation with Rabelais, however, we must first stop a moment and give some consideration to Michelet's place in the new science of historiography in the nineteenth century.

Michelet's concept of the Renaissance was in many respects an offspring of the theories the sixteenth century held about itself. French humanists had accepted from the Italians the notion of a break in historical development between the collaspse of the Greco-Roman cultural tradition and its revival in the sixteenth century.[3] Michelet too clearly reflects this basic distinction. The Romantic period, however, brought about certain additional value judgments. Historians began to study the national past and to fix in people's mind the habit of thinking in terms of historical periods. This was combined with the idea of progress inherited from the eighteenth century and the positive assertion of certain emotional values hitherto neglected: sentimentality, idealization, intuition, and spontaneity, to name a few.

When Michelet undertook the gargantuan task of writing the *Histoire de France* in the 1830's, his objective was to integrate through history all the elements—political, economic, artistic, literary—which had formed the French nation. No one before him had ever attempted such a project. And his view of the medieval period (the volumes appeared from 1833 to 1844) was marked by the new wave of unrestrained emotionalism common to Romantic thought. His depiction is one of sentimental praise for medieval society and melancholy regret at its passing. By 1845, however, he began to turn away from this position and discredit the Middle Ages. By the 1850's his attitude had shifted to one of frenzied condemnation. Under the influence of Quinet and the students taking his courses during these years, and especially under the influence of the attacks of the Catholic party against the university and himself, Michelet turned against the Middle Ages, the Church and Monarchy, and abandoned the history of France at the end of the fifteenth century in order to devote himself entirely to religious and social questions and to the writing of the history of the Revolution. Consequently, when he turned once again in 1853 to the history of France, he was light-years away from his original position. Whereas in his study of the Middle Ages he had seen in the Church the one refuge of liberty and in the Passion a universal symbol of man's effort to rise above himself through his own inner resources, he henceforth found in the Renaissance the principles of a new faith through free thought.

Michelet was probably the first to attempt a synthesis dealing with the Renaissance as a distinct phenomenon in general European history. Prior to him, the concept of rebirth was limited to special disciplines (e.g. art, literature, the classics). His approach was encyclopedic and lyrical, and his judgments were imbued with the political sentiments of a mid-nineteenth-century democrat who believed in the progress of the people. Events and individuals served as symbols, in one way or another, of this larger idea.

Such is the case in the visionary fashion in which he characterizes "l'immense et fécond Rabelais" (X, vi).[4] "Homme de toute étude," he writes, "de tout art, de toute langue, le véritable *Pan-ourgos*, agent universel dans les sciences et dans les affaires, qui fut tout et qui fut propre à tout, qui contint le génie du siècle et le déborde à chaque instant" (X, 367). Like Michelet, Rabelais had an all-encompassing interest in art, philosophy, religion, and science. Michelet's insistence on the heroic aspects of Rabelais, however, goes beyond mere intellectual affinity. He had come to realize that the common man alone through his own means could not progress. He now insists on the role of individuals who will symbolize and give voice to the inner will of the people.[5]

Thus, Michelet labels Rabelais the hero of the century and places at the beginning of his study of the Renaissance the words of Rabelais which are found engraved on the door of the visionary Thélème (called by Michelet *Temple de la Volonté*): "Entrez, qu'on fonde ici la foi profonde" (the modern spelling is Michelet's)—that is, a call to participate in the founding of a new faith in which man would begin to discover himself and from which would begin "l'heureuse réconciliation des membres de la famille humaine" (IX, 7).

In his chapter on Rabelais, Michelet—like Chateaubriand, Hugo, Taine, and Guizot, among other contemporaries—first pays tribute to Rabelais's enormous contribution in terms of the development of the French language. Rabelais more than anyone else took the complicated linguistic legacy of the Middle Ages, added to it a whole new scientific language and combined the two into one harmonious whole. "La langue française apparut dans une grandeur qu'elle n'a jamais eue, ni avant ni après" (X, 367: Michelet's reference to "après" reflects his view that Montaigne and the end of the Renaissance were introspective and unheroic).

Michelet finds Rabelais beyond comparison—superior to both Ariosto and Cervantes, both of whom he considers tied to the past in their work: "... tous deux rient sur un tombeau, sur la patrie défunte, et la chevalerie inhumée. Tous deux regardent au couchant. Rabelais regarde l'aurore" (X, 368). Moreover, he continues, *Gargantua* and *Pantagruel* should not be compared to the *Divine Comedy*. Not only does the latter work not lend itself to comparison, being limited to the confines of a systematic theology, but "répétons donc pour Dante ce que nous disions pour les deux autres. Il regarde vers le passé. Si sa force indocile échappe parfois vers l'avenir, c'est comme malgré lui, par des hasards sublimes de génie de passion, par un égarement de son coeur" (X, 369).

Nor does Michelet see any influence on Rabelais of such works as Thomas More's *Utopia* or Eramus's *Praise of Folly*.[6] Modern scholars make the point that there is little in Rabelais that is not already anticipated in Erasmus,[7] but Michelet insists on the uniqueness of Rabelais's genius: "Il n'a rien emprunté qu'au peuple, aux vieilles traditions. ... Navigateur hardi sur la profonde mer qui engloutit les anciens dieux, il va à la recherche du grand *Peut-être*. Il cherchera longtemps. Le câble étant coupé et l'adieu dit à la légende, ne voulant s'arrêter qu'au vrai, au raisonnable, il avance lentement, en chassant les chimères" (X, 370).[8]

This general view of Rabelais's uniqueness prevailed for a long time, whereas modern scholarship has come to consider the syncretistic range of Rabelais's thought as deeply rooted in the philosophical and religious issues of his own time.[9] Nevertheless, Michelet, like most French Romantics, believed Rabelais represented the first great revolt of free thought against tyranny and tradition. He was drawn to what he took as Rabelais's rejection of the past and his assertion of faith in human progress and perfectibility.

Specifically turning to Rabelais's famous *Gargantua* and *Pantagruel*, Michelet writes: "Le sphinx ou la chimère, un monstre à cent têtes, à cent langues, un chaos harmonique, une farce de portée infinie, une ivresse lucide à merveille, une folie profondément sage" (X, 367).

The words echo strangely those of La Bruyère (see n. 2), but the intent is altogether different. Michelet arranges his apparently contradictory terms to depict a movement from the grotesque to the sublime. The images generate conversions: the "chaos" becomes "harmonique," the "ivresse" becomes "lucide," and so on. This use of the oxymoron has little to do, it seems to me, with the popular late Renaissance habit in which an attempt was made to fuse contradictory experiences into a unity, nor with the eighteenth-century practice of rationally viewing such expressions as antithetical and representing divisions of experience. With Michelet the paradoxical qualities he associates with Rabelais suggest a deeper meaning. The metaphorical language is contained and controlled by the larger structure of Michelet's historicism. Rabelais is at once the superlative representative of his generation, but his work traces only one step along the evolutionary path of man's spiritual development. Such a position permits Michelet both positive and negative judgments in his evaluation of Rabelais.

More precisely, Michelet's remarks on *Gargantua* and *Pantagruel* center on Rabelais's ideas on education: "... à l'apparition du Gargantua, tous crièrent d'horreur ou de joie. Peu comprirent que c'était un livre d'éducation. Peu divinèrent le mot caché, qui est celui d'Emile: 'Reviens à la nature.' ... Contre le Moyen Age qui dit: 'La nature est mauvaise, impuissante pour te sauver,' il disait: 'La nature est bonne; travaille, ton salut est en toi'" (X, 372). Michelet is not, it seems to me, suggesting that unbridled instinct and desire are justified, but rather the belief that unspoiled human nature is essentially and potentially good. He constantly emphasizes what he perceives to be the moral aim of Rabelais. And while he does not quote Rabelais directly in support of his interpretation, his reading demonstrates an understanding of Rabelais's thought as some perceive it today.

Patricia Ward, in a recent article, has studied the stylistic procedures followed by Michelet in describing the sixteenth century in relation to the waning Middle Ages.[10] She stresses—and the point is not always made strongly enough—"the generative nature of [Michelet's] descriptive structures ... on the *Geist* of the Renaissance as Reform" (Ibid., 141). Renaissance and Reform are synonymous. The term Reform should not, I believe, be limited only to protests against religious abuses, but applied here to all forms of activity. The subject of educational reform was a constant concern of Michelet. How to educate the masses into a new, higher fraternal awareness was, for example, the topic of a series of impassioned lectures he gave at the Collège de France in 1847-1848.

Michelet is then led to a lengthy comparison of education in *Gargantua* and *Emile*. He finds an essential difference. Rabelais "ne part pas comme *Emile* d'un axiome abstrait. Il part du réel même de la vie, des moeurs de ce temps, de sa pensée grossière" (X, 373). Moreover, Michelet delights in the fact that Rabelais depicts critically the scholastic system of education still prevalent in the early Renaissance. "Il croit, *contre le Moyen âge*, que l'homme est bon, que, loin de mutiler sa nature, il faut la développer tout entière, le coeur, l'esprit, le corps" (X, 374). Rabelais's superiority over his successors, Montaigne and Rousseau, is evident, Michelet states, for Rabelais "croit contre . . . Montaigne et Rousseau, que l'éducation ne doit pas commencer par être raisonneuse et critique. Rousseau, Montaigne, tout d'abord, mettent leur élève au pain sec, de peur qu'il ne mange trop. Rabelais donne au sien toutes les bonnes nourritures de Dieu" (Ibid.). This humanistic as opposed to scholastic education corresponds more nearly to the various aptitudes of the modern child, Michelet argues. It stifles nothing. Most important: "Cette éducation porte fruit. Gargantua n'a pas été formé seulement pour la science. C'est un homme, un héros. Il sait défendre son père et son pays. Il est vainqueur, parce qu'il est juste, et courageux avec l'esprit de paix". (X, 375).[11]

But finally, Michelet asks, does Rabelais merit our unrestrained praise? Is the moral ideal of the author—an ideal of "peace," "justice," and "humanity"—complete? "Nulle éducation n'est solide," he answers, "nulle n'est orientée et ne sait son chemin, si d'abord elle ne pose simplement, nettement son principe religieux et social" (X, 376-77). To Michelet, Rabelais does this no more than do Montaigne, Fénelon, and Rousseau. His ideal is the same ultimately as theirs: *l'honnête homme*. This is an "idéal faible et négatif, qui ne peut faire encore le héros et le citoyen" (Ibid.). In the last accounting, Rousseau raises only "un gentilhomme," and Rabelais worse yet, "un roi" (Ibid.).[12] Such indulgences are the antithesis of liberality and a barricade against innovation. "Et le peuple, qui se charge de l'élever?" (Ibid.), he asks. The democratic ideal and the heroic ideal embodied in Gargantua represent a paradox. But the principle generated here is the same as that expressed by the stylistic use of specific oxymorons. Rabelais taken as a symbol of the Renaissance must be judged rough and incomplete when seen against the larger perspective of progress within history: "Ce grand esprit avait donné du moins un beau commencement, un noble essai d'éducation, une lumière, une espérance" (Ibid.).

Michelet's characterization of Rabelais in his study of the Renaissance is in many ways unsatisfactory. First of all, while his efforts to rehabilitate Rabelais are important, the text he produces is finally more interesting for what it reveals about his own system than for what it tells us about Rabelais. And second, a complex subject serves as a generalization to construct an historical synthesis of an age. It was, as Michelet insists in his Introduction to the

Renaissance in the *Histoire de France*, a period that witnessed "le jet héroïque d'une immense volonté" (IX, 13). But as Michelet concludes, the Renaissance and Rabelais represent only a transitional stage in man's development: "Cette France de Gargantua, principal organe de la Renaissance, est-elle au niveau de son rôle? Avec ce cerveau gigantesque, a-t-elle un corps? a-t-elle un coeur? a-t-elle cette vie générale, répandue partout, que l'Italie avait dans son bel âge? La France étonne par d'effrayants contrastes. C'est un géant et c'est un nain. C'est la vie débordante, c'est la mort et c'est un squelette. Comme peuple, elle n'est pas encore" (X, vi).

University of Kansas

NOTES

[1] I am here following L. Sainéan, *L'Influence et la réputation de Rabelais* (Paris: Librairie Universitaire J. Gamer, 1930).

[2] La Bruyère, *Œuvres complètes*, ed. Julien Benda (Paris: Editions Gallimard, 1951), p. 78: "Marot et Rabelais sont inexcusables d'avoir semé l'ordure dans leurs écrits: tous deux avaient assez de génie et de naturel pour pouvoir s'en passer, même à l'égard de ceux qui cherchent moins à admirer qu'à rire dans un auteur. Rabelais surtout est incompréhensible: son livre est une énigme, quoi qu'on veuille dire, inexplicable; c'est une chimère, c'est le visage d'une belle femme avec des pieds et une queue de serpent, ou de quelque autre bête plus difforme; c'est un monstrueux assemblage d'une morale fine et ingénieuse, et d'une sale corruption. Où il est mauvais, il passe bien loin au delà du pire, c'est le charme de la canaille; où il est bon, il va jusques à l'exquis et à l'excellent, il peut être le mets des plus délicats."

[3] See the excellent synthesis by Wallace K. Ferguson, *The Renaissance in Historical Thought* (Cambridge, Mass.: Houghton Mifflin, 1948), Chaps. V and VI. For these ideas in Rabelais, see *Œuvres complètes*, ed. P. Jourda (Paris: Editions Garnier Frères, 1962), I, 258-259: "Le temps estoit encores tenebreux et sentant l'infelicité et la calamité des Gothz, qui avoient mis à destruction toute bonne literature . . . Maintenant toutes disciplines sont restituées, les langues instaurées . . . Tout le monde est plein de gens savans, de precepteurs très doctes, de librairies très amples, qu'il m'est advis que, ny au temps de Platon, ny de Ciceron, ny de Papinian, n'estoit telle commodité d'estude qu'on y veoit maintenant . . ." (*Gargantua* in a letter to his son in Paris). Subsequent references to Rabelais will be from this edition.

[4] Jules Michelet, *Histoire de France* (Paris: A. Lacroix, 1877). All references will be to this edition and indicated by volume and page number in the text. I preserve Michelet's spellings and punctuation.

[5] For example, from the Preface to the Renaissance: "L'histoire est celle de l'âme et de la pensée originale, de l'initiative féconde, de l'héroïsme, héroïsme d'action, héroïsme de création" (IX, iv). And again his conclusion to the Introduction to the Renaissance: "Un grand mouvement va se faire, de guerre et d'événements, d'agitations confuses, de vague inspiration. Ces avertissements obscurs, sortis des foules, mais peu entendus d'elles, quelque'un . . . les prendra pour lui seul, se lèvera, répondra: 'Me voici!' " (Ibid., 122).

[6] Michelet is critical of both authors: "Erasme est un homme d'esprit, mais froid, de peu de verve, qui ne trouve le paradoxe qu'en sortant du bon sens. Il touche à l'ineptie lorsque, dans sa liste des fous, il met l'*enfant!* Quand il voit dans l'amour, dans le mystère sacré de la génération, *une folie ridicule!* Cela est sot et sacrilège" (X, 369-70). And, "Thomas Morus est un romancier fade, dont la faible *Utopie* a

grand'peine à trouver ce que les mystiques communistes du Moyen Age avaient réalisé d'une manière plus originale. La forme est plate, le fond commun. Peu d'imagination. Et pourtant peu de sens des réalités" (X, 370).

[7] See Raymond Lebèque, "Rabelais, the Last of the Erasmians," *Journal of the Warburg Institute*, 12 (1949), 91-100.

[8] On the theme of humanity and progress in Rabelais, see Pantagruel's destiny, *Œuvres complètes*, I, 614: "A ceste destinée ne povons nous contrevenir, car elle est passée par les mains et fuseaulx des soeurs fatales, filles de Necessité. Par ses enfans (peut estre) sera inventée herbe... moyennant laquelle pourront les humains visiter les sources des gresles, les bondes des pluyes et l'officine des fouldres, pourront envahir les regions de la Lune, entrer le territoire des signes celestes et là prendre logis ..." For a fuller discussion see Jerry C. Nash, "Rabelais and Stoic Portrayal," *Studies in the Renaissance*, 21 (1974), 81-82.

[9] See Marcel de Grève, *L'Interprétation de Rabelais au XVIe siècle* (Genève: Droz, 1961), for a thoughtful study of this relationship, and especially M. A. Screech, *Rabelais* (Ithaca: Cornell University Press, 1979).

[10] Patricia A. Ward, "Encoding in Romantic Descriptions of the Renaissance: Hugo and Michelet on the Sixteenth Century," *French Forum*, 3 (1978), 133.

[11] Michelet is paraphrasing in broad outline the episodic developments in Gargantua's life: Chapter XIV deals with how "Gargantua feut institué par un sophiste en lettres latines" (*Œuvres complètes*, I, 59), and Chapter XXIII, with how his father, seeing that the scholastic instruction he receives is leading nowhere, places him with Ponocrates who instructs him "en telle discipline qu'il ne perdoit heure du jour" (Ibid., p. 87). The training serves him well when he is recalled to help defend his father's territory against Picrochole's invasion, and especially afterwards, as in Chapter L, "La contion que feist Gargantua es vaincus" (Ibid., p. 182), where he expresses with humanistic eloquence ideas of peace and justice with regard to the distinction that is to be made between the guilty and the innocent in the treatment of conquered peoples. And again, Gargantua's later advice to his own son in Paris: "Science sans conscience n'est que ruine de l'âme" (Ibid., pp. 261-62).

[12] Michelet comments in another context concerning Gargantua as a king symbol: "La centralisation, qui commence, immense et confuse encore, n'est guère comprise des foules que comme la force infinie d'un individu. Point de vue populaire, enfantin, que Rabelais va reproduire... dans ses rois géants.... C'est l'adoration de la force, l'obscurcissement du droit" (IX, 310-11). And again: "Ces vieilles histoires de géant, loin de pâlir, s'étaient fortifiées à l'apparition de la royauté et du gouvernement moderne. Le phénomène étrange, diabolique ou divin, d'un peuple résumé dans un homme, la centralisation royale, comment la figurer? comment représenter ce Dieu? C'est un géant apparemment, qui mange les gens *en salade? Car un roi ne vit*

pas de peu" (X, 373). These last remarks which Michelet has put in italics are a good example of his tendency to paraphrase Rabelais within his own narrative rather than quote him directly (e.g. *Œuvres complètes*, I, 143: "Comment Gargantua mangea en sallade six pelerins").

THE "MAD" CHRIST OF ERASMUS

AND THE LEGAL DUTIES OF HIS BRETHREN

M. A. Screech

Erasmus refuses to let himself be tied down to one country or to one culture. There is hardly an aspect of the western Renaissance, in any country from Spain to Poland or from Scotland to Italy, in which his name does not appear. If he had been a lesser writer, the fact that he first published his *Moriae Encomium* in Paris would doubtless have linked his name mainly with France. But he published so much of such fundamental importance after the *Moriae Encomium* that we must inevitably expect him to appear in studies on the Renaissance in Italy, England, Germany, Spain, as well as France. Certainly it was in France, in the *Praise of Folly*, that he first gave his Europe-wide readership an insight into his theology of divine madness.

Erasmus worshipped a God who, by his incarnation, emptied himself of his manifest deity, sometimes even appearing to his fellow men as a raging lunatic.[1] This was no mere figure of speech for Erasmus—a theme to be sported with, say, in the *Praise of Folly*, but to be firmly set aside in his more sober theological writings. On the contrary: the most firmly expressed examples of this concept of Jesus as an ecstatic lunatic are to be found, precisely, in the theological writings.

A key text of the Gospels where the "madness" of Christ is concerned is the third Chapter of Mark. There we are shown Jesus accused—by "his own people"—of being mad.

> And when his kinsmen(?) heard of it, they went out to lay hold on him: for, they said, he is beside himself. (Mark 3, 21)

(The Scribes followed this up, in the next verse, by saying that "He hath Beelzebub".)

These stormy accusations are followed by the equally stormy scene in which Jesus' "brethren and his mother" wait outside, whilst Jesus, indoors, acknowledges not them but his true mother and brethren:

> And he looked round about on them which sat about him, and said, "Behold my mother and my brethren". (Mark 3, 34)

These points are traditionally weakened for English readers, since the

Authorised Version translates Matthew 3, 21 as though it were Christ's 'friends' who 'went out to lay hold on him', not his kinsmen. The Greek reads: *hoi par'autou*, a phrase probably meaning his "relations", his "kinsfolk", although the Revised Version still sticks to "his friends", despite the marginal note referring the reader to Christ's "mother and brethren" in verse 31. But the œcumenical Revised Standard Version refers to Christ's "family" in verse 21; so does the New English Bible. In some ways the clearest of all the English renderings where the points at issue here are concerned is that of the variant of the New English Bible:

> When his family heard of this, they set out to take charge of him; for people were saying of him, "He is out of his mind".

That is a version which Erasmus himself could have approved of, since he believed that Jesus' kinsfolk had come out with the set purpose of restraining their relative whom they believed to be raving mad.

The Vulgate is fairly clear, but Erasmus makes things clearer still in his own *Novum Instrumentum*.

Vulgate	*Novum Instrumentum*
Et cum audissent sui exierunt tenere eum:	Et quum audissent qui ad illum attinebant exierunt ut manus injicerent in eum:
dicebant enim, in furorem versus est.	dicebant enim, in furorem versus est.

In his annotation Erasmus glosses *hoi par'autou* so as to make it absolutely obvious that those persons *qui ad illum attinebant* were indeed Jesus' relations—the same no doubt as appear a few verses later—"his mother and his brethren" (verse 31):

> *Hoi par'autou: qui ad illum pertinebant, & ex illius erant familia, seu cognatione.* Itidem paulo inferius *ta par'autou* vertit *sua*. Sentit enim, *cognatos & affines ejus.* (LB5: 162, note 19)

The word *cognati* proves to be important for understanding Erasmus' concept of Christ and his apparent madness. Important too is the slipping, unheralded, from the *cognati* of this note to the *agnati* of the following note but one, where we are told that these relatives went out to 'lay hold' of Jesus in order to restrain him:

> Nam id est agnatorum, si quis commotae mentis esse coeperit. (LB5, 162, note 21)

Erasmus, influenced at least partly by Theophylact, Archbishop of Achrida (Bulgaria), believed, indeed, that these kinsmen had come out with chains. They did this, thinking that they were doing their duty: raving lunatics have to be restrained by their kinsmen.[2]

That they saw this as their legal duty is a point made again in the *Paraphrases* (*ad loc.*):

> Itaque quoniam erant cognati, juxta leges humanas, putabant esse sui officii, ut mentis impotem, & a spiritu quopiam arreptum, vinculis coercerent. (LB7, 183E)

Anyone who despises the world and wholeheartedly embraces the heavenly philosophy must expect similar treatment from the worldly-wise, who will naturally accuse him of being weak in the head (*mentis impos*), a fool, a madman.

Erasmus' phrase *juxta leges humanas* proves to mean more than at first may meet the eye. These *cognati* or *agnati* of the incarnate Lord were not being merely officious or vicious. They were acting in accordance with Roman Law. A wealth of legal and literary erudition underlies Erasmus' terminology; what he means can be explained without too many technicalities. The key lies in the word *agnati* and, to a lesser extent, with *cognati*.

All systems of law need some method of requiring care to be taken of certain sorts of people who are mentally ill. Roman Law is no exception. The basic law figured in the Twelve Tables. It gave rise to a well-known proverbial saying.

To deal with the proverb first. Marcus Porcius Cato (the Censor) is cited by Columella in his *De re rustica* (I, 3, 1) as attaching a great importance to a wholesome climate and a fertile area when looking for a farm to buy. For Cato anyone who bought a farm without first satisfying himself on both these scores must be mad:

> Porcius quidem Cato censebat inspiciendo agro praecipue duo esse consideranda, salubritatem caeli et ubertatem loci; quorum si alterum deesset, ac nihilominus quis vellet incolere, *mente esse captum atque eum ad agnatos et gentiles deducendum.*

The phrase in italics is the relevant one. Cato believed such a feckless purchaser of a farm to be "out of his mind"—*mente captus*—fit therefore to be taken away to the care of his *agnati* (his blood relations) or to his *gentiles* (the members of his same *gens*).

From the subject of Cato's remark Columella might seem to be alluding to M. Porcius Cato's *De agricultura*, but there is nothing in that work remotely resembling this assertion that the rash cultivator of a bad farm ought (as we would say) to have his head examined.

In fact Columella is quoting Cato as he is also cited by Varro in his *De re rustica*, I, 2, 8. The allusion in Varro comes after a reference to a lost work of Cato's entitled *Origins*:

> An non M. Cato scribit in libro Origenum . . . (etc.)

Varro tells his reader that Italian farmers look out for two principal qualities when choosing a farm: i) whether they will get a fair return for their labour, and, ii) whether the climate is healthy.

> Quorum si alterutrum decolat et nihilominus quis vult colere, mente est captus *adque adgnatos et gentiles est deducendus.*

So much for the proverb in antiquity. Now for the law.

This particular law of the Twelve Tables is alluded to by Cicero in *De inventione* (II, 50, 148):

> SI FURIOSUS ESCIT AGNATORUM [*OR*, AGNATUM] GENTILIUMQUE IN EO PECUNIAQUE EJUS POTESTAS ESTO.

Cicero alludes to it again in the *Tusculan Disputations*, III, 8, 11, when explaining that the Latin language distinguishes between certain kinds of madness better than the Greek does. In Greek the two main categories of madness, *mania* and *melancholia* are quite insufficient for the purposes of Roman Law. The Laws of the Twelve Tables do not put constraints on those who are merely "insane" (*insani*) but on those who are raging lunatics (*furiosi*):

> Itaque non est scriptus *si insanus* sed *si furiosus escit.*

The man who is merely *insanus* can at least look after his own affairs in the context of everyday life. But *furor* is another matter. It totally blinds the mind. And even the wise can fall into such a madness:

> Stultitiam enim censuerunt constantia, id est sanitate, vacantem posse tamen tueri mediocritatem et vitae communem cultum atque usitatum, furorem autem esse rati sunt mentis ad omnia caecitatem. Quod cum majus: esse videatur quam insania, tamen ejus modi est, ut furor in sapientem cadere possit, non possit insania. (*Tusc.* III, 5, 11)

Furor—not *insania*—is the kind of madness attributed to Jesus by his kinsfolk in the Vulgate rendering of Matthew 3: *In furorem versus est.* That Christ was held to be "raging mad" explains, moreover, the chains which Erasmus believed that these kinsfolk bore in their hands: in Antiquity as during the middle ages and the Renaissance, madmen were restrained above all with chains during their periods of raving lunacy.[3] Jesus' family thought that they had to deal with a man who was violently mad. (Erasmus apparently believed that these kinsmen of Christ, Jews though they were, were fulfilling their apparent duty under the laws of the occupying power.)

It is at this point that Erasmus' slide from *cognati* to *agnati* assumes special importance, for whilst it could be disputed whether the *cognati* had such a right and duty, there is no doubt whatsoever that the *agnati* did. The point is made not only in the Laws of the Twelve Tables but in the numerous editions of Justinian's *Institutes*. Normally, children and young persons were only in care of their guardians until the age of twenty-five. This limitation did not of course apply to those who were raving mad: cf. *liber 1, titulus xxiii,* § *de curatoribus* of the *Institutes*:

> Furiosi quoque et prodigi, licet majores viginti quinque annis: tamen in curatione sunt adgnatorum ex lege duodecim tabularum. Sed solent Romae praefectus urbi vel praetores, & in provinciis praesides, ex inquisitione eis curatores dare.
> (*Institutiones:* ed. Haloander and Contius, Paris, 1567, p. 25vᵒ— or any other edition, *ad loc.*)

Erasmus apparently preferred to use the term *cognati* most of the time, when treating the misguided behaviour of Christ's relations in Mark 3, because of the all-embracing nature of the term. *Agnati* are relations on the father's side only: the category embraces all those who were, or who had ever been, under the legal authority of the *paterfamilias*. But the Gospel of Mark refers in verse 32 of Chapter 3 to Christ's "mother and brothers": *hè mètèr sou kai hoi adelphoi sou.* The term *cognati* was wide enough to include mothers and all relations, on both the father's and the mother's side. Perhaps Erasmus felt justified in extending the rights and duties of the *agnati* to the *cognati* because the actual law of the Twelve Tables had been very wide in its terminology, alluding not only to the duties of the *agnati* but also of the *gentiles*—all, that is, who belonged to the same 'line' (*gens*). It was normally held—in order to make the genealogy of Christ in Matthew relevant to Jesus and his mother— that both Mary and Joseph were of the same line.

The distinction between *agnati* and *cognati* was well known to Jurisconsults. It is frequently made in the glosses to *liber 1, titulus xv* of the *Institutes*, entitled *De legitima agnatorum tutela.* In the Plantin edition of the *Institutes,* 1575, for example, one reads, col. 77:

> *Cognati.* nomen ergo cognationis generale est: agnationis nomen speciale. nam omnis agnatus est cognatus: sed non convertitur: ut hic & *j. de. leg. agn. j. respon. &, ff. eo. l. sunt autem.*

Folly is central to Erasmus' theology, so central that he had perhaps ceased to be surprised by it. Ecstasy of a mad-seeming kind he believed to be characteristic of chosen Christians as it had been for Jesus himself. That neither Jesus' mother nor his brethren should have recognised his role in the divine plan as the incarnate Son of God but have taken him to be insane in Mark 3 is in keeping with the kenotic theology which Erasmus consistently expounded. Some of the theologians who followed him were worried, however. And few seem to have grasped the import of his glancing allusions to the legal duties of the kinsmen.

An example of an exegete who was profoundly influenced by Erasmus yet seemingly unaware of this legal point being made, but troubled by the crassness of Jesus' relatives, is Augustine Marlorat ('Du Pasquier'), the learned Austin friar who became a minister of the Eglise Réformée. (He was hanged at Rouen in October 1562 when his religious enemies seized the town). Marlorat wonders at the "depravity" of Christ's *cognati* who talk of insanity when they ought to have been amongst the first of the 'workers-together with the Lord'. But the lesson is clear: salvation is not through flesh and blood, but from grace from above:

> Mirum est quòd in Christi cognatis tanta fuerit pravitas ut Christum insanire dicerent, qui ad promovendum Dei regnum primi adjutores esse debuerant. Quum vident aliquod jam nomen ille esse partum, titillitat eos ambitio, ut Jerosolymae celebrari cupiant: hortantur enim ut illuc

ascendat, quò se melius ostentet (Joh.7.a.3.4.). Nunc quia vident partim exosum esse primoribus, partim multis calumniis obnoxium, contemni etiam à magna parte, ne quid damni vel invidiae, vel dedeceris redundet ad commune genus, injicere illi manum cogitant, & domi constringere, tanquam hominem mente alienatum: atque ita fuisse persuasos, ex verbis Evangelistae liquet. Vide primum quanta sit humani ingenii caecitas, quòd tam perverse judicat de manifesta Dei gloria. Certè virtus Spiritus sancti manifestè refulgebat in omnibus Christi dictis ac factis: quòd si aliis fuisset obscura, consanguineos propter familiarem notitiam quomodo latere poterat? Sed quoniam agendi ratio quam Christus tenet, mundo non arridet, adeóque favorem illi non conciliat ut potius exponat multorum odiis, ecstaticum esse fingunt.[4]

It is by no means certain that Erasmus would have agreed that these relatives had wickedly contrived their actions against a Jesus taken to be mad. For Erasmus, Jesus was an *extaticus*. So too were Paul, Peter and many privileged saintly Christians. Jesus' relations acted ignorantly, failing to distinguish God-given "madness" from mental illness. But at least, unlike the Scribes, they did not accuse Jesus of being possessed by Beelzebub. His *cognati* acted in good faith. Some relations do the same today. Erasmus warns his readers that their own families may well believe them to be mad, if they are one of the privileged followers of Christ who are touched by the divine (LB7, 183 EF). (Marlorat may have been moved to interpret the rôle of Jesus' *cognati* as he did under the influence of another adage—one collected by Erasmus—*cognatio movet invidiam*).

But despite Marlorat's divergence from Erasmus over the rôle of Christ's *cognati* he realised as clearly as Erasmus himself that those who reject the world's madness will be judged mad by those who revel in it:

> Et crassa caro pro inanis habet quicunque cum mundo insaniente non ineptiunt. (Marloratus: *ad loc.*)

The apparent failure of at least some of Erasmus' contemporaries to spot the allusion to Cato and his legally based proverb certainly weakens the force of what Erasmus had to say about the ecstatic *furor* of Jesus in his *Annotationes in Novum Testamentum*. Erasmus may be in part to blame for this failure, in that he never included *Ad agnatos et gentiles deducere* amongst his own *Adagia*. This omission was made up for by two scholars of an Erasmian bent, John Alexander Brassicanus and Gilbert Cognatus, Erasmus' confidential clerk and pupil. In J. A. Brassicanus' *Proverbium symmicta* the proverb is given as, *Ad gentiles & agnatos deducendus*. In Gilbert Cognatus it is, closer to the classical sources, given as *Ad agnatos & gentiles deducendus*.[5]

Both authors link the proverb with its sources in Latin literature and Roman Law. They form good guides, therefore, towards what Erasmus meant by the "madness" which had apparently taken hold of Jesus in the chaotic events outlined in Mark 3. It was not a mere *insania*—such a form of folly cannot affect a wise man, as Cicero had pointed out (*Tusc.* III, 5, 11). It was such a *furor* as can affect even the wise. It was that kind of divine *mania* which the laws of men can mistake for raving madness: *ekstasis.*

The folly that Erasmus praised in the *Praise of Folly* is much more profoundly disturbing because of this.

University College London

NOTES

[1] Points such as these are developed in *Ecstasy and the Praise of Folly*, (London: Duckworth's, 1980); especially relevant where this article is concerned is Chapter 4, § 3: "The madness of Christ: an excursus".

[2] *Ibid.* pp. 71-2.

[3] *Ibid.*

[4] Augustinus Marloratus: *Novi Testamenti catholica expositio Ecclesiastica. ex universis probatis theologis (Quos Dominus diversis suis Ecclesiis dedit) excerpta, à quodam verbi Dei ministro, diu multumque in theologia versato* . . . Henricus Stephanus, illustris viri Huldrichi Fuggeri typographus. 1560; p. 284 (col. 2); on Mark 3, 21.

[5] For convenience I have used *Adagia, id est proverbiorum, paroemiorum et parabolarum, quae apud Graecos, Latinos, Hebraeos, Arabas, &c in usu fuerunt, Collectio absolutissima* . . . , 'Typis Wechelianis, Sumptibus Joannis Pressii', 1643; cf. p. 699.

THE DEVOTIONAL AESTHETICS OF A HUMANIST:

NICOLAS DENISOT'S *CANTIQUES*

Jerry C. Nash

It is a curious phenomenon of literary history when a writer achieves universal acclaim and unanimous praise in his own time, only to be forgotten by later generations and even centuries. This literary scenario is especially extraordinary in the case of a Renaissance humanist who excelled in poetry, painting, architecture, the teaching profession, classical philology, politics, mathematics, engineering, and espionage: who was praised as a first-rate poet by such leading literary figures of his day as Ronsard, Du Bellay, Baïf, Belleau, Jodelle, Magny, Muret, Michel de l'Hospital, and Montaigne among others; who organized and contributed to the *Tombeau* published in 1551 honoring the death of Marguerite de Navarre; who won the esteem and confidence of the English under Edward VI and served as preceptor of Latin, Greek, and French to the daughters of the powerful Duke of Somerset—Anne, Margaret, and Jeanne Seymour; who was sent by Henri II to live in Calais, under the pretext of being a painter, and who sent sent back to the French King secret drawings showing how best to attack the city and retake it from the English; and finally, for our specific purposes in this study, whose major collection of devotional poetry published early in 1553, during the peak of and contrary to the amorous orientation of the prevailing Pléiade poetry, contributed significantly toward establishing and promoting the poetic trend in Christian verse which came to dominate the poetic activity at the end of the sixteenth century. I am speaking of course of Nicolas Denisot, known literarily during his time by his anagram "Le Conte d'Alsinois," and of his widely read *Cantiques du premier advenement de Jesu-Christ* published in 1553 by la Veuve Maurice de la Porte in Paris. Like many other devotional poets of the French Renaissance, Denisot, in spite of the tremendous popularity and importance which he once enjoyed, is little known today, with no study in English ever devoted to his poetry, and has been virtually passed over in our modern critical concern with the Pléiade poets. This essay is an initial step toward correcting this oversight, a task in keeping with the renewed critical interest especially of Terence C. Cave and Michel Jeanneret in those religious poets overshadowed by the Pléiade.[1] As interesting and intriguing as the biographical side of Denisot is,[2] my comments here will be limited to Denisot's poetry with the hope of giving some indication of the remarkable poetic range and artistic beauty of a very good Renaissance devotional poet worthy of our attention in his own literary right as well as in the larger historical context of the development of French poetry in the sixteenth century.[3]

Denisot's *Cantiques* are fourteen in number composed in varying ode lengths with several, shorter *chants* appearing among the cantiques and serving to relieve the sustained concentration of the sequence. Each cantique is introduced by an "Argument," an heraldic device announcing a biblical motif which the poem will develop. As might be expected, the sequence has a definite musical purpose. In his "Dédicace," Denisot urges his readers to sing the cantiques aloud: "... de chanter cette petite Musique, que simplement j'ay faict notter à une voix, a celle fin que telle chose se peust autant chanter en solitude, qu'en toute compaignie vertueuse" (p. 4). Accordingly, the first stanza of each poem is handsomely set to music.[4] These cantiques of 1553 contain the sustained, rhetorical, and often complex patterning of elevated humanist art and do not have much in common with the composition of the simpler and more popular medieval "noëls," though Denisot does in a couple of instances, for the sake of certain effects, approach the medieval mode (he had previously written ten such "medieval" short lyrical pieces also on the devotional theme of the Nativity[5]). It is not idle to stress that the techniques and poetic principles employed by Denisot in his devotional poetry are derived from the very same presentational arts of the trivium—grammar, logic, and rhetoric, the stock in trade of the humanist culture of the 1550's—being used by the Pléiade poets for amorous ends. For one trained alongside Ronsard and Du Bellay at the Collège de Coqueret under the Hellenist Dorat, there could hardly have been a rejection of Pléiade poetics. What we in fact find is an adept transference of them to serve the new themes and motives of Christian poetics. In one of his introductory pieces to Denisot's poems, Belleau informs us:

> Le sujet n'est point d'Amours,
> Le trait n'est point variable,
> Ny fabuleux le discours,
> Mais eternel & durable.
> Icy ne sont point chantez
> D'un son pippeur les mensonges,
> Bois meuz, fleuues arrestez,
> Ny d'un mont cornu les songes.
>
> Icy l'on voit seullement
> Descouuertes les merueilles
> Du Sacré Aduenement,
> Digne des saintes oreilles. (p. 14)

In introductory pieces also written by Muret and Jodelle, we find the same call for a new emphasis and direction in the poetic activity of the Pléiade in the 1550's. Thus Muret urges his fellow humanist poets to abandon the old themes of love and follow Denisot in singing Christ. He too is calling, not for a change in technique, but for a change in poetic perspective, in "matiere":

> Diuins esprits, vrais ornemens du monde,
> Qui la liqueur d'Hippocrene epuisés,
> Et notre siecle a merueille induisés
> Par votre veine heureusement feconde,
> Las, n'est-ce asses emploié sa faconde,
> A vous monstrer d'amour martirises?
> Autre matiere à voz chans elisés,
> D'ou plus de fruit, & plus d'honneur redonde.
> CHRIST vous semond a chanter ses honneurs:
> Courage donc! soies-en les sonneurs,
> Ne chantés plus que de l'amour diuine,
> Emploiés la votre esprit tout entier,
> Et d'un accord ensuiués le sentier
> Ou Denisot le premier s'achemine. (p. 16)

As we all know, a devotional poem is not a devotional treatise or exercise, and we also know that one of the reasons is that devotional poetry relies on the very same affective stylistics for communicating its "experience" or "emotion" as does amorous, lyric poetry. Nothing except the "object" being addressed has changed in the two poetic experiences (though there are profound implications involved here, as we shall see). Since the purpose of both the devotional poet and the lyric poet is to move the reader, to incite him to praise and higher contemplation, their means can hardly be different. In Renaissance love poetry, this experience of emotion in the presence of beauty is the essence of the aesthetics of human love. The same principle applies to the devotional experience, and even more so: emotion and beauty are not only its essence, but also its final objective and its final triumph.

The whole notion of what constitutes poetic beauty rests, of course, in the eye of the beholder. However, there are common characteristics and depths of meaning to be found in a few masterpieces of poetic love whose very success we would all agree resides in the recording and disclosure of the poetic experience of beauty. Diotima's speech in Plato's *Symposium* points to the aesthetically ascending journey to be attempted later by such love poets as Dante, Petrarch, and Scève. All three will aspire in their poetry to understand and to capture that perfected state of primordial beauty through the inter-mediary of the human objects of their contemplation:

> When a man has been thus far tutored in the lore
> of love, passing from view to view of beautiful

> things, in the right and regular ascent, suddenly
> he will have revealed to him, as he draws to the
> close of his dealings in love, a wondrous vision,
> beautiful in its nature; and this, Socrates, is
> the final object of all those previous toils.
> First of all, it is ever-existent and neither
> comes to be nor perishes, neither waxes nor wanes;
> next, it is not beautiful in part and in part ugly,
> nor is it such at such a time and other at another,
> nor in one respect beautiful and in another ugly . . .[6]

Dante begins to experience this kind of enraptured ascent occasioned by a transcending beauty when he comes under the influence of the power of Beatrice's gaze. Her radiance, perceived as a reflection of the divine, leads the poet by degrees higher and higher (*Paradiso*, XV, 32-36):

> Poscia rivolsi alla mia donna il viso,
> e quinci e quindi stupefatto fui;
> ché dentro alli occhi suoi ardea un riso
> tal, ch'io pensai co' miei toccar lo fondo
> della mia grazia e del mio paradiso.[7]

Petrarch experiences this same wondrous and soul-consuming image of beauty in the person of Laura. Her beauty is also perceived by the poet as illuminated by the divine (R72):

> Gentil mia donna, i' veggio
> nel mover de' vostr'occhi un dolce lume
> che mi mostra la via ch'al ciel conduce;
> et per lungo costume
> dentro là dove sol con Amor seggio,
> quasi visibilmente il cor traluce.[8]

And Scève often embodies this profound poetic perspective in his intense and transcending contemplation of the beauty of Délie. She not only illuminates this world but provides a glimpse of the divine beauty. At times, Scève even comes very close to effecting the perfect union of the two desired spheres of existence, the mortal and the eternal, body and soul (D367):

> Asses plus long, qu'vn siecle Platonique,
> Me fut le moys, que sans toy suis esté:
> Mais quand ton front ie reuy pacifique,

Seiour treshault de toute honnesteté,
Ou l'empire est du conseil arresté
Mes songes lors ie creus estre deuins.
Car en mon corps: mon Ame, tu reuins,
Sentant ses mains, mains celestement blanches,
Auec leurs bras mortellement diuins
L'vn coronner mon col, l'aultre mes hanches.[9]

All of these poetic encounters involving personal experiences of human beauty have at least one thing in common: they celebrate and attempt to glorify the sudden and marvelous way in which human love takes hold of the poet's soul and guides him into higher spheres and into the "shining center" of creation and contemplation. How, as Scève describes this ascent to the beatific vision, the transcending power of love "renaist soubdain en moy celle autre Lune/*Luisante au centre,* ou l'Ame a son seiour" (D 106).

But in spite of these memorable and praiseworthy poetic aspirations to participate in the divine through contemplation of forms of human beauty, the experiences being recorded and analyzed by these poets are recognized by them to be incomplete and lacking. To return to the rest of Diotima's speech: "But tell me, what would happen *if* one of you had the fortune to look upon essential beauty entire, pure and unalloyed; not infected with the flesh and colour of humanity, and ever so much more of mortal trash? What *if* he could behold the divine beauty itself, in its unique form" (p. 207)? Petrarch will concede the same point, that in spite of the extraordinary forms of beauty illuminating this earth through the glory of Laura, there can be in the final analysis no true transfiguration of man here and now (R349):

O felice quel dì che del terreno
carcere uscendo lasci rotta e sparta
questa mia grave e frale e mortal gonna.
e da sì folte tenebre mi parta
volando tanto su nel bel sereno,
ch'i veggia il mio Signore, et la mia donna!

The same conclusion on the ultimately indefinable, unattainable, and thus limited nature of the love poet's attempt at beatific transcendence is reached by Scève in many of his dizains, in 166, 267, 410, and stated most poignantly in D96:

A contempler si merueilleux spectacle,
Tu anoblis la mienne indignité,

> Pour estre toy de ce Siecle miracle,
> Restant merueille a toute eternité,
> Ou la Clemence en sa benignité,
> Reuere a soy Chasteté Presidente
> Si hault au ciel de l'honneur residente,
> Que tout aigu d'oeil vif n'y peult venir.
> O vain desir, ò folie euidente,
> A qui de faict espere y paruenir.

Perhaps we appear to have strayed somewhat from Denisot, or have we? That change in poetic perspective, in "matiere," mentioned earlier as a felt need regarding the direction poetry should take is justified precisely on the same grounds as recognized, as we have noted above, by Petrarch and Scève: the ultimate inadequacy and inability of the current effort to attain poetic transcendence and finality with the theme of human love. Since human love by definition had to remain only an image of the divine, the two spheres of the mortal and the eternal would always remain separate. What was believed missing was the true principle of transcendence permitting the joining or uniting of the two spheres which some poets were proclaiming could only be found in Christ as the object and means of poetic contemplation. Jodelle also tells us this in his introductory ode. After having systematically debunked the amorous motives and myths of pagan antiquity and in particular the misguided lyrical talents of Orpheus, Amphion, and Arion, he embraces the new theme of Christ as the only one capable of bestowing total enlightenment:

> Dequoy me sert le Parnasse,
> L'Helicon Pegasien,
> Ou encor ie m'abbreuuasse
> Comme vn resueur ancien:
> Si cette saincte Fonteine,
> De grace & de doulceur plaine,
> Sourd pour m'arracher d'esmoy;
> Si cette saincte naissance
> Me donne la congnoissance
> Et de mon Dieu, & de moy? (p. 10)

Whether or not these poets actually believed they could acquire in their devotional poetry the experience of transcendence is of little importance. What is important is that they fervently felt that with a new "matiere" centered on Christ, they could come closer to achieving it.[10] Denisot is even more pointed in this matter of rejecting human love and embracing Christ than Jodelle:

Les carquois & les fleches,
Les amorces & meiches
De cest aueuglé archer
Ne soit plus la matiere
D'escrire coustumiere,
Pour noz traictz decocher.

Ce Dieu qui par le vuide
A son vouloir nous guide,
Seigneur de l'vniuers,
Soit la source & la force,
La fonteine & l'amorce
Du meilleur de noz vers. (VIII, pp. 71-72)

In fact, one of the central concerns of Denisot's poetry is the strategy of denouncing and banishing the old in preparation for this New Perspective. Sometimes the portrayal of this struggle of the old *versus* the new reaches cosmic proportions which we associate with later Baroque poetic art. In Cantique X, Denisot explodes the error of the past with its false gods and idols ruling everywhere in the universe with a deadly vengeance:

Ce fut lors mesmement aussi
Que soubz cest assotement cy,
On vit les sages de la Grece
Prendre Minerue pour deesse,
Qu'en Athenes on adoroit:
Qui des chansons & des allarmes,
Qui des estudes & des armes,
Le Pouuoir à soy retiroit.

Ce fut lors que Thir adora
Iunon, & que l'Ephese honora
L'image de Diane archere.
Ce fut lors que d'Amour la mere
Tint Paphe, Cipre, et autres liens.
Bref, ce fut lors qu'au monde vindrent,
Et toute sa rondeur obtindrent,
Cent mille milliers de faulx dieux.

Mais ce iourd'huy le Dieu puissant,
Qui roulle d'vn bras punissant
L'horrible traict de ces tempestes,
Faisant peur aux plus haultes testes,
S'est abbaissé pour rabaisser
De ces dieux orgueilleux l'outraige,

>   Faisant tomber chacun Image
>   Qui venoit son droict offenser. (pp. 91-92)

The old sacrifical practices of pagan idolatry are castigated in especially bold and contemptuous terms and are corrected in favor of the new meaningful simplicity of Christian devotion:

>   La main sanglante encore
>   N'est celle qui adore
>   Le grand Dieu immortel;
>   Ny la beste muglante,
>   Soubz le cousteau tremblante,
>   Craignant le coup mortel.
>
>   C'est la simple priere,
>   La congnoissance entiere
>   De sa perfection. (VIII, p. 70)

The description of the triumph of the Infant Christ over Satan is, to be sure, expressed even more forcefully and vividly. The language and imagery employed here are as graphic and violent as any Baroque description we find later in D'Aubigné, as we can see in Cantique VI:

>   Au berçeau ie voy
>   Vn petit Hercul,
>   Qui sans nul effroy,
>   Sans atteinte nulle,
>   Le vainqueur se faict
>   D'vn serpent infait:
>   Tout enflé d'enuie,
>   Sa gorge froissant,
>   Qui va vomissant
>   Et venin & vie. (pp. 51-52)

Quite often, as the passages above show, the basic conflict of the two forces is rigorously depicted by Denisot through the affectively dramatic device of antithetical composition, with the whole process resulting in the burying of the corrupt and fallen past to prepare for the redeeming emergence of the New. Denisot presents in axiomatic terms this new concept of the triumphant march of the divine power ever progressing in its natural expansion in Cantique I:

Y a-il durté si fiere,
Horreur de quelque matiere
Qui ne commence à mouuoir,
Pour estre la deuanciere
Deuant ce diuin pouuoir? (p. 20)[11]

This contrastive narration is continued and related directly to the theme of the Nativity by the end of Cantique I. Denisot's prevailing pattern is that of the inrush of harmony against discord, light against darkness, Logos against Chaos, with the opposing forces typically depicted in terms of a battle. Moreover, Denisot always forces us to see the new symbol from the perspective of a fallen state, and thus to be simultaneously aware of the symbol, its antithesis, and the tremendous and awesome force of the new power which will effect the long-awaited transformation:

La guerre estoit denoncée,
Nature estoit courroucée,
La Mort tenoit contre nous,
Pour l'ordonnance offencée
De Dieu qui nous est si doulx.

Mais la paix vniuerselle
A ceste couche nouuelle,
De ce sainct aduenement,
A vaincu la mort rebelle,
Soeur de nostre damnement. (p. 22)

The sharp juxtaposition of old and new, of Chaos and Logos, is further employed in reference to the theme of the Cross in Cantique VII. The portrayal again stresses the tension in the poet's mind between his intense desire for harmony and order and the awareness of present discord and disorder. Denisot forces us to contemplate both states simultaneously and thus to be constantly aware both of their thematic antagonism and of the formal tension between them. But as the antithetical portrayal develops and unfolds, its resolution ultimately reflects the transforming process again of creating order out of disorder, which is the purpose of the poetry and the longing of the poet's spirit:

Qui [l'Enfantelet] doit vn iour de sa croix
Faire vne telle ouuerture,
Qui, malgré tous les abboys
De l'infernale closture,

Brisera tous les effortz
De ceste bande orgueilleuse,
Pour noz peres tirer hors
D'vne force merueilleuse. (p. 65)

The development of the poet's meditation on the opposing forces in cantiques similar to the above prepares the way for the ultimate clarification, confirmation, and triumph of religious faith. The structural and thematic tension of opposites, bringing wholeness out of chaos and transforming corrupt and condemned flesh into dynamic spirit, is exultantly expressed in the *Chant* appearing between Cantiques VIII and IX:

C'estoit au temps passé
Que la loy de rigueur,
La race de Iesse,
Retenoit en langueur.

Mais d'icelle est sorti
Vng rameau florissant,
Qui a seul amorti
Le Lyon rugissant.

C'est l'Enfant nouueau né,
Qui, pour nous tirer hors
Du malheur ordonné,
Nous plege de son corps.

*   *   *

O l'honneur de Syon!
O parfaicte bonte!
O saincte Passion,
Qui la mort a donté! (p. 74)

This transforming process has also made possible the undistracted and serenely joyful contemplation of the poet's full religious longing for the experience of transcendence. The unique focus of the poems and of the poet's attention now shifts from conflict and tension to the quintessentially radiant beauty and power of the Logos incarnated in Jesus Christ:

Esprits diuins, chantez de la Nuict saincte,
C'est ceste Nuict que la Pucelle enceincte
Nous a produict le VERBE precieux. (IV, p. 37)

Christ's descent in the form of human flesh is perceived through the poet's ascent to the divine vision. The poetic upward gaze responding to the religious downward act pivots around the paradoxical brilliance and beauty of the mystery of the Incarnation: the Word which has become flesh in the second person of the Trinity in whom we can see, as Denisot says, "Dieu, la chair, & l'esprit" (XI, p. 96)! The traditional biblical and poetic images of the Logos such as light and life superseding death and night, the sun and its radiance, dance, music, song, and the harmony of the spheres are now at the very artistic center of Denisot's poems. The heavens, in perfect harmony, salute and praise the glorious Coming:

> C'est ceste Nuict que l'on a veu les cieux
> Tous decouuers, & bien cinq cens mil anges
> Chanter à Dieu eternelles louenges. (IV, pp. 37-38)

Cantique II opens with a burst of musical imagery. The sweet sounds of celestial music are heard everywhere, and especially in the innermost regions of the poet's heart and soul, the main stress being on "soul":

> O quelle voix Angelique!
> Quel accord melodieux
> Dont on oit mesme les cieux
> Bondir de ceste musique!
> Reueille toy, ô mon coeur,
> O mon Ame, ie t'appelle
> Pour voir la saincte Chappelle
> De tout le celeste Choeur. (p. 26)

The purpose of these verses, and of many others charged with an intense exhilaration and excitement, is to communicate a joyous affirmation of life seen through renewal and revival. The newly found joy and sweetness that the poet feels stem from the renewed assurance of his soul's immortality, and of that of the whole world. This central theme of life's renewal through the Incarnation is resoundingly expressed in Cantique XI:

> Ores chacun se peult dire
> Affranchi, rien ne tenant
> D'Adam, de Nature & d'Ire,
> Mais de Dieu: car maintenant
> Le monde se renouuelle,
> Nous avons race nouuelle,
> Dieu vient habiter en nous,
> Dieu vient pour nous sauluer tous. (p. 97)

Denisot employs many poetic variations and agents for communicating his personal sense of extreme joy and happiness. The two spheres of heaven and earth, heretofore separated and in discord, are entirely united and in perfect accord in their common praise and rejoicing: "Tout caressoit cest Enfant,/Le Ciel, La Mer & la Terre" (VII, p. 63). Denisot's devotional love lyrics convey not only the poet's personal feelings of spiritual revival, recovery, exceptional responsiveness, but also an assured note of serene trust in God, by both man and nature. This is ingenuously and yet beautifully portrayed and sung in Cantique XII, and quite appropriately so for the characters the poet is addressing: "Petit Cantique pastoral, de la reiouissance des Pasteurs . . .":

> Dansez en ceste prée
> Peinte de mille fleurs,
> Et d'esmail diaprée
> En cent mille couleurs.
>
> Et vous, ô brebiettes,
> N'ayez crainte des loups,
> Paissez donc camusettes
> Soubz cest vmbrage doulz.
>
>   *   *   *
>
> Bergers, quelle harmonie,
> Quelle musique es cieulx,
> Quelle voix tout vnie
> S'accord oncques mieux? (pp. 106-07)

The poet is often so overwhelmed by the emotional effect of the realization of the awakening of his own soul and of the whole created order that he yearns to ascend to an even higher spiritual plane. One of Denisot's deepest and most characteristic aspirations, at the very heart of his spiritual experience, is to ascend to a state of rapture, of ecstasy:

> Io, quest-ce que i'oy?
> Quelz feuz estranges!
> Voyez-la, ie les voy:
> Mille & mille Anges!
>
> Mon Dieu, mon Dieu, quel chant,
> Chant qui, en sorte,
> Va mon ame allechant:
> Qu'il la transporte! (XIII, p. 110)

His overriding desire is to surrender completely both soul and poetry to the highest service of God and thus to be absorbed and to participate in that higher glory, indeed to be an agent for its transmission:

> Qu'a la celeste oreille,
> En doulceur nompareille,
> Puisse voler ma voix,
> Oeillade ma pensée,
> Seigneur, encommencée
> Au secret de tes loix.

> * * *

> Et les yeux que i'addresse
> Tout droict a ta haultesse
> Seront les astres beaux,
> Que tu feras reluire,
> Pour l'oraison conduire
> Aux celestes flambeaux. (VIII, pp. 72-73)

Poetically and spiritually moving as the above themes and images are of life supplanting death through Christ, of dance, music, song, and the uplifting harmony of heaven and earth, Denisot's poetic talent and his faith approach their apogee when he depicts his two central perceptions of the incarnate Christ: the paradoxical visualization of light emanating from darkness and the sun and its radiance, both images being metaphors recognized by the poet of God in Christ. Denisot always views Christ as both immanent and transcendent, both God the Son and the earthly Jesus, through whose death man is reconciled to the Father, that is, redeemed:

> O filz de Dieu coëternel au Pere,
> En qui ce monde entierement espere
> Par ta venue estre viuifié,
> Et par ton sang vn iour iustifié,
> Seigneur, Seigneur, donne luy ceste grace
> Qu'en tout, par tout, ta volunté se face. (IV, p. 41)

Often Denisot's contemplation of Christ and of the Godhead is one of full radiance whose divine illumination he always responds to and yearns for, which is the subject of Cantique VI: "Cantique de la beaulté du Soleil, apparoissant le iour de la Natiuité, monstrant assez l'ineffable pouuoir de l'autre Soleil de iustice":

> Quel estonnement
> Vient saisir mon ame,
> Dessous l'ornement
> De la saincte flame
> Qui, du quart des cieux,
> Perce de ses feux
> Le voile nocturne,
> Son bel or trainant
> Ia, ia ramenant
> L'âge de Saturne. (p. 49)

This entire poem is constructed around the repetition and interpenetration of light-obsessed imagery: the initial reference to the sun and its dazzling impact upon the poet's soul, subsequent references to warm sunshine, to the rays of the sun brightly coloring the face of the earth, to the visible light of stars and of jewels (diamonds and pearls), in short, myriad reflections created by and radiating the divine and ultimate source of Light that links heaven and earth, and which wholly engage the sustained, creative attention of the poet:

> Voiez l'Orient
> Qui ça, qui là, dore
> Ce teint variant
> Que mon oeil adore.

> *   *   *

> Voyez ces couleurs
> Tant entrelacées
> Y former des fleurs.

> *   *   *

> Voyez le troppeau
> Des petitz nuages,
> Ainsi comme une eau
> Qui flotte aux riuages,
> De rang s'amassant,
> Et se compassant,
> Monstrer en peinture
> Maintz portraictz diuers. (pp. 50-51)

An even more artistically and thematically heightened sense of luminosity, of Christ incarnate, is achieved when Denisot treats the representation pictorially in chiaroscuro: through light which is made more radiant and visible by darkness setting it off. The poet's perception of this central paradox of light in darkness, of perfect clarity revealed at midnight, and then of light triumphant over darkness, is beautifully modulated in his apostrophe to Night in Cantique IV:

> C'est donc la Nuict des Nuicts la plus heureuse,
> La Nuict qui donne à toute ame amoureuse
> Cest heur de voir par foy son Createur,
> La Nuict qui donne à l'oeil du corps cest heur:
> Voir & toucher son Dieu en ce bas monde,
> Né de la Vierge à nulle autre seconde.
>
> Heureuse Nuict deuant le iour premiere,
> Nuict non pas Nuict, mais parfaicte lumiere,
> Qui luist tousiours & tousiours reluyra:
> O malheureux celluy qui te dira
> Doresnauant obscure, noire, ou sombre,
> Quand ton beau cler se faict maistre de l'ombre! (p. 38)

This poetically crucial image and principle of Christ as the midnight sun—constantly repeated in this poem and elsewhere as light shining forth from night, as the physical body containing but not eclipsing the luminous soul, as Christ's flesh enclosing and yet radiating the divine—must be appreciated for the way in which they illuminate the religious tenet on which Denisot's poetry and faith depend. For Denisot, night is a very special time of revelation. The day-in-night paradox is a mysterious and powerful symbol of the incarnate Christ as embodiment of the immanent and transcendent God: He is to be found in the darkest recesses of physical creation or matter in the form of the perfected light of its soul, and it is the latter which leads to the God beyond. Denisot's synthesis of the immanence-transcendence dualism, of heaven and earth, of matter and spirit, in the soul of man projects the highest religious optimism: the ultimate prospect of communion with God as opposed to damnation. Denisot's poetry and his faith share the same experience of quietly drawing one out of oneself, of pointing the soul—the "oeil du corps" from Cantique IV which is able even in this dark world to "voir & toucher son Dieu"—toward the supreme and ultimate longing for unification and perfection. This transcending movement is facilitated through the poetic portrayal of the deep religious experience of the soul's spiritual ascent:

> Du flambeau
> Qui nouueau
> Nous estonne,
> Et nous donne

Saufconduit,
Ceste nuict
A la ioye
Tousiours coye. (IX, p. 78)

Voyez ces nuës d'argent,
Esclairans la nuict obscure,
Ou le Dieu de la nature
Plus d'vne clarté nous rend. (XIV, p. 102)

Denisot's longing for inclusion in that bright essence and exceptional clarity of the soul in the dark night reveals the very high degree which he required of his religious faith and his poetic art. Denisot the poet understood Jesus quite literally and executed faithfully his commandment: "Thou shalt love the Lord thy God with all thy heart, with all thy soul, and with all thy mind" (Matt. 22:37). Nothing more can be asked of a devotional poet. It is hoped that the above discussion has added one more convincing reason to the claim that the Renaissance took its poetry and its relation to religion very seriously. In judging the individual efforts to sustain and to heighten this relationship, we should not underestimate the quite substantial contribution which Denisot made to "ce siècle qui veut croire."[12]

University of New Orleans

NOTES

[1]Cave, *Devotional Poetry in France c. 1570-1613* (Cambridge: Cambridge University Press, 1969); Jeanneret, *Poésie et tradition biblique au XVIe siècle* (Paris: José Corti, 1969). See also René Bady, *Humanisme chrétien dans les lettres françaises XVIe-XVIIe siècles* (Paris: Fayard, 1972).

[2]There is unfortunately no biography of Denisot. For a sketch of his life, see the French doctoral *thèse* by Clément Jugé, *Nicolas Denisot du Mans, essai sur sa vie et ses oeuvres* (Paris: A. Lemerre, 1907); and also, recently published by Enea Balmas, "Un poeta francese in Inghilterra nel Cinquecento (con documenti inediti)," in Mario Curreli and Alberto Martino, eds., *Critical Dimensions: English, German, and Comparative Literature Essays in Honour of Aurelio Zanco* (Cuneo: Saste, 1978), pp. 21-38.

[3]There is no extant manuscript of Denisot's *Cantiques*. My quotations will be from the 1553 first edition (112 pp.) mentioned above, a copy of which is housed at the Bodleian Library of the University of Oxford (280. C. 56.). All editing and italics are mine. I wish to thank Professor I.D. McFarlane, who first introduced me to the poetry of Denisot and who was most helpful to me in securing material on the poet during a brief research stay at Oxford in the summer of 1977. A word of thanks is also due Monsieur Louis Renard, Director of the Municipal Library of Saint-Calais, who was also very cordial and helpful during my visit there to inspect the 1610 manuscript copy of the anonymous *Recueil des Noelz vieux et nouveaux faictz par plusieurs autheurs* (Saint-Calais No. 4465, with Denisot's *Cantiques* beginning on page 165). This turned out to be a handwritten copy of the Paris 1553 first edition, in itself further indication of Denisot's popularity.

[4]The early nineteenth-century French composer Alexandre Boëly wrote a number of organ pieces (like Bach's *Orgelbüchlein*) based on the melodies for Denisot's cantiques.

[5]These were originally published in 1545 and were reprinted in 1847. The reprint edition can be found at the Bibliothèque Nationale Réserve Ye 3812: *Noelz, par le Conte d'Alsinoys* (Le Mans: Chez A. Lanier, 1847).

[6]W.R.M. Lamb, ed., *Plato* (Cambridge, Mass.: Harvard University Press, 1961), V, 205. Though the distinctions to be developed in this section between love poetry and devotional poetry may be pursued in any number of critical works dealing with the subject, I found the following especially useful: Anthony Low, *Love's Architecture: Devotional Modes in Seventeenth-Century English Poetry* (New York: New York University Press, 1978), Chapter I: "Poetry and Devotion," pp. 1-11; Nicholas Arseniev, "The Religious Meaning of the Experience of Beauty," *Comparative Literature Studies,* 2 (1965), 315-22; J. B. Broadbent, *Poetic Love* (New York: Barnes & Noble, Inc., 1964), Chapter 7: "Religious Love Poetry," pp. 88-128.

[7]Natalino Sapegno, ed., *La Divina Commedia* (Firenze: La Nuova Italia Editrice, 1970), Vol. III.

[8]Raffaello Ramat, ed., *Rime e Trionfi* (Milano: Rizzoli Editore, 1957).

[9]I.D. McFarlane, ed., *The Délie of Maurice Scève* (Cambridge: Cambridge University Press, 1966). In his Introduction, McFarlane provides ample discussion and examples of what he calls Scève's "fixity of gaze," those supremely quiet moments of enhanced lucidity in triumphant adoration of the Beloved. Though critics have always asserted that religion plays no part in the *Délie,* there are certainly moments approaching "religious experience" in the *Délie,* ones which radiate the religion of art and the poetic meaning and experience of Beauty. This idea is discussed further in my "The Notion and Meaning of Art in the *Délie,*" *Romanic Review,* 71 (1980), 28-46.

[10]Many of these poets also felt that, in addition to the old theme of human love, the linguistically impure medium of language itself was an obstacle to reaching higher contemplation. This criticism runs throughout Denisot's first cantique which begins:

> Seigneur Dieu, ouure la porte
> A mon ame demi-morte,
> Donne luy a ceste-foys
> Ta grace, *affin que plus forte*
> Au ciel se hausse ma voix. (p. 17)

This view of the inadequacy of language may also help to explain why so much devotional poetry, and Denisot's *Cantiques* in particular, relies so fundamentally upon the ancillary aesthetics of music and painting to help convey its experience. The dynamics of reader response to the interrelation of visualization and musicalization in Denisot's devotional lyrics is a separate and complex subject which deserves and requires fuller treatment in a future study. For now, see Jean Plattard, "Nicolas Denisot, poète et peintre," *Revue bleue,* 14 (1911), 442-45; and Elisabeth Gautier-Desvaux and Vidiane Koechlin-Schwartz, *Noël au Perche* (Saint-Mard-de-Réno: Société historique et archéologique de l'Orne, 1977). For general reading in this area, the following is indispensible: Rensselaer W. Lee, "*Ut Pictura Poesis:* The Humanistic Theory of Painting," *Art Bulletin,* 22 (1940), 197-269.

[11]Cave in his *Devotional Poetry in France* has already concluded that antithetical portrayal of the Christ Child is one of the two salient characteristics of the Nativity meditation (the other being sentimentalization; cf. pp. 51-52). Though this technique, basic to presenting the Christ Child, is also used by Denisot, an extended handling of it is one of his best affective means for preparing the way for such subsequent depiction: through arousal of the textual tension of opposing forces which is then triumphantly resolved by and in the Christ Child.

[12]Lucien Febvre's conclusion to his seminal *Le Problème de l'incroyance au XVIe siècle* (Paris: Albin Michel, 1962), p. 491.

ANATOMY OF A MORAL:

SEDUCTION IN SIXTEENTH-CENTURY

FRENCH COMEDY

Donald Stone, Jr.

When the sixteenth century wrote about comedy, it added very little to the simplistic definition of the genre established in antiquity by the rhetoricians Donatus and Diomedes. Everyone agreed that comedy was a mirror of life, its characters, taken from the middle class, its ending, happy, and that here was a genre "in which," according to Donatus, "it may be learned what is useful in life and what, on the other hand, is to be avoided."[1] Jacques Grévin's association of comedy with a "discours fabuleux . . . par lequel on peult apprendre ce qui est utile pour la vie, et au contraire cognoistre ce que lon doit fuir"[2] constitutes just one instance among many in which the ideas of Donatus reappear, almost word for word.

Grévin's text also underscores a problem that faces all students of the French Renaissance: how to square such definitions of the moral aim of comedy with its immoral content. According to one astute reader of Turnèbe's *Les Contens,* the play might be summarized as "la représentation plaisante de la séduction d'une jeune fille de bonne famille."[3] Moreover, examples of what we would call "pre-marital sex" occur in no fewer than six French comedies of the century,[4] including *Les Esprits* whose author Pierre de Larivey maintained, following Donatus' dictum, that in his plays he had placed diverse lessons, "blasmant les vitieuses actions, & louant les honnestes."[5] It will be the contention of this study that to equate the plots of these six plays with seduction can mislead and that without always providing a clear-cut portrait of human motivation, the comedies in question do lend support to contemporary claims regarding their didactic value.

We have chosen to study the plays as a group because of the number of traits they share. Taken singly, these traits might or might not appear significant, but when repeated, they give an unmistakable shape to the subject at hand and that shape proves to be rich in its implications. In speaking of "shape," we hasten to add that the term is not used to describe the familiar contours of the comic mode. To be sure, the tension, basic to comedy since ancient times, between parents and children over acceptable behavior, especially in affairs of the heart, returns in nearly all of the plays. So, too, the portrait of the servant as a wily source of schemes to abet a master in love. The contours we are referring to, however, those which will permit us to discuss the moral content of the plays, emerge at the next level of development as the French playwrights determine in what way these traditional features will be expanded upon.

On occasion, the texts do lead us to think the worse regarding the lover's motivation. The lawyer of *Les Esbahis* exclaims, with respect to his impending visit to his beloved,

> si je puis entrer dedans,
> Il y aura du passetemps
> Ou par amour, ou par contrainte. (p. 164)

In *Les Escoliers* Sobrin tries to bargain with the only person who can help him gain access to the lovely Grassette: the man she loves in preference to Sobrin. As part of his plea for assistance, Sobrin says to his rival:

> Si d'elle je ne jouys,
> Accablé de maux et d'ennuis,
> Vous verrez en peu de journées,
> Venir la fin de mes années. (p. 180a)

Camille in *Les Néapolitaines,* about to put his stratagem into action, admits: "Aussi bien m'est-il impossible de vivre si je ne donne allegeance à ceste flamme vehemente" (11.1861-63). Each lover employs an unequivocal vocabulary. One confesses to a willingness to use force if necessary; the others, with such words as "allegeance" and "jouys,"[6] suggest that their concerns are of a purely physical nature. Moreover, since Sobrin, like Camille, knows that his love is not requited, the adventure he contemplates would seem to merit the term seduction.

Characteristic of these plays is the fact that just as the reader begins to feel confident regarding his analysis of the action, the text complicates that analysis and adds an alternate set of givens. We are not invited, for example, to see the lovers as immoral and unappealing individuals. Sobrin, faced with parental outrage, remarks:

> J'ay encore gravée en mon coeur
> Une paternelle douceur
> Qui m'a esté fort indulgente,
> Jusqu'à la journée presente. (p. 172a)

The young men in *Les Esprits* exhibit a similar capacity to act without malice, despite the misfortune created by Severin's avarice. Though Desiré suddenly finds himself in possession of Severin's coins, Fortuné says to him (with reason), "encore qu'ils soyent en vostre puissance, je ne pense pas que les vouliez retenir, cognoissant à qui ils apartiennent" (IV, i, 11. 9-11).

Some care is even taken to show the youths' behavior as dependent upon a situation not of their making. While Severin's brother regrets the trick that has been played on the miser, Fortuné observes: "On ne pouvoit faire autrement" (IV, iii, 1. 20), and the play's portrait of the insenstive Severin justifies the remark. In the case of Camille, when he finally explains his behavior, we learn that the reason for the seduction is his concern over the reputation of the girl and her mother:

> D'un costé, l'amour et mon devoir m'incitoient à
> l'espouser, de l'autre, sa honte m'en retiroit, à
> cause de la vie desbordée de celle que j'estimoy
> veufve et sa mere. On dit qu'aux meres ressemblent
> les filles le plus souvent. (11. 2402-2405)

Camille's words show him to have a definite sense of duty. Moreover, duty and love are linked (not opposed) in his mind as incitements to marry. No means here to label Camille a reprobate, concerned only with satisfying the demands of the flesh.

These facts will eventually be brought to bear on the issue of seduction. The lovers know the world and the practice of taking one's pleasure before abandoning the deflowered girl. More than one young man in our plays declares that he does not subscribe to such unprincipled behavior. Basile is the most insistent: "Non, non l'amour que je luy porte n'est tel que celuy de plusieurs hommes envers les femmes, lesquels aussitost qu'ils en ont eu la jouyssance ne les voudroient jamais voir" (*Les Contens,* 11. 451-45). The lawyer in *Les Esbahis* swears to be Madelon's servant forever, even though a cousin ("le gentilhomme") advises him to direct his attentions elsewere. Only Filadelfe of *Les Corrivaux* loves and leaves. Of his reason we will hear later.

If such words of fidelity, spoken even before the couples have slept together, undercut our potential impression of the young lover as immoral and insoucient, so must the attitude of the girl. In four plays (*Les Contens, Les Esbahis, Les Corrivaux, Les Esprits*) the text makes explicit that the young man's love is fully reciprocated.[7] In *Les Escoliers* the girl agrees to the rendez-vous believing it to be with the man she adores. Twice in the plays passing reference is made to the girl's attempt to resist her lover's advances, but the descriptions fall far short of portraying a violent struggle. Her hesitation suffices to protect the girl against any suggestion of *paillardise* but does not permit the charge of rape to be leveled against the young man.

Into this network of somewhat contradictory statements about the central couple is set the traditional portrait of the lovers' parents. Its development may vary in degree and nature. *Les Esprits* and *Les Contens* devote considerable space to tracing the parents' character; in *Les Esbàhis* such attention shifts to a depiction of the familiar *senex* in love, but in each case the older generation receives a resolutely (yet not uniformly) negative treatment.

As in ancient comedy, money can play a decisive role in the representation of the parents. A father's avarice is central to the plot of *Les Esprits.* It plays a part in *Les Corrivaux.* Resolution of the lovers' difficulties regularly follows a promise of restitution or discovery of such lost identities as endow the poor with respectable riches. Nevertheless, our plays willingly go beyond these stock elements and, in particular, make much of the older generation's inability to grasp both the quality and the needs of the young.

Geneviefve's mother Louyse *(Les Contens)* and Madelon's fiancé Josse *(Les Esbahis)* are defined immediately by such ignorance. As *Les Contens* opens, Louyse insists on considering her daughter to be a child, unfamiliar with the ways of the world even though the audience learns from the same scene that Geneviefve and Basile have already once deceived the mother. Later, at the very moment that Louyse is about to find the house door open (and observe the young couple together), she completes a portrait of Geneviefve as a girl who does nothing but "dire ses heures ou prier Dieu en son petit oratoire, à genoux devant un crucefis et une Notre-Dame-de Pitié" (11. 1672-74). Similarly, when we meet Josse, who has already lost one wife, we hear him assert, "Je suis sage par mon malheur" (p. 120), and yet from further remarks in his speech we realize that such wisdom tells him that Madelon knows nothing of love (the same Madelon who is in fact deeply enamoured of a young lawyer). Elsewhere adult blindness can be more starkly presented.

Grassette's father fumes at the mere suggestion that his daughter may be in love: "Quoy! ma fille! Que ma fille ayme!" *(Les Escoliers,* p. 171b). In the same play, Sobrin's father has destined him for a life of study and for that he reminds us, he has spared no expense. Now the boy has fallen in love! "Est-ce d'un bon enfant l'office?" he asks, "Et quant tu dois les lettres suyvre/Le breuvage d'amour t'enyvre!" (p. 168a). Two scenes later the son gives vent to his own feelings in a long monologue that interestingly enough, begins with the question "Mais est-ce l'office d'un pere/D'estre à son enfant si sévère?" (p.170a). Sobrin goes on to lament his lack of taste for the cloistered life and his lost youth. The clash of "offices" could not be more clear. It can, however, be made to relate even more closely to the problem of love and marriage, and through the servants that link is forged.

To Fleurdely's father (who has ordered that Fleurdelys may not leave the house during his absence), the nurse Alizon replies by chiding him for his refusal to marry the girl, using such barbs as "il me semble que vous la faites trop jeusner" and "il vous est advis que tout le monde est aussi froid que vous" *(Les Corrivaux,* p. 89). A similar sequence occurs in *Les Esbahis* when Madelon's servant proves merciless in her asides and brings old Josse to brag of his vibrant sexual prowess. After he leaves, she vows that Madelon will not marry "ce vieil fantasme renfroigné" and speaks of Madelon's father Gérard, who "N'en debvroit rougir de grand honte/D'en tenir un si peu de compte" (p.130).[8]

Given that the servants prove so adept at driving home the failings of the adults, both comic and serious, we may feel inclined to rely on their judgments to guide us through each play. Yet here again the works reveal their rich (and complex) shape. If, on the one hand, the servants favor the lovers and underscore the parents' foibles, on the other hand, their attitude toward life and the schemes they are hatching lays bare a moral cast that cannot be equated absolutely with the views of the lovers.

The servants generally assume an immoral stance. In *Les Corrivaux,* Restitue, pregnant and abandoned, tells her nurse of her situation. The nurse remains unperturbed: "Hé Jesus Maria, nous avons esté (ce me semble) jeunes, & amoureuses nostre part comme les autres" (p.62),[9] and the bedding is dismissed as "petites follies en amour" committed unthinkingly (p. 64). Basile's servant Antoine argues for a meeting with Geneviefve by pointing out that in that way his master will be "prenant gentilement un pain sur la fournée. Pour le moins auriez-vous tousjours cela sur et-tant-moins. Et puis, si Eustache la prenoit, à son dam" *(Les Contens,* 11. 362-65).[10] As Marion and Julien discuss how they will effect a similar meeting, Marion makes clear that she expects Madelon to accept easily to sleep with the lawyer:

> Ell' ne sera pas si farouche,
> Que dessus le coing de sa couche
> Elle ne soubtienne aisément
> La peine d'un si doux tourment.
> *(Les Esbahis,* p. 150)[11]

In none of these cases does the servant speak the work 'love' or imagine the arranged meeting in terms other than simple sexual gratification. Thus, although the servants are often eloquent in defending the rights of the young to love and marry, their basic moral stance is as extreme in its way as that of the adults they censure.

The same tendency can be observed through other attitudes expressed by the servants. From them we also hear remarks on the folly of marriage (*Les Esbahis,* pp. 135-36), the wiles of women (*Les Néapolitaines,* 11. 1238-43), and the silly pursuit of a single beloved (*Les Corrivaux,* p. 76). Here are attitudes no less opposed to the principles that motivate the lovers than those expounded by the older generation. In that the young couples act in accordance with neither set of values, their defiance of parental intolerance ends not in licence but in an expression of love as society sanctioned it: fidelity and marriage. For this fact alone, the comedies earn the moral worth attributed to them in their own day.

The fact is all the more significant since, as with the question of the lovers' initial motivation, the text can lead us to see in love a force that knows no restraint, respects no law. If, for example, Filadelfe has abandoned Restitue before the play opens, the reason lies in the power of love: "HA je sçay bien, Restitue," he tells himself, "que je te fay tort portant amitié à autre que toy: Mais quoy? qui est celuy qui ne connoit les forces d'amour?" (p. 69). Sobrin agrees: "Bref amour tant tant me commande,/Qu'il faut que son serf je me rende" (*Les Escoliers,* p. 170b). The lawyer of *Les Esbahis* draws courage for his meeting from "l'amour audacieux" (p. 163) which, not uninterestingly, in turn attacks his beloved. As the lawyer describes the event, at first Madelon resisted his advances,

> Amour pourtant la surmontoit,
> Amour pourtant en fut vainqueur,
> Couvrant ses yeux d'une rougeur.
> Avecques une honneste honte:
> "Amour, dit-elle, me surmonte;
> Adieu l'heur de mes jeunes ans!" (p. 194)[12]

After the lover has succeeded in sleeping with his beloved, love's imperious hold is reiterated. In no fewer than four of the plays, a lover expounds on the joy he feels after the bedding (*Les Escoliers,* p. 183b; *Les Esbahis,* p. 173; *Les Contens,* p. 125; *Les Néapolitaines,* p. 46). The vocabulary employed— "jouissance," "contentement"—recalls other speeches quoted above and yet at this juncture, much in the way that references to "jouys" and "contrainte" are counterbalanced by the insistence on fidelity, these passages are often neutralized by the introduction of eloquent pronouncements in the petrarchist vein.

At one moment in *Les Esbahis,* the lawyer regrets Madelon's apparent infidelity. His outburst also defines his attitude toward her:

> Ma Madelon, que j'aimoy mieux
> Ny que mon cueur, ny que mes yeux,
> Qui pour son amour acquérir,
> M'a faict cent fois le jour mourir,
> A qui, comme un vray serviteur,
> J'avoy du tout voué mon cueur. (p. 137)

In *Les Contens* Basile and Geneviefve pronounce a long exchange filled with such sentences as:

> B.—Je suis maintenant assez content, puisque j'ay l'heur de vous voir. Mais aussitost que je vous auray perdu de veuë, je demeureray plus estonné et confus que celuy qui en une nuict d'hyver chemine par mauvais païs, le vent luy ayant estaint sa lumiere.

> G.—Si ce que vous dites est vray, je desire de pouvoir entrer dans vos yeux sans vous faire mal et y demeurer perpetuellement, à celle fin que vous soyez tousjours content, voyant devant vous celle qui ne vit d'autre viande que du souvenir de vos perfections. (11. 2811-2820)

In his edition of this play, Professor Spector sees the function of such speeches as "d'assurer les spectateurs, et les jeunes amoureux eux-mêmes, qu'ils n'ont vraiment pas commis de péché, qu'ils ne se sont pas conduits autrement que ne devaient faire, en de telles circonstances, un jeune chevalier et sa dame" (p. 1 xv). Since the plays do emphasize the power of love and, on occasion, make reference to the girls' acquiescence as recompense for the lover's service or pity for his torment,[13] the courtly analogy may not be dismissed out of hand. Yet is the suggestion that the lovers have slept together in accordance with courtly licence fully consonant with the text?

It is interesting to note that the two plays which offer the finest examples of petrarchist vocabulary *(Les Esbahis, Les Contens)* prepare the bedding in the same fashion: the lover, feeling that his beloved will soon become the bride of another, agrees to an extreme measure in order to prevent the undesirable marriage. In the case of Euvertre of *Les Corrivaux,* a father's avarice forbids

him to wed. Having thus failed to secure Fleurdelys by acceptable means, he
resolves to kidnap her (pp. 81-82). In *Les Contens*, such urgency and despair
reach poignant dimensions when Basile describes the state of the unhappy
Geneviefve:

> Je suis bien seur que la pauvre fille, pour la bonne affection qu'elle me
> porte, ne s'accordera jamais de prendre celuy que sa mere luy veut donner,
> si ce n'est par contrainte, dont elle prend telle fascherie, ainsi que je sceus
> hier d'elle, qu'elle en est pire que folle. (11.306-310)

These words speak eloquently of the parents' capacity to provoke crises and
unhappiness. (*Fascherie* here has the usual strong connotation of 'trouble,
grief, vexation.') The speech also reminds us once more that the lover is not
presented as a complacent seducer. Basile knows that Geneviefve's mother
finds him unacceptable. The beginnings of the union of Basile and Geneviefve
as sketched here embrace her affection for him and his awareness of her
unhappiness. Such devotion and concern are, not unexpectedly, repeated in
the petrarchist passages but in one significant aspect these passages do not
reflect the courtly code: the couples do not see their love as incompatible with
or worthy to exist outside the institution of marriage.

Once Sobrin has weathered the storm of Grassette's anger, he promises
to wed her:

> J'atteste. . .
> Qu'un mariage bien-heureux
> Fera un seul corps de nous deux. (p. 184b)

In *Les Esprits,* the text is explicit regarding the longstanding hope of Desiré
and Fortuné to marry the object of their affection. Similarly, at the return of
Feliciane's father, we learn of Urbain's statement that "en despit de tout le
monde, il la veut espouser" (V, iii, 11.13-14). In *Les Contens*, Basile insists
before Louyse that he did not ravish her daughter, "puisqu'il luy a pleu
m'accepter pour son mary"(11.3181-82).

To a twentieth-century audience, Basile's words may occasion surprise.
The couple has slept together; no wedding ceremony was performed and yet
Basile can reject the charge of rape and say that Geneviefve accepted him as
her husband. To grasp the sense of the statement we must understand that
despite the vigorous debate in the sixteenth century over clandestine marriages
and a parent's right to annul such a union, the Church held fast both before and

after Trent in affirming that the essence of marriage resided in the consent of
the parties. Similarly, although they determined to put an end to clandestine
marriages by requiring that the words of consent be spoken before the parish
priest and two witnesses, the Tridentine fathers categorically refused to admit
that parents could interfere in the sacrament of marriage.

The comedies further reflect that contemporary discussion over marriage
by placing some emphasis on promises that may have been made by the
lovers. Poor abandoned Restitue is soon asked by her nurse if "quelque
promesse de mariage" exists between her and Filadelfe (*Les Corrivaux,* p.64)
and the lawyer of *Les Esbahis,* believing himself betrayed by his beloved,
reflects on a broken promise:

> Ha, Madelon, qui l'eust pensé,
> Que nostre amour encommencé,
> Voire asseuré par le serment,
> S'assujetist au changement?
> Ha promesse mal asseuree! (pp. 136-37)

In canon law such promises were taken seriously, all the more so since "Par le
seul fait de la *copula carnalis* intervenant entre les fiancés les fiançailles se
transformaient en mariage véritable."[14] Unfortunately, Restitue did not
obtain such a promise. On the other hand, the existence of a "serment"
between Madelon and the lawyer and Basile's statement that Geneviefve was
pleased "to accept [him] as her husband" set before us facts that once again
may be used to exonerate the lovers. Depending on whether one did or did not
believe in the supremacy of canon law over civil law, or in a parent's right to
overturn a marriage formed *solo consensu,* the coupling was or was not to be
condoned and in *Les Contens* one character is most insistent about how we
should view the problem.

As Geneviefve's mother reacts in an ever more irrational and comic
fashion to what has happened to her daughter, it becomes clear that Girard will
speak the words of wisdom that eventually effect the happy solution. Part of
the confrontation between the two characters is contained in a crucial
exchange that occurs in Act IV. Girard is the father of Eustache whom
Louyse believes to be the foul seducer. She will take him to justice. Although
astounded that his son would commit such an act, Girard says to Louyse: "Je
ne pense pas qu'Eustache soit si meschant d'avoir eu affaire à elle que
premierement il ne luy ayt promis foy de mariage." Louyse, still bent on
exacting justice, replies: "Il se peut bien faire, mais il n'y a si beau mariage
qu'une corde ne defface" (11.2223-27). As this response places Louyse on

the side of those who maintained that parents could break their children's marriage, so Girard's oncoming retort contains a central argument used against the parents: "Cela est vray entre gens barbares et qui voudroient user de toute rigueur. Mais entre chrestiens ceste maxime ne peut avoir lieu, d'autant qu'il est escrit qu'il n'apartient pas à l'homme de separer ce que Dieu a conjoint" (11. 2228-32). The reference is to Mark 10:9, a verse well debated at Trent and one instrumental in reassuring the fathers that the sacrement of marriage could not be confused with a civil contract, that is, with a contract over which civil authorities (and parents) could exercise any control.

Although not as specific as it will be in certain late sixteenth-century short stories,[15] this echo of contemporary debates on marriage woven into the familiar fabric of comedy is doubly important for our investigation. It reveals new aspects of the authors' ongoing elaboration of the comic tradition, and the elaboration in question relates directly to the plays' insistence upon the devotion of the couple and their willingness to express their love in a way that is compatible with the laws of both nature and God.

Further examples of this technique are provided by the portrait of the young lover. The inclusion of a man who is either a literal rival of the *jeune premier* or who represents an alternate attitude toward love occurs frequently in our plays. Some, but not all of the characters are stock comic types (Dom Dieghos in *Les Néapolitaines* and Panthaléone in *Les Esbahis,* Rodomont in *Les Contens*). Their ludicrous behavior provides good laughter but it also makes the hero appear all the more attractive and acceptable. (And it should be added, especially in the light of the importance of the petrarchist passages, that the contrast between the comic lover and his rival emerges most concretely at the level of language. Both Panthaléone and Rodomont are capable of grandiloquent passages, and after each speech a servant's aside mocks the voice that has just spoken—*Les Esbahis,* pp. 147, 195; *Les Contens,* 11.1125-26). The more serious foils (Eustache in *Les Contens,* the "gentilhomme" in *Les Esbahis,* or Corbon in *Les Escoliers*) predictably underscore the more serious dimensions of loving and being loved. Spector's description of Eustache as "débauché et cynique" (p. 1iii) suits the "gentilhomme" as well; both, therefore, make the devotion and fidelity of the *jeune premier* appear all the more impressive. The curious opposition between Sobrin and Corbon in *Les Escoliers* marks the most revealing development in this context, however.

Initially Corbon eschews the servitude of love and expresses a preference for virtue and knowledge, making us believe that he has been created to exemplify moral rectitude of the highest order. (Certainly the period wrote often enough of the dangers of passion and of the rewards of virtue and learning.) But Corbon soon exhibits less admirable traits. Having obtained from Sobrin a *bénéfice* in return for helping in the seduction of Grassette, Corbon muses on his decision. He would have been foolish not to seize the occasion:

> C'est folye à celuy qui pense
> Estre avancé par sa science.

> *   *   *

> J'eusse long temps suivy l'estude,
> Tant est grande l'ingratitude,
> Sans qu'il m'en fust or advenu
> Pour quatre sols de revenu.

> *   *   *

> Vertu est pauvre et importune
> Mais les biens sont pour la fortune. (p. 183b)

He recognizes that Sobin's plan is "quelque peu mal 'honneste" but profit is so pleasing to man that it is preferred to a good reputation (Ibid.). The aura of scholarly dedication evaporates. Corbon's venal ambition takes charge, allowing him to recognize, yet dismiss the impropriety of Sobrin's scheme. This devaluation of the character plays a part in Grassette's change of heart. Furious against Sobrin, she eventually accepts his love (and actions) and brands Corbon as "desloyal et traistre," adding,

> . . .ore fais-tu paroistre
> Des hommes la fidelité.
> O ciel contre moy irrité! (p. 184a-b)

The vocabulary reminds us of the lawyer's outrage at Madelon's supposed betrayal of their love. Suddenly elaborate tones and grandiloquent constructions appear and in each instance they interject echoes of that high code which rescues love from the world of base instinct. Is not Grassette saying—and without this the action would remain unresolved—that Corbon has, by aiding Sobrin, betrayed the love she expressed for him (whereas by implication Sobrin's actions, though seemingly improper, can be accepted since they demonstrate the force of his affections)? Although subtlety does not usually characterize these comedies, the contrasts in *Les Escoliers* between a scholar who prefers love to study and a scholar who prefers money to virtue and morality, between impetuous, yet true and abiding sentiments and self-centered, unscrupulous motivation rejoin other contrasts we have examined in unveiling the richness of the total portrait of lovers and loving provided by these plays.

In analyzing French Renaissance comedy, we can never fully escape the influence of the *comedia erudita* on their plots. The same stupidity, avarice and indifference that classical comedy attacked in the older generation define here, too, some of those tendencies that comedy was understood in the sixteenth century to teach us to flee. It is also possible to remark that to both the ancient and Renaissance mind marriage constituted a particularly useful way to right impetuous wrongs. In their comedies Grévin and Turnèbe give somewhat humorous intimations as to why marriage could save the day. When rivals learn that their beloved is no longer a virgin, their usually honey-coated language gives way to another tone. "Quoy," exclaims Josse, "que je prenne une paillarde?" (p. 185). "Sans mentir," says Rodomont, "je l'ay aymée pendant qu'elle estoit fille, d'aussi bonne amour que jamais gentilhomme ayma. Mais depuis que j'ay descouvert qu'un autre estoit le mieux venu en son endroit et qu'elle avoit laissé aller le chat au fourmage, je ne suis pas deliberé de m'en rompre jamais la teste" (11.3027-32). Here is ample justification for the concern expressed from time to time that the beddings may become public knowledge, but more important, these allusions to the fate of fallen girls underscore yet another means employed to stress the moral worth of the young lovers. Although many of the works show extreme parental satisfaction that a marriage can be arranged to save face, most also make clear that the lovers have all along hoped for no more. For them the marriage is a desired event, not an expedient to protect their reputation. Thus, when Fortuné declares to Desiré near the end of *Les Esprits* that it is decided to marry him to Laurence, he answers, "Je ne desire autre chose" (V. vii, 1. 5).

To be sure, the moral is more completely drawn in some of the comedies than in others. Although the text of *Les Corrivaux* takes care to explain why Filadelfe leaves Restitue, it effects their reunion through a simple directive from Filadelfe's father to which the young man responds, "que j'en suis ayse!" (p. 147). Between Corneille's description of her mistress's despair at having been violated and the announcement of the arranged marriage, no further indication is given in *Les Néapolitaines* of the girl's feelings. Where greater elaboration occurs, however, the lovers emerge, in counterdistinction to both parents and servants, as individuals who experience passion as desire *and* duty, as urgency *and* a ritual of faithful service. To the sixteenth century comedy was a "mirror of life." Did it quite realize to what extent, by mixing in the comedies of the day the notions of imperious love and petrarchist fidelity, it had made comedy reflect two polar concepts of its broader literary production? The question is no less intriguing than the problem with which this study began.

Harvard University

NOTES

[1]Quoted in H. W. Lawton, *Handbook of French Renaissance Dramatic Theory* (Manchester University Press, 1949), p. 13.

[2]Lawton, *Handbook,* p. 55.

[3]See Norman Spector's introduction to his critical edition of *Les Contens* (Paris: Didier, 1964), p. liv.

[4]The plays and the editions quoted below are: François d'Amboise, *Les Néapolitaines*, ed. Hilde Spiegel (Heidelberg: Carl Winter, 1977); Jacques Grévin, *Les Esbahis,* in *Théâtre complet et poésies choisies,* ed. Lucien Pinvert (Paris: Garnier, 1922); Pierre de Larivey, *Les Esprits,* ed. Donald Stone, Jr. (Cambridge, Mass., 1978); Jean de La Taille, *Les Corrivaux,* ed. Denis L. Drysdall (Paris: Didier, 1974); François Perrin, *Les Escoliers,* in *Le Théâtre français au XVIe et au XVIIe siècle,* ed. Edouard Fournier (Paris, n.d.); Odet de Turnèbe, *Les Contens*, ed. Norman B. Spector, 2nd ed. (Paris: Didier, 1964).

[5]*Les Six Premières Comédies facécieuses de Pierre de Larivey* (Paris, 1579), sig. a2^v.

[6]In *Les Esprits,* Fortuné uses the same verb "jouir" to describe his borther's initial attitude toward Feliciane (IV, iii, 1. 104).

[7]In *Les Esprits,* I, v, 11. 103-107; II, i, 11. 34-37; IV, ii, 1.27; *Les Esbahis,* pp. 152-53; *Les Corrivaux,* p. 67; *Les Contens,* 11. 305-307.

[8]Perhaps the most curious example of parental obstinacy is provided by Louyse's opposition to Basile as a suitor for her daughter. The text gives no clear explanation for this behavior but intimates that Louyse was once interested in him herself. Spector's introduction to the play contains an excellent discussion of this aspect of *Les Contens* (pp. 1iv-1vii).

[9]In Plautus' *Bacchides* a similar remark is made by a parent. The transfer of the idea from a parent to a servant constitutes a small but telling tendency of the French plays to relegate morally questionable sentiments to the world of the servants.

[10]In Antoine's colorful language "prendre un pain sur la fournée" = "anticiper sur le mariage"; "cela sur et-tantmoins" = "en déduction."

[11]In *Les Contens,* Antoine insists that Geneviefve will be easy "bien qu'au commencement elle face semblant d'y resister. Car une fille ne veut jamais accorder de parolles ce qu'elle laisse prendre de fait, et est bien aise d'estre ravie" (11. 1620-23).

[12]On one occasion in *Les Contens,* Basile suggests similar resistance on the part of Geneviefve: "Mais je te puis dire que tout ce que j'en ay eu a esté plus de force que de son bon gré." Subsequent conversation between Basile and Geneviefve produces no reference whatsoever to the "force" Basile speaks of.

[13]See *Les Esbahis,* p. 174 and *Les Néapolitaines,* 11. 1196-1203.

[14]A. Esmein, *Le Mariage en droit canonique* (Paris, 1891), I, 142. Note also the language used by Basile to Geneviefve: "un peu devant que je vous eusse espousée" (11. 2871-72) and by Gerard to Louyse: "Asseurez-vous. . . que Basile a espouzé vostre fille. Et qui plus est, a consommé le mariage" (11. 3072-74).

[15]See my "Marriage, Style, and French Fiction at the Turn of the Seventeenth Century," *Stanford French Review,* 3 (1979), 211-21.

BÉROALDE DE VERVILLE

AND THE SELF-DESTRUCTING BOOK

Barbara C. Bowen

I *The Book and its Critics*

The *Moyen de Parvenir*,[1] unlike many sixteenth century works, has never been entirely neglected. Royer[2] and Saulnier[3] between them list 38 editions of it, between the disputed date of the first (1610?) and 1940. Its influence on *Tristram Shandy* was recognised long ago, and until the twentieth century it was read and enjoyed by those who appreciate dirty stories, and ignored by those who do not.

Modern critical views of the book have been entertainingly varied. Its most recent critic, Ilana Zinger,[4] dismisses her predecessors with: "Tous les essais d'interprétation du *Moyen de Parvenir* n'ont débouché que sur des hypothèses vagues." This is unfair. Certainly the earliest critics were circumspect about the aims of the *Parvenir*. La Monnoye,[5] in the early eighteenth century, naively describes it as "une représentation naïve des conversations ordinaires." In 1841, Jacob[6] (who was convinced that the *fond* of the book was by Rabelais) says that it has no aim or conclusion, and in 1896 Royer makes no statement about its purpose.

Since then, however, hypotheses have multiplied, and one would rather call them 'dogmatic' than 'vague'. Sainéan,[7] in 1927, asserts that the book's main subjects are eroticism and alchemy. In 1944, V.-L. Saulnier,[8] in what is still the most balanced general view of the *Parvenir*, stresses its debt to antiquity and its provocative incoherence: "Le but de tout le *Parvenir*, c'est de dérouter le lecteur." He defines "le béroaldisme" as "un pantagruélisme du samedi soir: ne se formaliser de rien." A year later he goes considerably further,[9] enlarging his definition to "une sagesse de mesure et de tact, de vertu souriante et de charme savouré" (p. 8), and placing Béroalde at the mid-point between Montaigne and the Chevalier de Méré.

After Saulnier there is a long gap in Béroalde studies, which begin to flourish again in the 70's. Janis Pallister[10] developed some of Saulnier's ideas into a definition of Béroalde as a baroque author, concentrating on the themes of time, mutability, death and folly. Since then hypotheses have accumulated, especially in an interesting MLA Session in San Francisco in December 1979, organised by Michael Giordano.[11] Armand Renaud here claimed that the book is both a paradigm and a spoof of the alchemical quest, and Janis Pallister that it is a "how-to-be-your-own-doctor" book. Whereas in 1971 she had emphasized Béroalde's doctrine of laughter and implicit acceptance of life,[12] she now describes it as a "book of the utmost cynicism."

Also in 1979 appeared Ilana Zinger's study,[13] which analyses in detail some of Béroalde's comic techniques. She concludes that the main genre sources of the *Parvenir* are the Banquet, the Dialogue, and the "recueil de contes," and manages to attribute to Béroalde both satire of churchmen (Catholic and Protestant) and alchemists, and a complete lack of didactic intent.

Of all the recent critics, two seem to me to have genuinely helpful things to say about the *Parvenir*. André Tournon, in a 1978 article,[14] describes it as an "anti-discours" in which "la facétie, généralisée, prend une fonction structurale." The *cadre* is *gratuit*, only 15% of the *répliques* of interlocutors are genuine verbal exchanges, and "la règle est de manifester le plus haut degré d'incohérence possible" while keeping the text legible. Along rather similar lines, Gerald Prince,[15] in the 1979 MLA Session mentioned above, focused on what the book does to itself; not just its lack of normal structure, but its constant contrasts between *oral* and *écrit*. "Le livre se dé-livre," as he puts it in a suggestive phrase.

At the risk of adding yet another "hypothèse vague" to those already proposed, I should like to suggest that while Tournon and Prince are definitely going in the right direction, they have not gone far enough. It is my contention that the central concern of Béroalde's book is indeed the book, both in a destructive and in a constructive sense.

II *The Author and the Book*

All critics of the *Parvenir* have underlined its incoherent, "décousu" aspects, but none seems to have realised how consistently Béroalde sets about disappointing his readers' assumptions about what a book is and what it does. Renaissance readers had expectations of a book very similar to ours. They assumed that it would be 'about' something definable; would belong to a familiar genre; would have a beginning, middle, and end; and that if it was divided into chapters or sections, these would have recognisable content. More generally, they would assume as we do that a book is controlled by its author; that it is a container from which the reader extracts something; and that a book is written in some variety of 'literary' language, which is different in nature from spoken language.

Of our many expectations about what a book will be and do, perhaps the most important is that it will be 'about something'. Much argument, some of it eccentric, has been expended on the title, *Le Moyen de Parvenir*. The reason for this title is surely very simple: a great many books are 'how-to' books. The Renaissance did not have titles quite like "How to Succeed in Business Without Really Trying," but many of its books are 'ways to' something; a better knowledge of rhetoric or arithmetic, more competence as a poet, or further progress in the spiritual life. In one volume of Montaiglon's *Anciennes Poésies Françoises* there are two such titles: *Le Moyen de soy enrichir, profitable & utile à toutes gens* (p. 85), and *Le Médecin Courtizan, ou la nouvelle & plus courte manière de paruenir à la vraye & solide médecine* (p. 96).

Béroalde plays with his readers by giving us as many different and contradictory definitions as possible of his "moyen de parvenir." Sometimes the advice given or implied is practical: "Le principal mot du guet du MOYEN DE PARVENIR, est d'auoir de l'argent" (II 227), or *parvenir* is specifically related to stealing (I 165) or to fraud in general (II 22). On other occasions the *moyen* is left vague, or expressed very generally: "Le moyen de paruenir comprend tout, & est composé des quatre elements de piperie auec leur quinte essence" (I 155). On one occasion only, it looks completely serious: at the Crucifixion everyone present was guilty of Christ's death in some way, except for "les pauures femmes qui l'ont pleuré, & ainsi ont trouué le moyen de paruenir" (I 111).

Throughout the book, in fact, Béroalde plays around with his title, and with readers who want a book to help them in some practical way. But this is only the first of many such disconcerting techniques. Much more than a modern reader, a Renaissance reader assumed that a book would belong to a familiar literary genre. Critics of Béroalde have usually stressed the dialogue and the symposium as sources, and as Ilana Zinger says,[17] it was already common to mix them as in the *Heptaméron* and Bouchet's *Serées*.

But by emphasising Béroalde's debt to Lucian, or to Petronius, we can lose sight of the complexities inherent in both dialogue and symposium. As David Marsh usefully sums it up,[18] there are four separate dialogue traditions: the genuinely Platonic, the symposiac, the Lucianic and the humanist, all of which can have considerable variation in tone and technique. The Renaissance is the great age of dialogue—indeed, to quote André Chastel,[19] "it is scarcely an exaggeration to define humanism as the demand for dialogue." Béroalde is fully aware of all this, and of the fact that didactic works on almost any subject were frequently written in dialogue form. A glance down his list of interlocutors confirms that there are representatives of all four traditions among them, but undoubtedly the symposium is most often in question.

The Ancients had a particular respect for the symposium as a genre, because of Plato, but by the end of Antiquity it could hardly be called a genre any more. To Plato's very serious, philosophical *Symposium* had been added Lucian's *Dialogues of the Dead*, in which celebrated figures of the past make satirical remarks on the present; Athenaeus' *Deipnosophists*, where a large number of characters discuss at great length minutiae related to food, cooking and other areas of daily life; Petronius' *Satyricon*, a hilarious mixture of semi-pornographic fiction and conversation on all possible levels; and Macrobius' *Saturnalia*, a serious, wide-ranging discussion among scholars and gentlemen. Rabelais' insertion of a semi-comic, semi-serious symposium into the central section of the *Tiers Livre* indicates his awareness of this multiple tradition.

Indeed, the sixteenth century as a whole was aware of it. Closer in time to Béroalde, we find a handy summary in Guillaume Bouchet's "Discours" which serves as prologue to his *Serées*.[20] He stresses in particular two aspects of the banquet which Béroalde will make fun of: its sociability and the ideal number of banqueters. The only two specific numbers he mentions are Xenophon's nine and Plato's twenty (e 2), both rather far from Béroalde's total of about 400. Bouchet also stresses that the banqueters must be able to sit at the same table and to hear each other. With regard to sociability, Bouchet demands a mixture of serious conversation and "discours plaisans & recreatifs" (a 8?—the folios are numbered very strangely). He would even excuse "quelque parolle un peu libre," but not, presumably, the entire banquet of *parolles libres* provided by Béroalde. All these prescriptions for a banquet can be found in antiquity, especially in Aulus Gellius and Plutarch, who no doubt got them from Cicero. All these authors stated, for instance, that more license in jesting is permitted in banquets than elsewhere, although, like Bouchet, they would certainly not have approved of the extreme license of jesting in the *Parvenir*. In fact Béroalde's guests, by the crudity of their subjects and especially of their language, are implicitly denying the whole concept of *urbanitas* which, in 1610, was well on its way towards classical *honnêteté*.

I do not agree with Tournon that the banquet frame is *gratuit*. It makes clear to us at the outset that this is an anti-banquet; we have an impossibly huge number of guests, including real people of all historical periods, obviously made-up names, and non-names (Quelqu'un, L'Autre). These interlocutors are usually interchangeable, despite a few *répliques* which are suitably attached to speakers (Solon says "si iamais ie fais des loix . . . ," I 69, and Apulée remarks in II 210: "I'ay esté asne comme chascun sçait").

The other genre most often quoted in connection with the *Parvenir* is the collection of short stories, and here again oversimplification is common. The Renaissance knew at least two varieties of *conte*, the full-length anecdote and the shorter verbal joke, common in Italy since Poggio's *Facetiae*. These *motti* (which Laurent Joubert and Bouchet call *rencontres*) are what we find in Des Périers' *Nouvelles Récréations et Joyeux Devis*. Moreover, tone varies from one collection of *contes* to another; Marguerite de Navarre's stories, though sometimes dealing with 'low' subjects, are invariably couched in lofty style, while Noël Du Fail's are pseudo-bucolic, and so on.

There are other aspects to the fact that a book belongs to a recognisable genre. It also necessarily has a relationship to the books which precede and follow it; to its sources, analogues and the works it influenced. The *Parvenir* rejects this relationship: "Tous les autres pretendus liures, cayers, opuscules, libelles, fragmens, epitomes, registres, inuentaires, copies, brouillars, originaux, exemplaires, manuscrits, imprimez, esgratignez; bref les pancartes des bibliotheques, soit de ce qui a esté, ou est, ou qui iamais encore ne fut, ou ne sera, sont icy en lumiere profetisez ou restituez" (I 49-50), and on the other hand all other books are "signez, ou marquez, ou paraphrasez, ou predictions de cestuy-cy" (I 54, and cf. I 214 and II 171). All temporal connections between the *Parvenir* and other books have been abolished. The theme of time, which Pallilster sees as an indication of baroque pessimism, is rather a means of reinforcing the 'this can't be a book' theme.

Yet another aspect of genre is the distinction between text and gloss, as in Montaigne's complaint that "tout fourmille de commentaires; d'auteurs, il en est grand cherté" (III 13). Indeed, this separation of text (authentic and venerable) and gloss (unnecessary or actually misleading) might be called the foundation of humanism. But in chapter 10 ("Circoncision") Béroalde tells us about "l'antiquité de ce volume," and that "le Gentilhomme qui le transcriuit pour votre auancement en toute sagesse a tout escrit d'vne suite, meslant sans distinction glose & texte."

Surely Béroalde is deliberately making it difficult, if not impossible, for his reader to come to any basic conclusions about his book. Is it a symposium? A Dialogue of the Dead? A *recueil de contes*? What are the major influences on it? Is it an original text or a commentary on some other text? Béroalde forces us to answer both 'All of the above' and 'None of the above' to these questions.

Similar remarks apply to the internal structure of the *Parvenir*. We expect a book to have a beginning, middle and end; Béroalde's begins with "Question I" (there never is a "Question II"); chapter 11 is "Pause dernière," which begins: "Or commençons de conclure;" chapter 13 is "Conclusion;" while the last chapter, 111, is called "Argument." The first word of the first chapter is "Car," while in the last occur the phrases: "Passons outre, ie sens desia que ce liure nous eschappe," and "Et afin que ie puisse vn iour commencer ce volume . . .".

The 111 chapter headings in the Royer edition have no connection whatever with their content, *pace* Janis Pallister. A large majority are designations of written texts, whether logical ("Axiome," "Demonstration"), philosophical ("Problème," "Distinction"), theological ("Parabole," "Sermon VI"—there are no other sermons), legal (a large number, including "Instance," "Exploit" and "Bail"), literary ("Journal," "Histoire," "Emblesme"), or general ("Mappe-monde," "Liure de raison," "Dictionnaire," "Kalendrier"). The only ones which appear to have no connection with writing are "Cérémonie," "Vidimus," "Occasion," "Plumitif," "Risee," "Coyonnerie," "Respect," "Couuent" and "Folie"—not a large number out of 111. To give the names of written texts to episodes of a banquet is to confuse the *oral* with the *écrit*, once again.

There seems, moreover, to be no reason to divide the *Parvenir* into chapters at all. Stories run over several chapters; there are frequent *rappels* of remarks made several pages back, and a chapter seldom begins with an entirely new subject. Béroalde has created a sizable book (580 pages in Royer's edition) which is as unlike a book as possible. One can indeed (as has been claimed for Montaigne) open the *Parvenir* anywhere and start reading.

*   *   *

But one of the main subjects of this non-book is precisely the book, what it is and what it does. And here again Béroalde's aim is to upset and make fun of his readers' expectations. Have we always assumed that an author is in complete control of his work? Then he will confide to us: "Ie sens desia (in the final chapter!) que ce liure nous eschappe," or "Que ie dirois de belles choses si ie les sçauois" (I 58). While at one point Aristotle claims that "ces menus propos" contain "toute la mouëlle de doctrine vniuerselle" (I 131), a few chapters later (I 175) L'Autre will tell us that "ce liure . . . iadis fut fait en belle rithme croisee: mais celui qui l'a transcrit sans y auiser, meslant ce qui estoit decà & delà, a fait qu'il n'i ait, ce semble, ne rime ne raison . . .". Doubt is cleverly cast on Béroalde's authorship, and on the difference between an author and a speaker, by an interlocutor who quotes as witness "Veruille qui me l'a dit, ainsi qu'il l'a escrit" (II 150). Some critics, inspired partly by this remark and partly by the differences in style between the *Parvenir* and Béroalde's other works, have tried to claim that he did not write it.

But Béroalde is more interested still in another premise about books: that they are containers from which the reader extracts the content. Walter Ong and Marshall McLuhan have explained exhaustively that whereas a medieval book says something, a Renaissance book contains something. "The whole mental world has gone hollow," as Ong sums it up.[21] Béroalde plays about constantly with the container/contained relationship. Sometimes his book is a "bréuiaire" (I, 43 and 45), sometimes a glass ("Verre & volume sont equiuoques," I 44). Like Diogenes' barrel in the Prologue to the *Tiers Livre*, it is "inextinguible": "Vous liriez icy quatre iours tous entiers, que vous ne vous souleriez aucunement" (II 237). Sometimes it is a more impressive container: "ce beau petit abondant moule de perfection exemplaire" (I 54), or even "un globe d'infinie doctrine . . . tout farcy de science mystigorique & concluante" (I 36). In the same chapter he refers to it as a "docte monument"—a rather different type of container.

As these quotations indicate, the early part of the book is particularly rich in these eccentric analogies. In a single chapter (12: "Vidimus") the book is: a breviary; a universal *object* containing "la lanterne de discretion & la lampe de beatitude;" "la grosse clef d'ordonnance, à laquelle pend le trousseau de toutes clefs;" "LE CENTRE DE TOVS LES LIVRES;" and "la parole secrette qui doit estre descouuerte au temps d'Helie." The reader, like Rabelais' reader, is encouraged to "crocheter, voir & chercher ce qui est sous ceste escource de veloux & d'or entortillé de paroles quelques fois de soye, & quelquefois de fil . . .". This is a new slant on the old bone-marrow *topos*; if the book is the container the *paroles* should be inside it, not outside it as part of the decoration on the bark/binding.

Eccentric analogies are by no means confined to the book as container. The words it contains are compared to food, excrement, rags, seeds, farts, pearls, *noix de muscades*, and things which need to be 'fixed' by gluing or freezing. In a passage already quoted (I 131) *menus propos*, 'words', become the container: "contenans & comprenans toute la mouëlle de doctrine vniuerselle;" *moüelle* and *escorce* have again changed places. This double meaning of *menus propos* is one of Béroalde's many allusions to literary genres, quarrels and clichés of his time. Quintilian and Du Bellay had talked about style as the sheath for substance, but it takes Béroalde to apostrophise mediocre poets "suant iour & nuict apres pour desgayner vne pauure parole"

(I 128). Or he defends the *richesse* of the French language, so dear to the Pléiade, by pointing out that French has more synonyms than any other language "pour remarquer la copulation qui est cause que tout est producit, ergo, elle est la plus produisante" (I 227).

But the book and its contents are in turn part of a larger subject: the nature of, and connection between, reading, writing and speaking. And once again, Béroalde appears intentionally to upset and confuse our assumptions: which are in this case that a book is written in literary language, which is at least in some ways different from spoken, and that reading is an intellectual activity, quite different from the physical activities of eating, drinking and eliminating. Since a banquet, where people eat, drink and talk (usually about sex or scatology), is both the subject and the form of his book, Béroalde is able to combine all these topics in a remarkably confusing and suggestive way.

Most obviously, the book and the banquet are conflated and confused. "Verre & volume sont equiuuoques" means that reading and drinking are analogous (an old *topos*); but the confusion is deeper than this. When someone says: "Or sur tout prenez garde à quelques petites gentillesses qui sont ici redittes, & les calculez auec leur distance, & sous ceste proportion vous trouuerez vn grand notable secret..." (I 133), does his *ici* mean 'at this banquet' or 'in this book'? In many other passages he talks about the secrets (often related to the Philosophers' stone) contained in the book, but since the book is the recital of the banquet can we distinguish them? Some chapters later, Illiric asks the author (?): "Puis que tu fais tant le resolu, qu'auois tu affaire de nous nommer icy?" (II 198), where *icy* is equally ambiguous. But if the book and the banquet are identical, what becomes of the traditional distinction between *oratio* and *sermo*, written language and spoken language?

The final metaphor for the book which Béroalde leaves us with, in the last chapter, is of an anamorphosis: "ces peinctures qui monstrent d'un, & puis d'autre." But despite this emphasis on metamorphosis, the equivalence between reading and eating is fairly constant. Truth is the wine drunk at the banquet (I 15), and therefore also the resulting excrement (I 217). At the beginning of the banquet we are told that: "Il y auoit gens apostez à ce qu'ils eussent egard que personne ne chommast, sur tout qu'il n'y eust point de parole perduë, & qu'aucun mot ne tombast ou fust egaré ou eschappé" (I 23). So talking and eating are analogous, as were reading and drinking; someone is later described as "ayant sauouré les propos auec les oreilles" (I 15).

The constant discussion of natural functions is not merely making fun of the *bienséance* traditionally required at a banquet. In one discussion of *sales paroles* someone asserts that: "Si on ostoit ces paroles d'ici, ce banquet seroit imparfait . . . Il faut suiure Nature, ainsi nostre discours le suit" (II 76). No ancient theoretician, not even a Stoic whose motto was *secundum naturam*, would have said this about either a book or a banquet; Béroalde is using scatology, sex and three-letter words to make of his symposium something natural, not artificial. Which is much the same thing as demolishing both the book and the banquet.

III *The Book and the Word*

In all these ways, and more, Béroalde systematically (except that nothing he does is systematic) upsets our preconceived ideas about what a book is and does, and about reading, talking and writing. Our conclusion might well be that the *Parvenir* is what Stanley Fish calls a self-consuming artifact; that the only point of the book is its own destruction. But I believe that, much as he loves demolishing, he also cares about affirming, and that though the book may lie in ruins round our feet by chapter 111, something more important is still standing.

It has been said, over and over again, that every chapter of the *Parvenir* contains a dirty story and/or some obscene language. This is not quite accurate—a few chapters contain neither. But no-one has noticed (although Ilana Zinger makes a pertinent remark in passing[22]) that almost every chapter also contains reflections on, and discussions about, language. Not only can Béroalde play with language as no-one else except Rabelais can; we find in the *Parvenir* all of the language subjects which preoccupied the sixteenth century, whether in the domain of literature or of ethics.

Béroalde very obviously delights in playing about with words. He is fond of punning—what Saulnier calls *faux lapsus*—although many of his puns are feeble by our standards, because of their clumsiness, not their obscenity. *Entregeant/entre-jambes* (I 62) is not bad, but *apacalipse/apoplexie* (II 148) is poor, and *endèlechie/endroit où l'on chie* (I 39) frankly awful. But all of these puns, and there are dozens of them, show Béroalde doing what he does best: treating words as things. And I wonder if the Latin phrase *Nunc ipsa vocat res* on the title page, on which Janis Pallister has expended prodigies of ingenuity, is not important here. Strictly speaking, things cannot call; only words can. Béroalde is very good at pointing out how words should, or should not, function as things.

Like Rabelais, he particularly enjoys jolting us into an awareness of the clichés we use without thinking about them. "Dittes vous pas bon jour monsieur? Il est donc vostre sieur, & partant vous le maistre du chantier où l'on sie" (I 9); "Or Laurence ne faisoit pas l'Amour, il est tout fait" (I 65); or the misunderstanding of the servant girl who, when asked by her mistress: "Où allez-vous si vite?" replied: "Ie m'en-vois chez nous, six cons" (II 232); such remarks force us to stop and think about our everyday language. And the constant emphasis on obscenity is part of this concern for the nature of language. There are several discussions about *sales paroles*, and some banqueters object to them. Licofron says: "Il faut auoir bien du coeur, & encor en soupant, pour supporter telles paroles & tant ordes" (I 198), but the general conclusion seems to be that: "Les paroles ne sont point sales, il n'y a que l'intelligence" (II 76). Witness the doctor who, on a journey, told his wife that he wanted to kiss her "entre cu & con." She was shocked, but it turned out that they were between two streams called respectively *Cu* and *Con*. "Voila de belles paroles, elles sont claires, comme eau" (II 81).

Like Montaigne, Béroalde disapproves pride in one's name, since "les noms sont ils pas communs" (II 198). And again like Rabelais, he makes fun of people who are unaware that language can signify on several levels at once. This can involve *paroles sales*, as in the case of the innocent Prioress instructing a nun how to sing the Latin word *conculcavit:* "La, ma mie, chantez bien: là tenez moi ce con ferme, con; là apres, cul, haussez moi ce cu; apres à ce cas, entretenez-moi ce cas; puis à ce vit, là tenez moi ce vit bien long" (II 245). But obscenity is not necessary to make a point; a naive (or malicious?) Genevan wife-beater, instructed by the Consistoire "qu'il y ait de la mesure en vos actions," beats his wife with an *aune*. Reprimanded again, he is told: "Remonstrez lui auec l'Escriture saincte." He therefore sets about her with "vn gros Nouueau Testament couuert de bois & ferré," and finally, when ordered "qu'il n'eut plus à chastier sa femme que de la langue," he uses "vne langue de boeuf fumee" (II 214-16).

Obscenity is also part of the whole question of euphemism and periphrasis. Besides the astonishing number of synonyms for genitals—of which *cas* and *cela* are the most frequent—there are also many different periphrases for them, and for the sexual act. Béroalde can be as inventive as Rabelais, if not as onomatopoetic. In any case, again, "il ne faut pas tousiours dire ces parties-la honteuses, dautant qu'elles ne le sont que par accident, & faisant autrement vous feriez tort à Nature qui n'a rien fait de honteux" (I 39-40). More important is the whole question of how to speak. Most interlocutors object strongly to "langage courtisannifié" (I 9); to people who "vous paillardez lanternierement sur l'eloquence" (II 242). Budee neatly sums it up: "Ie hay ces paraphrases, il faut donner dedans" (I 104). The sexual implications of these last two quotations recur, and there is frequent equivalence of *bouche* and *cul*, which corresponds to the exchange of metaphors noticed above.

As one would expect in a satire, most of Béroalde's comments on language are negative, and he is especially fond of satirising abuses of language. Churchmen, both Catholics and Protestants, are blamed for misusing *la parole* in different ways. About the celibacy of Catholic priests we are told (I 235): "De fait on les nomme morts pour autant que l'outil qui perpetue la vie leur est bouclé par la vertu de certaines paroles conferantes ordre supernaturel." Rabelais' changing of the name Galemelle to Gargamelle is cited as evidence that he was a bishop, since only bishops and archbishops can "changer le nom en muant vn peu de la substance" (II 201). And a Reformer accuses himself: "O nous miserables reformez de proferer tant de paroles oiseuses, dont nous rendrons conte . . . " (I 53).

Other misusers of language include hypocrites, who "ne sçauent dire les choses par leur nom" (I 173), and "ces escorcheurs de latin, ces escarteleux de sentences, ces maquereaux de passages poëtiques qu'ils produisent & prostituent à tous venans; gardez-vous de ces entrelardeurs de Theologie alegorique, de ces effondreux d'argumens, & de tous ceux qui aiguisent les remonstrances sur la meule d'hypocrisie" (I 51).

Most, if not all, of these individual satires imply a positive counterpart— a right use of language to instruct and to signify. Rufin says of the banquet (I 111): "Nul ne parle ceans pour scandaliser ains pour edifier & corriger s'il est besoin;" a remark I believe should be taken seriously. People who are *scandalisez* by *sales paroles* have misunderstood the purpose and function of language, and need correcting. There are many other remarks which imply positive use of the spoken word. In the first chapter we are told: "Promettre est facile, mais effectuer difficile" (I 6), and this is reinforced on the next page by satire of people who have tried to "trouver vne glu qui peust congeler les parolles & les faire tenir." Like all the humanists, Béroalde knows that silence is sometimes wiser than speech (I 18), and that "si tout le monde auisoit aussi bien à ses paroles, il n'y auroit pas tant de procez perdus, ny au croc." "Il ne faut pas dire les secrets" is a humanist commonplace, which Béroalde enlivens by giving a trivial reason for it (I 131): "De peur qu'estans publiez on n'en recognoisse la vanité; cependant que l'on ne les entend pas, on en est en admiration."

As words can readily be confused with things, so can they be with action. The moral of the charming story about Marciole and the cherries is that the concupiscent guests have been too ready to swear to their pleasure in terms of money—which they did not intend to be taken literally. "Il n'y a rien au monde de si beau, ie ne voudrois pas pour cent escus n'auoir eu le contentement que ie reçoy" says one (I 29), and the others follow suit. The narrator describes them: "Trop bauards ils se deslauoient les badigoinces de ce qu'ils auoient à dire." So justice is done when Monsieur la Roche forces them each to pay the amount they had named: "Par la double, digne grande corne triple du plus ferme coqu qui soit icy, vous payerez chacun ce que vous auez dit...". In a quite different context, the humanist longing for words to be as efficacious as deeds is nicely characterised (I 302): "Pensez-vous que Ciceron soit aise qu'on dise de lui: 'Voila des epistres qu'il a faites'? Non non, il veut que l'on croye qu'il est auec vne belle espee faisant le tiercelet d'Empereur."

These are just some of the judgments made and implied, in the *Parvenir*, about right and wrong uses of the spoken word. In context, the remark: "Vous estes bien cruel de regarder à des paroles, et non à l'intention" (II 86) is ironic, but it could summarise all the abuses Béroalde makes fun of. And whereas his remarks about the book are always highly suspect ("ce qui doit estre dit, doit estre ici" I 303), other statements about books in general are often very sensible. We have seen him claiming that text and gloss are indistinguishable, in the *Parvenir*, but he agrees entirely with Montaigne on the general subject of the capriciousness of glosses (I 147): "Plusieurs interpretent les escrits & paroles des autres selon leurs sens: ainsi les Moines yurognes interpretent les epigrammes de Aeneas Siluius & de Beze en yurognerie, les Sodomites en Sodomie, les amoureux en amour, les auaricieux en richesses . . .". On many of these subjects the *Parvenir* turns out to be surprisingly close in tone to the *Palais des Curieux*.[23] That work's first stated aim is to "discourir de quelques façons de parler" (p. 10); it contains many reflections on the functions of language; and it ends with praise of *la parole* (582-4).

*   *   *

"Ie ne vis iamais tant parler" says Aloilol (II 226) towards the end of the book. The reader's reaction might well have been along these lines: "Tu causes, tu causes, c'est tout ce que tu sais faire." I have tried to show in this article that Béroalde's *paroles* are at once the substance, the form and the purpose of his book. Written words are suspect, so he creates an anti-book which is at the same time an anti-symposium. But once the book has destroyed itself, what remains is the spoken word, infinitely more comic and infinitely more important. The *Parvenir*'s nonexistent interlocutors, talking at their anti-banquet, finally make it quite clear what the author is for as well as what he is against. Béroalde would surely reverse the terms of the old proverb, and say: "Les écrits s'en vont, les paroles restent."

University of Illinois (Urbana)

NOTES

[1] I am using the edition of Charles Royer (Paris, 1896), reprinted by Slatkine (Geneva, 1970, 2 vols. in one). References in the text are to the page numbers in this edition.

[2] Pp. liii-lxii.

[3] "Etude sur Béroalde de Verville: Introduction à la lecture du *Moyen de Parvenir*," BHR, 5 (1944), 209-326.

[4] *Structures Narratives du Moyen de Parvenir de Béroalde de Verville* (Paris: Nizet, 1979), p. 130. An article by the same author, "Typologie des chapîtres du *Moyen de Parvenir* de Béroalde de Verville," appeared in *RHR*, 10 (1979), 56-71.

[5] La Monnoye's "Dissertation" (1700?) is reproduced in several later editions of the *Parvenir*.

[6] In his edition of the *Parvenir*, reprinted in 1889 (Paris: Charpentier, p. xxvii).

[7] *Problèmes littéraires du seizième siècle* (Paris: Boccard, 1927).

[8] See note 3.

[9] *François Béroalde de Verville, Anthologie poétique*, ed. V.-L. Saulnier (Paris: Haumont, 1945), p. 8.

[10] *The World View of Béroalde de Verville (Expressed through Satirical Baroque Style in Le Moyen de Parvenir)* (Paris: Vrin, 1971).

[11] "Irony and Narrative Technique in Béroalde de Verville's *Le Moyen de Parvenir.*" The panelists were Tom Conley, Janis L. Pallister, Gerald Prince and Armand Renaud. I should like to thank Professors Pallister and Prince for letting me read their papers.

[12] P. 15.

[13] See note 4.

[14] "La composition facétieuse du *Moyen de Parvenir*," RHR, 7 (1978), 140-146.

[15] His paper was entitled "Récit et texte dans le *Moyen de Parvenir*" and has now appeared in *Neophilologus*, 65 (1981), 1-5.

[16]Vol. X.

[17]*Structures Narratives*, p. 151.

[18]*The Quattrocento Dialogue: Classical Tradition and Humanist Innovation.* Harvard University Press, 1980, pp. 5-8.

[19]*The Age of Humanism: Europe, 1480-1530*, tr. K. M. Delavenay and E. M. Gwyer (London: Thames and Hudson, 1963), p. 24.

[20]Guillaume Bouchet, *Premier Livre des Serèes* (Lyon: Ancelin, 1608).

[21]*Ramus, Method, and the Decay of Dialogue: From the Art of Discourse to the Art of Reason* (Harvard University Press, 1958), p. 121. Cf. also his article "System, Space and Intellect in Renaissance Symbolism," in *The Barbarian Within* (New York: Macmillan, 1962), 68-87, especially 74-5.

[22]"On est frappé de la place que Béroalde accorde au langage." *Structures Narratives*, p. 3.

[23]Paris: Guillemot and Thiboust, 1612.

SURNATUREL OU DIABLERIE:

HISTOIRES PRODIGIEUSES MAIS VÉRITABLES

Isabelle Armitage

Pierre de l'Estoile, sous le vocable d'histoires prodigieuses, relate quatre incidents hors du commun dont il affirme la véracité. Bien qu'après chaque titre on trouve la mention olographe "Extrait de mes Mémoires" elles semblent n'apparaître nulle part ailleurs que dans mon édition originale d'un fragment de manuscrit qui au bout de quatre cents ans, par les voies détournées de la Providence, a surgi parmi les oeuvres rares de la Bibliothèque de l'Université du Kansas.[1]

Pourquoi l'Estoile, qui avait la réputation d'être rationaliste et de se moquer des explications surnaturelles, avait-il choisi de consigner des événements fantastiques en insistant sur leur authenticité, alors que le plus souvent il affectait impartialité, indifférence ou scepticisme à l'égard des soi-disant prodiges?

Par exemple, en décembre 1574 il écrit non sans une certaine ironie à propos du cardinal de Lorraine, mort d'un refroidissement contracté à la procession des Battus, qu'une tempête s'étant déchaînée les

> "catholiques lorrains disaient que la véhémence de
> cet orage portait indice du courroux de Dieu sur la
> France, qui le privait d'un si bon, si grand, si sage
> prélat. Les Huguenots au contraire, disaient que c'était
> le sabbat des diables qui s'assemblaient pour le venir
> quérir; qu'il faisait bon mourir ce jour-là, pour ce
> qu'ils étaient bien empêchés. Ses partisans maintenaient
> qu'il avait fait une tant belle fin chrétienne, rien de plus."[2]

Ailleurs, le 10 février 1586, il raconte, sans commentaires, avoir vu un "homme sans bras, qui écrivait, lavait un verre, ôtait son chapeau, jouait aux quilles etc..." (H. III, 444). En décembre 1587 il rapporte une histoire prodigieuse qui courait à Paris selon laquelle par "une spéciale et singulière grâce de Dieu" une Allemande de 27 ans vivait encore alors qu'elle n'avait ni mangé, ni bu, ni dormi depuis sept ans (H. III, 512). Ici non plus l'Estoile ne cherche pas à influencer son public.

Par contre les quatre histoires qui avaient jusqu'à présent échappé à la publication requièrent avec insistance l'approbation du lecteur. La première

(IA, 113) est intitulée "Histoire prodigieuse mais véritable, en laquelle reluit plainement la Providence de Dieu; advenue l'an 1566" écrit de la main du scribe. Dans la marge l'Estoile répète, de sa main, "Ceste histoire est prodigieuse mais véritable et en laquelle reluit plainement la Providence de Dieu" suivi de la mention "Extrait de mes Mémoires." Au cours de la narration un gentilhomme Breton est obligé de prendre refuge pour la nuit dans une hostellerie qui s'avère une retraite de voleurs "ou on fait mestier & marchandise d'égorger les passans, & n'en estoit point revenu (à ce qu'on dict) de ceux qui y avoyent logé." L'auteur insiste sur le fait que le gentilhomme en question était "guidé, & conduit par une secrette providence de Dieu." En effet le vieillard soutenu par son sang-froid et aidé de son valet fait échec a ses quatre assassins présumés qui lui ont fait servir au dessert "quatre grandes dagues toutes nües" qu'il a pour mission de "digérer." "Bien donc, Messieurs, dit le Gentilhomme, puisqu'ainsi est qu'il me faut mourir, permettez-moi au moins de prier Dieu devant, & de boire encore un coup à vous devant que de mourir." Le verre de vin lui ayant été accordé il le leur jette aux yeux. Le valet en profite pour en abattre un à coup de pistolet, le gentilhomme en abat un autre, puis tous deux s'emparent des dagues pour achever les deux suivants. Après avoir coupé la gorge à la maîtresse du lieu ils épargnent la servante qui leur montre l'issue secrète leur permettant d'échapper à la douzaine de voleurs qui doivent arriver dans l'heure. L'histoire se termine à Moulins, auprès du roi qui pardonne au "bon vieillard" le port d'armes prohibées et lui accorde "raison & justice" de la requête pour laquelle il avait entrepris ce périlleux voyage.

Le titre de la deuxième histoire (IA, 115) l'introduit comme "encore plus prodigieuse; advenue en 1567" (c'est-à-dire trois ans avant l'Edit de Pacification de Catherine de Médicis). De la main de l'Estoile se trouve de nouveau la mention "Extraite de mes Mémoires." Il s'agit cette fois d'un "Gentilhomme de la Religion nommé la Loüe" qui doit passer la nuit dans un "nid de sorciers" et partager la couche d'un "Gentillastre du pays, qui avoit le bruit d'estre un grand sorcier." Au moment de s'endormir le gentilhomme voit entrer une procession étrange: "un homme avec son cornet ...et deux Damoyselles masquées. & habillées tout de noir que quatre gros limiers suyvoyent." Le gentilastre, tiré par le pied est mis à terre et dévoré par les chiens, puis la procession repart dans le même ordre sans "faire aucun mal à personne, ni même au Gentilhomme couché avec le sorcier" qui en est quitte pour une "peur et un effroy si grand, qu'il en fust plus de six mois après sans pouvoir revenir, & et en cuida mourir." L'Estoile nous dit "qu'un homme d'honneur et véritable l'a assuré l'avoir ouy conter plus de six fois par le Seigneur de la Loüe, Gentilhomme signalé & homme de bien au dire de tout le monde." Le narrateur, encore une fois endosse la responsabilité d'exactitude de son écrit à travers la réputation de probité faite au principal spectateur du drame.

"Autre sur ce subject, non moins prodigieuse que véritable, advenue à Paris en l'an 1558" est le titre de la troisième (IA, 116) reconnue elle aussi par l'Estoile comme extraite de ses Mémoires. La mort, encore une fois, y figure de facon prédominante. Le protagoniste est un "certain personnage homme docte et studieux, mais fort addonné à Magie, & à l'invocation des malings Esprits" malade, à la veille de sa mort il fait brûler des papiers par son logeur et lui remet une boite fermée à jeter à rivière sans l'avoir ouverte dès qu'il serait passé de vie à trépas. Bien que conscient de sa fin prochaine l'homme refuse de recevoir un prêtre et recommande qu'on le laisse seul même si l'on entend du bruit. Et, en effet, "l'heure de minuict estant venue, on oye un tel bruit & tintamarre en cette maison, qu'il semblait que tout deust fondre." L'homme est trouvé démembré, en quatre quartiers dans son lit. La boite est portée à la rivière et aussitôt qu'elle est jetée à l'eau le logeur "entendit comme plusieurs voix se plaignans & crians horriblement." Cette histoire, la plus effrayante des quatre, la moins susceptible d'explication rationnelle est celle dont l'Estoile dit "Mᵉ Matthieu Beroald mon maistre, pour l'avoir veu & pour estre parent de ceux qui logeoyent le dit personnage, asseure ce que dessus estre vray." Or l'année 1558, date de cette histoire est celle où, peu avant sa mort, Louis de l'Estoile avait confié son fils Pierre à Béroalde, lui demandant de l'instruire "en la piété et crainte de Dieu." A l'époque, Béroalde, théologien versé dans l'étude des langues anciennes, était professeur à l'Université d'Orléans; il devait plus tard se convertir au protestantisme et devenir ministre de la nouvelle religion à Genève. Il semble certain que l'Estoile respectait le jugement d'un homme auquel son père avait confié son éducation.

La dernière histoire (IA, 117) porte le titre laconique d'"Autre." Elle aussi provient des Mémoires. C'est une narration toute unie, concernant un soldat, appartenant à un gentilhomme normand, louant une chambre "inhabitée, & où personne ne pouvoit loger, à cause qu'il y revenoit quelque chose." Le militaire n'en tient pas compte, prend soin néanmoins de "boucher & coller toutes les fentes & ouvertures tant des fenestres que d'ailleurs" et garde auprès de lui son épée. A peine a-t-il fermé les yeux que "voicy comme une grande femme qui vient" elle l'empoigne au collet et il se défend à coups d'épée "tant qu'à la fin cela disparoist." Le lendemain matin la chambre est pleine de sang ce qu'il fait constater aux curieux qui s'affairent et retrouvent "à quatre lieux de là une femme sur le chemin gisant à terre, tirant à la fin, & ne parlant plus, qui avoit quatre ou cinq coups d'espée." Ce représentant féminin du mal est reconnu comme" la plus grande sorcière du pays, & eust-on opinion que c'estoit elle qui revenoit à ladicte chambre, et à laquelle le soldat avoit donné les dicts coups." "Ce que dessus est témoigné & creu en Normandie par plus de dix mille personnes." Telle est la conclusion de l'Estoile.

Pourquoi l'Estoile n'a-t-il pas inclus ces contes dans la rédaction définitive de ses Mémoires? Mais surtout quelle était l'attitude du public à l'égard de ces supposés prodiges? L'examen de cette dernière question nous aidera peut-être à répondre à la première. Dans son récent et volumineux ouvrage sur les prodiges,[3] Jean Céard demande ce que pensaient les lecteurs des "histoires qu'on leur racontait et des réflexions dont on les entremêlait." (JC, 479) Il répond que "les seules réactions connues viennent évidemment d'hommes cultivés, qui pour les uns, rejetaient avec mépris ces sottises, qui pour les autres plus nombreux, les accueillaient avec un amusement un peu moqueur et volontiers sceptique" et il ajoute en note "Pierre de l'Estoile est le type de ces lecteurs." (JC, note 105, 479) Cette assertion est dérivée de l'ouvrage de J.P. Seguin, *L'Information en France avant le périodique, 517 canards imprimés* entre 1529 et 1631, (JC note 40, 468) dans lequel se trouvent rassemblés un grand nombre de témoignages de l'Estoile. Le mémorialiste était-il moins sceptique qu'il n'espérait le paraître? Ou bien voulait-il simplement être fidèle à sa réputation d'impartialité? Nous ne pouvons que supputer avec un retard de quatre cents ans les mobiles d'un homme dont la curiosité nous a fourni tant d'anecdotes précieuses sur l'histoire de son temps.

Néanmoins l'Estoile a rédigé ces contes qui appartenaient á une tradition bien définie de la deuxième moitié du XVIe siècle, celle de Pierre Boaistuau auteur d'*Histoires Prodigieuses* publiées en 1560.[4] Ce livre eut un immense succès si l'on en juge par le nombre considérable de rééditions et de continuations par Claude de Tesserant, François de Belleforest et Arnauld Sorbin dont le *Tractatus de Monstris* constituera le cinquième livre des *Histoires Prodigieuses* en 1582. Boaistuau prétendait que son seul dessein était de rendre compte des prodiges, affirmant dans son *Advertissement au lecteur* "ce que je n'ay encore observé avoir esté faict d'aucun avant moy." (Cité par JC, 252) C'est un ouvrage sans plan qui n'offre pas de conclusion, son objet apparent étant de distraire un public qui se laissait charmer par l'étrange au milieu des inquiétudes quotidiennes. Néanmoins "toutes ces histoires sont autant de digressions à partir d'un thème unique," dit M. Céard citant Boaistuau, qui est "de faire apercevoir dans les mouvements étranges et les bouleversements des choses 'un secret jugement et fléau de l'ire de Dieu'." (JC 254) Alors que les réflexions des prédécesseur que Boaistuau cite dans l'avertissement (Camerarius, Polydore Vergile, Julius Obsequens, Cardan, Peucer, Rueff,Lycosthenes) étaient graves, qu'ils s'attachaient aux signes et aux menaces, lui ne cherchait pas à approfondir ni à découvrir la signification voilée. En fait son continuateur Sorbin reprochait à Boaistuau d'avoir été inspiré par la curiosité, et de ne chercher qu'à édifier, tandis que lui voulait amender, réformer—sans succès d'ailleurs, car sa pensée grave fut accueillie par un demi-silence. Il est intéressant de noter que dans les quatre histoires contées par l'Estoile seul l'élément d'édification semble présent. En effet, la première est une victoire du bien sur le mal, les trois suivantes traitent du sort peu enviable des sorciers hommes ou femme alors que les autres personnages sortent indemnes de l'aventure. A nous de conclure peut-être que les bien-pensants sont protégés des maléfices de sorciers qui à priori seraient des suppots de Satan.

En fait qu'entendait Boaistuau par la notion de prodige? Jean Céard répond que "le mot prodigieux" en premier examen est le simple équivalent de "monstrueux, estrange, merveilleux, admirable, mémorable." En deuxième examen "une lecture plus attentive fait voir que le mot de 'prodigieux' est volontiers utilisé comme une sorte de comparatif de supériorité." (JC, 255) Une supériorité qui peut fort bien s'exercer dans le domaine naturel. M. Céard ajoute qu'à la limite c'est la possibilité naturelle du prodige qui garantit son existence..." (JC 256) L'intérêt que porte l'homme aux phénomènes qui l'entourent étant fondamental, la créature humaine cherche à pénétrer le secret des choses, son incapacité à le faire "manifeste à la fois l'éminence du livre divin et la dépendance de l'homme à l'égard de son auteur." (JC, 257) C'est ainsi que pour Boaistuau le prodige devient une marque de la présence divine. Le naturel et le surnaturel sont juxtaposés, ces deux ordres de cause deviennent même synonymes d'inférieur et de supérieur. L'oeuvre de Boaistuau dans son ensemble explore la réserve de signes que constitue la création. Constituer un cabinet de "singularités" est un acte louable, la contemplation des monstres et des prodiges devant faire appel à notre réformation, car nous dit Boaistuau "Dieu par l'object des choses qui se présentent...nous fait sentir la violence de sa justice si aspre, que nous sommes contraincts d'entrer en nous-mesmes, frapper au marteau de nostre conscience, esplucher nos vices, et avoir en horreur nos meffaicts." (HP, ch. 17, 100-101) C'est bien la leçcon que l'Estoile semble vouloir appliquer dans la première histoire dont l'issue favorable est attribuée d'une facon insistante à la Providence de Dieu.

On reproche cependant à Boaistuau sa tendance à diluer le surnaturel dans le naturel (en cela d'ailleurs il ouvre la voie à la science de la nature qui ne viendra que bien plus tard avec Buffon). Son successeur Tesserand soumettra à Dieu seul l'apparition de monstres et de prodiges, donnant à la nature son autonomie propre, offrant ainsi un témoignage important du point de vue de l'histoire des idées (cf. JC, 326). Mais est-il possible de voir dans les prodiges uniquement la main de Dieu? Montaigne pour lequel Dieu est seul à connaître la raison de l'ordre du monde, s'il y en a une, arrive à la conclusion, qu'il n'appartient pas à l'homme de décider du possible et de l'impossible. Mais lui avait résisté à la tentation à laquelle ont succombé beaucoup de ses contemporains "de penser que le Malin s'emploie à corrompre l'évidence des signes divins et naturels." (JC, 493) Plutôt que de considérer les choses comme des énigmes, il les voyait comme des problèmes c'est ainsi termine Jean Céard que "l'homme de Montaigne ouvre l'âge moderne, l'âge de l'aventure solitaire de la connaissance." Pourtant avant d'en arriver à ces conclusions sur les prodiges et leurs causes naturelles, l'opinion publique attribuait l'impossible à la magie et à la sorcellerie.

Gabriel Pérouse dans un récent ouvrage[5] examine plusieurs aspects du problème et nous affirme que "la société française de 1550 apparaît au regard de Jacque Tahureau" (auteur de *Dialogues* en 1555 et de *Discours non plus mélancoliques que divers* en 1557) "profondément marquée par la superstition." Tandis qu'à la même époque du Fail la récuse vigoureusement, Guillaume Bouchet note que les marchands ont gardé la leur . . . la liste est longue. Yver écrit que "le bon ton commande d'avoir au moins sous le bras un tome de Boaistuau ou de Belleforest traducteur de Bandello." (GP, 194) M. Pérouse cite également Taburot, lequel dans le "Quatriesme livre des Bigarrures" traite des "Faux sorciers et de leurs impostures." Il semble que dans les cercles lettrés au moment de la *Démonomanie des Sorciers* de Jean Bodin, l'opinion chrétienne était que les diables avaient permission de nous nuire. Tabourot confirme cependant la vitalité de la superstition et s'emploie à "rabattre les estonnements des superstitieux" par des explications naturelles. (GP, 424)

Dans le monde obscur comment savoir où finit l'occulte naturel et où commence l'oculte démoniaque puisqu'ils ont suivi la même évolution si l'on en croit les preuves fournies par l'immense littérature démonologique de la deuxième moitié du XVIe siècle? demande Jean Céard citant Jean Wier, lecteur de Fernel: "Plusieurs choses se présentent parfois à nos yeux, lesquelles pour sembler estre plus que naturelles sont estimées illusions et ouvrages diaboliques: combien que pour certaines causes et raison assez évidentes, nature mère de toutes choses, les ait produites." (JC 353) Pour Wier, Satan, ange déchu ne peut rien faire sans l'aide de Dieu. Toute une théorie du monde occulte s'élabore selon laquelle le diable collabore avec la nature dans l'obscurité allant jusqu'à singer les opérations naturelles et à l'utiliser pour ternir l'oeuvre de Dieu. Bodin lui aussi se montre en faveur de l'occulte naturel dans la préface de la *Démonomanie*. On trouve dans un passage de l'ouvrage une situation qui rappelle celle de la troisième histoire de l'Estoile où au moment présumé de la mort de l'homme addonné à la magie on entend un bruit terrible dans la maison. Chez Bodin il s'agit d'un praticien de Lyon cherchant avec ses compagnons un trésor, dont il avait appris l'existence par sorcellerie, enfoui dans la terre, et qui entend "la voix d'un homme qui estoit sur la rouë près du lieu d'où ils estoient sortis, & entrerent dedans faisant un bruit si grand, que l'hoste pensait qu'il tonnast. Depuis il fist serment qu'il n'irait jamais chercher thresor." Bodin conclut "Ainsi void-on que les malings esprits ne veulent pas, ou pour mieux dire, que Dieu ne souffre pas que personne par tels moyens puisse enrichir." L'Estoile n'offre pas de morale, il se contente d'authentifier son histoire par le témoignage de Béroalde. Il ne commente pas non plus les deux autres histoires de sorciers. Au lecteur de déduire que si l'ordre de la nature est troublé, Dieu fait agir, ou laisse agir les malin démons pour manifester à l'homme sa colère et l'admonester. Ainsi les sorciers de Pierre de l'Estoile, par leurs fins effrayantes peuvent servir d'exemple à la démonstration de la colère divine.

Le lecteur du XXe siècle concluerait peut-être plus volontiers que ces histoires appartiennent à une forme bien déterminée de la littérature. Ainsi que nous le fait remarquer Michel Butor dans son *Essai sur le roman*,[6] bien que nous interprétions la réalité qui nous entoure à travers la fiction, que ce soit théâtre, cinéma, média ou littérature, "au milieu de tous ces récits grâce auxquels se constitue en grande partie notre monde quotidien, il peut y en avoir qui sont délibérement inventés." Ces inventions ont "des caractéristiques qui les distinguent d'emblée (des événements) auxquels nous avons l'habitude d'assister." En effet, ils font partie d'une littérature fantastique: ce sont des mythes, des contes, des histoires.

The Monterey Institute
of International Studies

NOTES

[1]Isabelle Armitage, *Fragment des Recueils de Pierre de l'Estoile, édition critique originale* (Lawrence: Kansas Humanistic Studies, 1976), pp. 113-17. (Cité ci-après: IA).

[2]Pierre de l'Estoile, *Journal de l'Estoile pour le règne de Henri III, 1574-1589*, ed. Louis-Raymond Lefèvre (Paris: Gallimard, 1941), p. 54. (Cité ci-après: H.III).

[3]Jean Céard, *La Nature et les prodiges, l'insolite au XVIe siècle en France* (Genève: Librairie Droz, 1977). (Cité ci-après: JC).

[4]Pierre de Boaistuau, *Histoires prodigieuses les plus mémorables qui aient été observées depuis la Nativité de Jesus Christ jusques à nostre siecle. Extraictes de plusieurs fameux autheurs grecz et latins mise en nostre langue par P.B.* (P.: 1560) 4°, XII. 173 folios. (Cité ci-après: HP)

[5]Gabriel A. Pérouse, *Nouvelles françaises du XVIe siécle, images de la vie du temps* (Genève: Droz, 1977), p. 172. (Cité ci-après: GP).

[6]Michel Butor, *Essai sur le roman* (Paris: Gallimard, Idées, 1969), p. 8.